VINTAGE FASHION

VINTAGE FASHION

A COMPLETE SOURCEBOOK

NICKY ALBRECHTSEN

Over 1,300 illustrations

T&H

Cover Detail of a colour block geometric print
on silk jersey, 1980s (see p. 132). Collection of
Nicky Albrechtsen.

1 Illustrators in the past were as important as
photographers today for conveying the styles of an
era and also how to wear them. Thirties fashion was
usually accessorized with hats, gloves and handbags.
More fashion from the thirties can be seen starting
on p. 32.

2 Suits from the late fifties were often designed in
printed fabrics, a far cry from the severe tailoring of
forties post-war fashion. More examples can be seen
on pp. 75 and 77. JULIAN ROSE. SILK. c. LATE 1950s.

3 This large bag is hand-made from printed silk and
decorated with silk fruit and vegetables. Probably
used originally to contain home knitting or sewing
(the fruit would have been used as pin cushions),
it can be used as a beautiful handbag today. Bags
are discussed in more detail starting on p. 182.
HANDMADE. SILK. c. 1920s.

4 This unlabelled handmade felt hat of French
origin dates to the forties. A selection of hats can
be seen starting on p. 154. HANDMADE. FELT WITH
VELVET CORSAGE. c. 1940s.

First published in the United Kingdom in 2014
under the title *Vintage Fashion Complete* by
Thames & Hudson Ltd, 181A High Holborn,
London WC1V 7QX

First published in the United States of America in
2014 under the title *Vintage Fashion Complete* by
Chronicle Books, 680 Second Street, San Francisco,
California 94107

This paperback edition published in 2023

First published in the United States of America in
2023 by Thames & Hudson Inc., 500 Fifth Avenue,
New York, New York 10110

Vintage Fashion Complete © 2014
Thames & Hudson Ltd, London
Vintage Fashion: A Sourcebook © 2023
Thames & Hudson Ltd, London
Text © Nicky Albrechtsen

Designed by Broadbase

British Library Cataloguing-in-Publication Data
A catalogue record for this book is available from
the British Library

Library of Congress Control Number 2023934850

ISBN 978-0-500-29720-9

Printed and bound in China by
C&C Offset Printing Co. Ltd

Be the first to know about our
new releases, exclusive content
and author events by visiting
thamesandhudson.com
thamesandhudsonusa.com
thamesandhudson.com.au

Contents

4

SUIT-DRESSES are next in importance. The print-and-plain one gives the effect of a three-piecer, but it is a dress with a jacket. The latter is cut like a suit jacket, with the new Schiaparelli shortness, the fitted lines, the one button. No. 9156.

BANDS OF CONTRAST edge the second suit-dress, at the hem, neck, and cuffs. This hem-border fashion was started by Molyneux, but it is only now getting underway. The jacket is the suit-type, too, with a slightly flared peplum. No. 9166.

For back views and yardage see page following last fashion page

SOME HAVE JA

1 Fashion in the thirties closely followed the Parisian couture houses, and dressmaking patterns from companies such as McCall's and Weldons informed women of the latest trends. These illustrations from 1937 show the trend for mixing plain colours with print; shorter length jackets, as shown by Schiaparelli; and plain border hems, as seen in the designs of Edward Molyneux. Thirties fashions are discussed on pp. 32–51.

2 A swing coat from Jacques Fath's winter 1951 collection, as illustrated by Durani. See pp. 70–89 for more fifties fashions.

3 A fifties advertisement for Braemar Knitwear, showing one of the beautiful illustrative campaigns used to promote this Scottish company's sophisticated styling and colour palettes. Knitwear examples can be seen on pp. 250–63.

Introduction

'FASHIONS FADE
STYLE IS ETERNAL'

YVES SAINT LAURENT

Vintage style, a phenomenon that has been sweeping through the mechanisms of fashion since the late nineties, shows no sign of faltering and has become a sought-after category in its own right. The term 'vintage' reflects a style that is not defined by a particular decade, fashion era or designer. It encompasses the collective fashions of past eras that are worn today simply because they are beautiful, and therefore always desirable. The appeal of vintage lies in the unique charm of individual garments; clothes that demand to be bought and worn.

Vintage includes the most exciting, the most attractive and, above all, the most wearable fashions from every past fad, trend or pivotal moment of clothing design. These fashions are appreciated for their craftsmanship and the individuality they can bring to a contemporary ensemble. For enthusiasts, this search for the best of the past has led to an increased understanding of bygone design and a willingness to explore all it has to offer.

By being labelled simply as 'vintage', these pieces defy the traditional categorizations of fashion into ready-to- wear and couture, and challenge judgments based on age and label alone. Therefore, rather than being placed simply within a framework of 20th-century fashion history, the vintage pieces selected for this book are also explored thematically. Restricting an item of clothing to a specific decade ignores how a piece lives beyond the date of its creation. Beautiful fabric was stored and treasured, so it is not unusual to find a fifties evening dress made from rare forties silk and fastened with ornate thirties Bakelite buttons. By combining the fashions of different decades we can understand how fashion trends evolve and how they can be adapted for contemporary style. For these reasons, the book has been divided into three sections: DECADES, ELEMENTS and HALLMARKS.

3

The first section of this book presents fashions by DECADES to familiarize the reader with the changing style of each era. This not only identifies the details that date garments but also helps with understanding the silhouettes that suit different body shapes. While many can instantly recognize the iconic styles of each period – whether that's the flapper girl, the mod or the hippy – fashion history is surprising, and each decade also reveals unexpected traits, details of tailoring, embellishments or textiles subsequently reworked by designers from later decades to provide new trends. A suit of the seventies will echo forties styling, while a belt from the eighties will be reminiscent of designs that accessorized feminine floral frocks in the thirties.

The ELEMENTS section focuses on the different genres of fashion, everything from swimwear to wedding dresses, as well as the all-important accessories – the bags, shoes and glasses – that accent a fashionable ensemble. By grouping these items collectively, they can be studied for their design and appeal without the hindrance of date. A hat may be chosen because it complements the contours of a face, and the fact it was designed in the sixties is an interesting attribute rather than an overriding stipulation.

Finally, the section on HALLMARKS highlights some of the favourite themes long associated with vintage fashion. Nautical, botanical, lace and the Little Black Dress have been reworked for every decade to become not only vintage staples today, but also inspiration for contemporary designers exploring fashion history for their own creations.

The majority of garments that are presented in this book have been selected from private collections, and represent fashions from every 20th-century decade, from the twenties to the eighties, that are worn and loved for their individual design appeal and the stories behind them. Many may look familiar, having inspired contemporary collections on both the high street and the catwalk or having been worn as covetable costumes in television dramas. Most are affordable and within the reach of the average collector, although some are real one-off handmade creations. Others were one of a commercial run but over time have become unique. What unites them all is their individual allure: a rare attribute in the fast turnover of fashion we've become accustomed to in the 21st century.

Today, sourcing vintage fashion is a way of creating an individual style. It need not be expensive but it can be an investment if chosen carefully. Like collectable art, vintage fashion will only increase in value if it is carefully looked after. But fashion is designed to be worn and should be enjoyed: there are few pieces so rare that they should only be looked at. While there are many labels of note for the true collector, what governs the price of an individual garment is above all its unique beauty as judged by contemporary standards. The ripped vests and shackled bondage trousers of seventies Punk are exemplary museum pieces, but it is the unlabelled bias-cut thirties silk evening dress that has fashionistas fighting for it.

1 This plaited leather design comes from the United States. Towards the end of the forties there was a fashion for jewel colours and the platform sole began to disappear. More forties shoe designs can be seen on pp. 174–5. LEATHER. c. 1940s.

2 Raffia embroidery is indicative of the fifties and often of the object being made in the United States. The style decorated weekend and holiday handbags and was emulated in thick embroidery thread on knitwear of the era. A large wicker basket like this was often made to carry precious summer straw hats when not being worn. Comparable bags can be seen on p. 191. WICKER. c. 1950s.

3 The shoulder cape was used with evening dresses of the thirties, a time when the more demure covered their shoulders. Often losing their dresses over time, the capes make fashion statements today worn over coordinating tops, or even contemporary dresses. There are more thirties shoulder capes on p. 41. SILK. c. 1930s.

1 This close-up detail shows a fifties nylon evening dress. Nylon was welcomed in the early fifties as a substitute for silk, and was pioneered as a fashion fabric by textile converter Zika Ascher. NYLON. c.1950s.

2 Slinky jersey was a favourite fabric of the seventies, seen mostly in the Grecian styles for the dance floor and associated with designers such as Halston. More eveningwear can be seen on pp. 264–81. MR DARREN. SYNTHETIC JERSEY. c.1970s.

The labels of couture will always be desirable – their quality and finish are enduring and their rarity a certainty. However, the unlabelled or handmade should not be discounted. Many couture labels were removed to avoid taxation when garments were privately exported. Moreover, much of pre-fifties fashion was handmade, providing unique, never-to-be replicated pieces.

For many the appeal of vintage lies in the mystery and romance of past ownership, while for others it is an opportunity to create an individual style statement. For the designer, it can be the inspiration of a rare colour combination, the brush stroke of a floral print or the ruffles on a nylon blouse. Archived design has always been a resource for the contemporary and, while there are those who criticize the 'plundering' of past collections, it would be a waste of centuries-worth of design if the finer details of fashion were not re-examined and reinvented. Even Coco Chanel famously remarked, 'I would shed tears the day no one copied me.'

Never before has the desirability of individual pieces been so widely publicized. A picture of Kate Moss wearing Vivienne Westwood's 1981 Pirate boots sparked frenzied internet sales for the originals before the design was eventually reissued. As fashion houses turn to their own heritage in order to stay at the forefront of fashion, it is clear that the power of old clothes cannot be underestimated.

Within the infinite variations offered by vintage fashion, there is something for everyone and the hunt for that perfect piece is part of the allure. There is nothing more thrilling than finding a stunning seventies maxi dress squashed on a rail between shrunken jumpers, or discovering a fifties brushed mohair coat, only to find the couture label hidden deep in a waistband. What is important for those looking to grow their vintage wardrobe is a knowledge of old fabrics and trimmings and a familiarity with the aftercare needed to prolong the life of a historical garment. A working guide is supplied at the end of this book not only to advise on general cleaning and storage but also to offer guidance on simple alterations and repairs to help decide if that ripped Ossie Clark is indeed worthy of purchase.

While the definition of vintage is quite fluid, what many fashion gurus recognize is that yesterday's fashion can be cutting edge, and that vintage garments can transform a style or simply blend with their distinctive chic into the modern wardrobe.

4 This late thirties pair of rayon pyjamas is combined with an embroidered bed jacket, creating a possible outfit for today's vintage fashionista. More examples of beautiful lingerie and nightwear can be seen on pp. 218–29.

5 This Christian Dior advertisement dates to the sixties and its line illustrations give the modern collector detailed information on styles of sixties shoes. See pp. 168–81 for more designs.

6 The oversized sunglasses of the seventies have been so emulated it is sometimes hard to distinguish between old and new. Spectacles and sunglasses are discussed on pp. 192–9. SILHOUETTE. TEXTURED PLASTIC. c. 1970s.

3 As the effects of lace were explored during the fifties, even prints of the period copied its transparent properties. More lace designs can be seen on pp. 348–61. COTTON. c. 1950s.

Souliers
Christian Dior

THAIS
en chevreau toucan,
bordure et
nœud chevreau noir
forme Roxanne,
talon 612,
prix 129 F.
◀ page ci-contre

NATHALIE
chevreau loutre,
applique et
nœud crêpe noir,
forme Cervinia,
talon 406,
prix 129 F.

Simplicity

Fashion Preview
May

4674

Part One

DECADES

THE 1920s

THE ALLURE OF COUTURE

'THE TWENTIES ARE MY ABSOLUTE FAVOURITE PERIOD FOR TEXTILE DESIGNS, PARTICULARLY THOSE FROM WIENER WERKSTÄTTE. THE CLOCHE HAT, THE SWEATER AND NECKLACES WITH EVERYTHING, EVEN PYJAMAS, MARKED A GREAT ERA FOR WOMEN AND SOME OF THEM EVEN GOT THE VOTE.' SUSANNAH BUXTON, COSTUME DESIGNER, *DOWNTON ABBEY*

The haute bohemian chic of the twenties is revisited regularly by fashion. An era that broke with tradition and moved away from the constraining flounced frills of the Belle Époque and the Edwardian 'S' bend, the twenties was the first decade to celebrate youth fashion, and its stylish pizzazz is unrivalled in the inspiration it provides for both the contemporary high street and the catwalks of couture. Dropped waists, handkerchief hems, ornate beadwork and layers of fringing are just a few of the signature elements that have been reworked and restyled throughout the subsequent decades. The original garments of the twenties are rare and have a fragility that is both attractive and real, but they also have a modern-day wearability that creates a great demand for original vintage pieces.

In reality, the fabulous flapper girls, the 'Bright Young Things' photographed by Cecil Beaton, documented by Evelyn Waugh and portrayed at the time in F. Scott Fitzgerald's novels, were a fashionable stereotype limited to the very fortunate few who were able to indulge in such a hedonistic lifestyle. Fashion represented class and social mobility at a time when a newly acquired freedom of dress and a private bank balance were the luxuries enjoyed by a recently formed female workforce in the post-war era. Even Fitzgerald, renowned for his representations of class through clothing, purchased a suit from the couturier Jean Patou for his wife Zelda as part of their efforts to fit into twenties New York society.

By the early 20th century, the first French couture houses had already established their dominance, making Paris the centre of style. Charles Frederick Worth, an Englishman who settled in Paris, introduced an early forerunner of the fashion show. Others followed his example and, by the twenties, many notable names of couture including Patou,

1 A close-up of louvre (horizontal) pleats probably made from the scrap box remains of a twenties lightweight linen summer dress. Tucks, pleats and inserted panels (godets) were all common decorative details of this decade.

2 Daywear fashions of the twenties show a more relaxed and sporty silhouette than ever previously experienced. Championed by couturiers Chanel and Patou, two- and three-piece combinations became the new vogue as hemlines rose and fell over the decade.

3 Women devoted much time to home sewing in the twenties and their efforts can be seen in the intricate embroideries and lace embellishments on otherwise simple dresses. HANDMADE. COTTON. c. 1920s.

4 The sailor tie is a frequent adornment on necklines from this era. HANDMADE. CREPE AND SILK SATIN. c. 1920s.

3

4

1 This page from a catalogue for luxury department store Harrods from the mid-twenties shows the outer glamour achieved during the decade through the use of over-sized collars and cuffs.

2 An evening coat fashioned from a metallic jacquard woven fabric demonstrates the decade's distinguishing large collar, cuffs and deep border trims, always in a contrasting fabric such as the velvet and fur used here. These dramatic evening garments, though rare and expensive, make prized possessions today. HANDMADE. METALLIC AND SILK COAT, WORN OVER CREPE DRESS WITH METALLIC EMBROIDERY. c. EARLY 1920s.

3 This French fashion illustration shows the variety of coats in the decade. 'Intricate cutting achieves the fashionable low fullness,' ran one of the editorial headlines of the era. The knee-length, wrap styles of mid-decade are completely compatible with contemporary fashions if you are lucky enough to find a coat from this era in a wearable condition.

Greenland
Seal

A Harrods Model
in beautifully
marked Greenland
Seal, richly collared
in Raccoon
79 Gns

The same style in Seal
Coney and Skunk
39 Gns
Or in Natural Mus-
quash and Beaver
35 Gns

Harrods

LE MIROIR DES MODES

EN VOYAGE

MANTEAUX PRATIQUES ET CONFORTABLES

Vionnet, Chanel and Lanvin had invited clients to private viewings in deluxe showrooms, a practice that eventually became a daily procedure during 'the season'.

The success of the couture house depended upon the loyalty of its patrons; celebrity endorsement was as important in the twenties as it is today. The youthful aesthetic of Jeanne Lanvin's clothes for women proved popular during the modernist era of the twenties and her signature design was the *robe de style*, a full-skirted, dropped-waist alternative to the defining *garçonne* silhouette of the era. Lanvin boasted the actresses Marlene Dietrich and Mary Pickford among her clientele, just as Worth had dressed the stars of the stage Lillie Langtry and Sarah Bernhardt. The rise of the film industry and the nightclub scene created glamorous stars, each associated with the styles of a different atelier. Jean Patou, Paul Poiret and Madeleine Vionnet all designed exotic ensembles for Josephine Baker, the American dancer who took Paris's Folies Bergère by storm.

In addition to early superstar patronage, a burgeoning new media became integral to the promotion of style: the fashion magazine, as we know it today, had been established in the United States in the late 19th century with titles such as *Harper's Bazar* (as it was then spelt) and *Vogue*, with other titles following suit. Reporting on Parisian-led fashion, elementary photography and fashion illustrations featured the work of couturiers and translated them into defining trends for its readers. Before photography became the norm, illustration was ubiquitous and it was an essential method of advertising the latest designs and dictating to women exactly how they should be worn. As well as in magazines, it was used in newspaper advertisements, department store catalogues and for the covers of dressmaking patterns. Many of the French couture houses had arrangements with pattern companies such as Vogue Patterns, Simplicity and Butterick to retail toiles (the tested garment shape produced by a designer in inexpensive fabric before the couture garment is made) for reproduction.

Unlike other decades, there was little middle ground between the eminent names belonging to the Chambre Syndicale de la Haute Couture and the private tailors and home dressmakers of this period. The average woman of the twenties was a proficient seamstress and unsurprisingly a vast amount of clothing from this era is handmade. It is this personalization of fashion that accounts for the era's appeal today and makes every garment found truly unique.

4 Nancy Carroll, an American actress of stage and screen, models daywear from the mid-twenties. The leopard-print lining of her jacket matches the trimming on her fashionable cloche hat.

1 An example of early knitwear that has been printed with Egyptian-style patterning. Egyptomania was a trend that inspired more subtle interpretations in Britain than the vibrant American versions. HANDMADE. RAYON. c. 1920s.

2 The discovery of Tutankhamen's tomb had an enormous influence on fashion, particularly seen in embroideries and decorative prints. In the United States, the trend was so popular it was eventually considered to be common and vulgar. The maker of this dress actually lived in Egypt. HANDMADE. RAW SILK. c. 1920s.

4

The affordable garments that can be discovered today echo the innovations of a handful of names. The fabrics and textile designs of the Viennese collective of artists and designers, the Wiener Werkstätte, laid the foundations for appealingly dramatic modernist geometrics, while the embroideries of Paquin and Vionnet (often created by the house of Lesage) were imitated on elaborate dresses, the Art Deco stylization of the period perfectly fitting this new way of dressing.

The twenties also experienced the rise of the department store. A sprinkling of department stores selling the first off-the-peg garments had emerged in the major fashion capitals in the late 19th century. The labels of these stores provide easy identification when determining the age of a garment, particularly as some changed name during the following decades. Marshall & Snelgrove, Whiteleys, Peter Robinson (now Topshop) in London; Le Bon Marché in Paris; and Macy's and Lord & Taylor in New York were all fuelled by the needs of a female workforce. Secretarial and retail positions offered new alternatives to domestic service. They were roles that demanded comfortable and presentable clothing that could be purchased from the stores, which also offered free alteration services. 'Women were peacocks when they had nothing to do. As they became more important their clothes were less noticeable,' recounted *Harper's*. 1918 saw a limited selection of women awarded the vote and this was extended to all women over twenty-one in 1928.

Gradually everyday fashion of the twenties became less aspirational and more practical and suited to a busy lifestyle. These garments, which are beautiful in their understated simplicity, quite often go unnoticed between the fragile feathers and sequins of flapper fashion that command high prices today. But it is the simple hand-embroidered cotton shifts and crepe dresses that should not be overlooked: their interesting printed infills (simple, sleeveless constructions made to 'fill in' the opening of a dress front) and exquisite lace collars and blouse fronts make for both affordable and desirable vintage wear today.

3 The simple styling of twenties garments created a blank canvas for the painstaking embroideries and embellishments that were the handiwork of their wearers. HANDMADE. SILK. c. 1920s.

4 Gabrielle Chanel was the designer responsible for adapting the fabric of underwear for fashionable outerwear. As early as 1914 she designed cardigan suits in the fluid, soft jersey worn for sportswear and casual daywear. HANDMADE. WOOL JERSEY. c. 1920s.

1 Twenties shift dresses are easy to wear today. Art Deco prints are simple and create a vintage look easier on the eye than the 'dressing-up' effect sometimes evoked by later eras. HANDMADE. RAYON. c. 1920s.

2 Dresses with what appear to be open fronts or deep necklines were designed to be worn over lace or printed silk sleeveless 'vest'-style blouses. These pretty undergarments were integral to the design of the dress. HANDMADE. CREPE AND LACE. c. MID-1920s.

3 The contrasting collar and cuffs of printed velvet of this twenties cocktail dress are resonant of the later seventies trend that also employed the bishop sleeve. HANDMADE. CREPE AND VELVET. c. 1920s.

4 The placement of elaborate embroideries took the jersey garment worn for relaxed daywear to new, sophisticated heights. HANDMADE. SILK JERSEY. c. 1920s.

5 Many odd little blouses, sleeveless and often elasticated at the waist, can be found dating to the twenties. Although they appear unfinished, they are in fact rudimentary blouses intended to be worn under jackets and V-necked dresses. Invariably made from highly decorative lace or printed fabric, these blouses would have been the focal point for an outfit. Worn today under cardigans and jackets they can achieve the same effect. HANDMADE. RAYON. c. 1920s.

1
2
3
4

1–4 Twenties eveningwear was in complete contrast to the understated and relaxed style of daywear. Jackets and dresses worn for parties and balls shone with decadent opulence. While vintage beaded evening jackets from any decade are good investment pieces, this particularly applies to those from the twenties and thirties. These fragile garments are often found with small rips and tears, or patches where beads and sequins have broken away. Lining silk and tulle garments is an effective way to control their fragility as the new fabric is able to support the heavy beadwork. Design inspirations included Art Deco or the recently discovered Tutankhamen's tomb. Here American film actress and fashion icon, Louise Brooks, is seen modelling a handkerchief evening dress from around 1925.

2 HANDMADE. SEQUINNED TULLE. c. LATE 1920s/EARLY 1930s.

3 SEQUINNED SILK. c. 1920s.

4 HANDMADE. BEADED SILK CHIFFON. c. 1920s.

5 The early twenties evening dress differed in style and length from the flapper dress of the mid-twenties. The ankle was the erogenous zone at the start of the decade. HANDMADE. SILK. c. 1920s.

6 The craze for dancing the tango, the shimmy and the Charleston had an overriding influence on twenties eveningwear. To allow ease of movement dresses were sleeveless, skirts were fluted or inserted with glittering panels, and hem lengths rose to the knee. HANDMADE. SILK CHIFFON. c. MID-1920s.

1

2

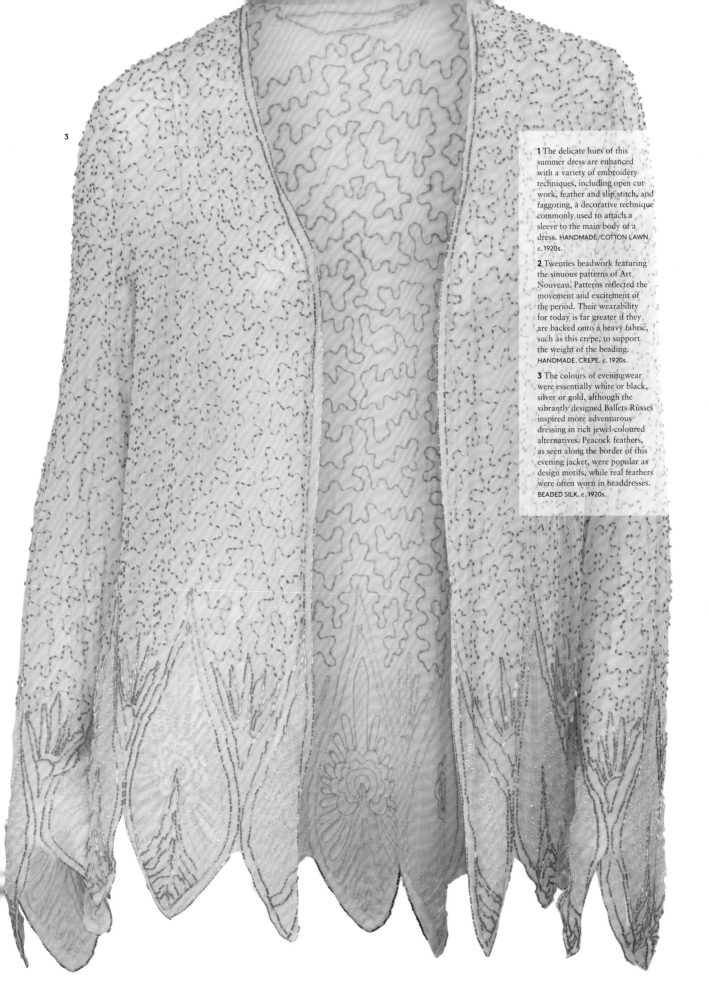

1 The delicate hues of this summer dress are enhanced with a variety of embroidery techniques, including open cut work, feather and slip stitch, and faggoting, a decorative technique commonly used to attach a sleeve to the main body of a dress. HANDMADE. COTTON LAWN. c.1920s.

2 Twenties beadwork featuring the sinuous patterns of Art Nouveau. Patterns reflected the movement and excitement of the period. Their wearability for today is far greater if they are backed onto a heavy fabric, such as this crepe, to support the weight of the beading. HANDMADE. CREPE. c.1920s.

3 The colours of eveningwear were essentially white or black, silver or gold, although the vibrantly designed Ballets Russes inspired more adventurous dressing in rich jewel-coloured alternatives. Peacock feathers, as seen along the border of this evening jacket, were popular as design motifs, while real feathers were often worn in headdresses. BEADED SILK. c.1920s.

1 Decorative fabrics were imported from the Far East to be used for both fashionable clothing and interiors. Department stores such as Liberty, London, carried 'aesthetic' fabrics used to create the fashions of the day. Founder Arthur Lasenby Liberty was influential in his encouragement of a simplicity of style that did not distort the body. HANDMADE. EMBROIDERED COTTON. c. 1920s.

2 An article in American *Vogue*, 1921, stated; 'Owing to this craze for dancing, dining in restaurants where dancing takes place either during dinner or after dinner, has become very popular, and it is in such restaurants that one sees the newest clothes.' This early twenties fashion plate from the United States illustrates a parade of the latest ensembles worn by ladies at lunch. The fashionable focus on a low waist and a contrasting waist is highlighted by this interesting selection of coats and wraps.

3, 4 Twenties daytime dressing was far more demure than twenties evening attire. While **3** shows a dress from the early to mid-decade, with the dropped waist and the sailor collar that continued in popularity from the turn of the 20th century, **4** illustrates the change in style by the end of the decade to a higher, natural waistline with an emphasis on the sleeves and a more fitted silhouette.

3 COTTON LAWN. c. EARLY 1920s.

4 HANDMADE. COTTON LAWN. c. LATE 1920s.

5 The beautiful embroideries used on twenties dresses were often given further decorative appeal by 'space-dyeing' effects. Seen commonly on scarves, the practice of dip-dying threads to create tonal hues is an identifying detail of the period. HANDMADE. COTTON. c. 1920s.

1 This delicate chiffon dress demonstrates the popular style of soft loose floral prints. These are more whimsical and painterly in style than those seen in the following decades. HANDMADE. SILK CHIFFON. c. 1920s.

2 A twenties French fashion plate illustrates the variety of hem styles that can be found in fashions of the decade, including godets of contrasting fabrics, soft fluting and the handkerchief hem known as a signature style of Vionnet. On hats, deep brims sheltered eyes from the summer sun before sunglasses became fashionable, while, without doubt, the style of the decade was the cloche worn in a variety of fabrics for every season.

3 A dress from the United States made from 'artificial silk' is printed with irregular oriental motifs, a popular print style for both loungewear and eveningwear. HANDMADE. RAYON. c. 1920s.

4 By the end of the decade sportswear and beach style had influenced daywear for women. Healthy outdoor activities and sports such as golf and tennis, cycling and even rollerskating demanded clothes that allowed freedom of movement. This playsuit is part of a two-piece ensemble with a wrapover skirt that can be removed to reveal the shorts below. LINEN. c.1920s.

4

5 6

5, 6 As the one-piece swimming costume ceased to be scandalous, Western women began to reveal their bodies while swimming and sunbathing. The promenade became a fashionable parade for the latest styles and created a whole new market for *après-swim* fashions.

1218

1221 1222

1218

1223

1219

1220

SUR LA PLAGE

1218 — Robe très jeune d'allure, en toile rose découpée en dents de scie, et formant des volants superposés sur la jupe, échancrée de toile blanche au col et aux emmanchures. Ceinture de daim blanc. Métrage : 5 m. 75 en 1 m.

1219 — Jumper en toile de soie blanche bordée de toile bleu marin et brodée de macarons en soutache du même ton, posée sur une jupe de toile blanche entièrement à plis couchés. Métrage : 5 m. 50 en 1 m.

1220 — Robe de jeune fille, en crêpe Lisette amande. La jupe, montée à froncès, d'une ampleur très floue et garnie de volants. Jabot au corsage ; col d'organdi. Métrage : 3 m. 50 en 1 m.

1221 — Robe d'une seule pièce, en serge blanche et rouge mélangées. Des panneaux plissés sont incrustés dans la jupe. Bandes appliquées à plat en garniture. Métrage : 3 m. en 1 m. 30.

1222 — Ensemble en toile citron et toile de Jouy imprimée de larges fleurs composant le corsage. La veste sans manches est toute droite ; la jupe composée de groupes de plis couchés. Métrage : 4 m. 25 en 1 m.

1223 — Coquette petite robe en crêpe imprimé de fleurettes et coupé d'une crêpe uni rouge vif. La jupe, ample et ronde, est montée à froncès. Le col fichu est noué devant. Métrage : 3 m. 50 en 1 m.

1218 1219 1220 1221 1222 1223

THE 1930s

FASHION ON FILM

1 The thirties highlighted the back as an erogenous zone, and swimsuits and evening dresses explored backless designs inspired by the work of Schiaparelli and Vionnet. SILK. c. 1930s.

VOTRE BEAUT

SEPTEMBRE 1934

Soyez belle, on vous épi

2

2 The September 1934 cover of the French magazine *Votre Beauté* featured a dress by Madeleine Vionnet, often referred to as 'the queen of the bias cut'. 'I never came across any fabric that disobeyed me,' she famously claimed, creating sensual drapery from silk, chiffon and jersey. She closed her atelier at the end of the decade, just before the onset of the Second World War.

3 This striking evening dress is made from silk taffeta, a stiff fabric that holds its shape. Both the hem and collar are reinforced with a concealed couching stitch to keep the bottom of the dress full and the collar firm. The puffed sleeve is typical of thirties styling, creating a soft fullness in contrast to the decade's slim-line silhouette. Puffed sleeves can be found in a huge variety of shapes on everything from knitwear to blouses from this decade. HANDMADE. SILK TAFFETA. c. 1930s.

'WHAT HOLLYWOOD DESIGNS TODAY, YOU WILL BE WEARING TOMORROW.'

ELSA SCHIAPARELLI

The thirties is often referred to as 'The Golden Age of Hollywood'. It was a pivotal point in fashion history, between two world wars and a time of economic hardship following the stock market crash of 1929. It was an era when the stars of the silver screen oozed charismatic glamour and were seminal influences on a cinema-obsessed public desperate to escape the privations of the times.

Released from the constraints of corsets, bodices and bustles by the *garçonne* style that had typified the twenties, women of the thirties were offered a more feminine form. It was a style that evolved, like the following forties, from a need for frugality. The era was not constricted by the 'make do and mend' mantra of wartime, but incomes did not allow for the abundance of decoration that had been enjoyed during the Jazz Age. A 'less is more' ethos was the defining silhouette, reflected even in the cost of a couture dress: by 1938 a simple day dress by Madeleine Vionnet could be bought for £19, a reduced sum compared to earlier in the decade but still roughly equivalent to the average British working woman's monthly wage – and collections from the Paris fashion house had diminished to just one hundred garments (compared with the several hundreds featured in each collection during the twenties).

Devoid of expensive beadwork and embroidery, dress style became all about silhouette and drapery, and fashion embraced the form created through the bias cut attributed to Vionnet. Both diminutive and full-blown printed florals were used to decorate dresses of chiffon, rayon and silk, while blouses can often be found exhibiting soft geometrics abstracted from Art Deco. Textile industry advances and increased mass production helped provide women with flattering and sensual fashions. In part, the thirties 'look' was achieved through the use of the 'slide fastener' (the forerunner of what we know as the zip or zipper today), previously a fastening reserved for shoes; the use of soft jerseys, previously only used for underwear; a return to the natural waistline, highlighted with coordinating or contrasting soft leather belts; softly draped décolletages with flowing bows and cowls; and, for the first time, a low cut back, as seen in the highly collectable evening dresses of the day.

3

1 Embroidery is a distinguishing decorative element of late thirties garments. Used as an all-over decoration or as a carefully placed detail, inspiration came from Art Deco motifs or intertwining florals. Very occasionally small figurative designs such as animals or novelty images inspired by the designs of Schiaparelli can be found, although these are rare. HANDMADE. EMBROIDERED CREPE. c. 1930s.

2 The thirties were the height of feminine fashions. This chiffon afternoon dress is constructed from layers of cut flowers taken from printed silk. HANDMADE. SILK CHIFFON. c. 1930s.

3 The 1935 September cover of the British magazine *Radio Times* shows a Victor Reinganum illustration of female variety singers. Variety shows continued to entertain huge audiences despite the rapidly increasing popularity of talking cinema.

3

4 While the silhouette of the thirties was slender with little added ornate decoration, fabrics became more elaborate and metallic woven jacquards gave a subtle sophistication to the decade's eveningwear. In the thirties couturiers enjoyed the use of embroideries and appliqués, as seen in the mix of techniques used by Schiaparelli to create her Circus collection. This jacket has been created from a woven fabric, with an area left free for a printed design that adds a rich contrast. HANDMADE. SILK JACQUARD. c.1930s.

Cinema was the arbiter of style and, despite the Great Depression, thirties fashion had glamour, led by the working relationship between French couture and the Hollywood desire for spectacular. The introduction of the Motion Picture Production Code in 1930 (also known as the Hays Code) followed a spate of badly made, risqué films and laid down strict guidelines dictating what was considered suitable viewing for the cinema-goer. Female costume became less about titillation, as had been seen in the skimpy skins of the *Tarzan* films, and more of a tool of allure with which to captivate audiences. Nothing was more tantalizing than the rags-to-riches stories of actresses plucked from the street and now promoted on screen dressed in Parisian couture. Coco Chanel costumed Gloria Swanson in the 1931 film *Tonight or Never* and was given a million pound contract to costume MGM's leading stars. The creations of Elsa Schiaparelli were seen on screen in over thirty films and Mae West models a Schiaparelli gown in nearly every one of her thirties films, reaching a spectacular zenith in 1937 with *Every Day's a Holiday*.

However, costume designers were seen as equal in status to the notable names of fashion. Gilbert Adrian of MGM, and Travis Banton and Edith Head, both of Paramount, were responsible for shaping many of the looks of the day. The latter forged the later famous alliance of Hubert de Givenchy and Audrey Hepburn. Adrian was the first designer to have an on-screen credit, given as 'Gowns by Adrian'. He interpreted the fashion of the moment for the screen to create the all-important signature looks for individual stars that, in turn, inspired the wardrobes of cinema-goers who worshipped the glamour of the big screen. Greta Garbo, for example, excelled in casual masculinity and was proud of her personal legacy, the right to wear trousers on screen. Adrian therefore insisted that 'the Garbo girl must never wear anything under the descriptive category "dainty"… such things are flappers and Garbo is not a flapper'.

These costume designers had huge followings of loyal fans who imitated screen style using film-endorsed dress patterns. A Butterick 'starred' pattern, for example, would illustrate Katharine Hepburn's latest screen costume, while a company named Hollywood Patterns used photographic portraits to launch new styles. Costume designers had their own labels aimed at the growing department-store and off-the-peg markets, and were also often responsible for the all-important, off-screen wardrobes of their stars. One of

Adrian's most commercially successful designs was based on a white organdie evening dress with voluminous ruffled sleeves worn by Joan Crawford's character in the film *Letty Lynton*. It sold over 500,000 manufactured copies in Macy's department store. Adrian eventually left MGM to set up his own fashion house in Beverly Hills.

Department stores allied themselves with the silver screen to ensure their continuing popularity. These stores marketed themselves to the rising middle class, offering affordable fashion, with many of their styles adapted directly from the screen in addition to the costume patterns licensed and sold for home dressmaking by companies such as Weldons. Shops such as Montague Burton and Debenhams in the UK began to engrave or embroider initials free of charge, a popular service that helps to date garments from this era.

But perhaps the most sought-after garments from the period are the sensual evening gowns and collectable beaded evening capes that are worn today with everything from jeans to dresses. Unlike their delicate daytime counterparts in chiffon and lace, the thirties evening dress was popularly made in heavy satin that needed little embellishment; a style that is often echoed in contemporary collections.

From a decade coined 'the Threadbare Thirties' emerged garments of understated, seemingly effortless glamour,

made for the ready-to-wear market in easy-care and affordable fabrics that reflected the styles seen on the silver screen as much as the latest offerings from the couture houses. 'Who did that look first, Hollywood or Paris?' asked British *Vogue*. With these two prodigious style dictators leading fashions within the adverse economic climate of the times, it is not surprising that the garments from this era retain a wearability that remains relevant to today's fashion. Slinky cardigan jackets, striped blazers and contrasting tailored styles can easily be adopted for a modern wardrobe. The aptly named 'cinema' or 'theatre' suit – a tailored suit designed in the style of daytime wear but executed with longer skirts in fabrics suitable for evening such as velvet and sateen – makes a contemporary statement. The trench coat that emerged from the mid-decade onwards may be utilitarian in style, but offered in lamés and velvets it creates forward-looking styling even now.

It is the elegant simplicity of thirties fashion that makes garments from this decade relevant and eminently wearable today. The new 'talkies' of the era became a catwalk for the working woman, fashion history recorded for today.

1 A flattering draped cowl neckline is a signature of thirties day and evening wear. Sleeves were elevated, with small shoulder pads often made from scraps of leftover fabric. These snippets of beautiful prints contrast delightfully with their garments. HANDMADE. METALLIC JACQUARD. c.1930s.

2 An American fashion editorial from 1933 shows the trend for summer halternecks and the wide trousers that were a natural development of the 'pyjama slacks' seen towards the end of the twenties. The halterneck, or 'vestee' as the article describes it, has been hand-crocheted as – surprisingly – have the matching shoes. The author suggests making the espadrille soles from the most hardwearing material that can be found in the scrap box!

3 The most prevalent colour for eveningwear was black, unless one aspired to the glamorous on-screen gowns that oozed sexuality in pale photogenic tones. Form and silhouette were the main focus of design and any decorative elements came from rows of buttons, elaborate belt buckles, small embroidery insertions or the print of a fabric. Thirties sleeves are fascinating and feature all manner of cutting and constructive techniques. CREPE. c.1930s.

4 Kate Moss wore a thirties silk dress to the opening night of the *Golden Age of Couture* exhibition at the Victoria and Albert Museum in 2007. The fragile train ripped during the evening when it was stepped on by another guest.

5 Open lace work, often in heavy cotton, was a thirties trend frequently worn over an underslip of contrasting colour to enhance the lace patterning. HANDMADE. COTTON LACE AND VELVET. c.1930s.

1 A devoré blouse relies on ruching and rows of covered buttons for decoration. The slight puff on the upper sleeve helps identify its age. HANDMADE. SILK DEVORÉ. c. 1930s.

2, 3 The elaborate chevron ruching and the frill on the lower sleeve help to give volume to the upper section of both of these velvet evening jackets. Large frontal bows or jabot collars (often referred to today as the 'pussy bow') are another identifying feature of thirties fashion for both day and evening garments. With clever drapery and seaming meaning very little other ornamentation was needed, statement fastening clasps in moulded Bakelite or metals became the focal point of a garment. HANDMADE. SILK VELVET. c. 1930s.

4–7 The elaborate and diminutive evening cape is one of the most sought-after garments from the thirties. Made to be worn over the simple bias-cut evening dress, a short cape or jacket was the focal point of a fashionably plain evening ensemble. Contemporary demand is so high for these rare, intricate and varied garments that there have been countless interpretations from both the high street and couture houses. Sequins from this era were often made from gelatine and should only be washed in cold water or dry-cleaned by a specialist.

4 HANDMADE. SEQUIN ON NETTING. c. 1930s.

5 HANDMADE. SILK CHIFFON AND SEQUIN. c. 1930s.

6 HANDMADE. SILK EMBROIDERY AND SEQUIN. c. 1930s.

7 HANDMADE. EMBROIDERED VELVET. c. 1930s.

1 During the twenties, the careful placement of floral sections was more common than use of a complete all-over floral print. By the thirties, florals were used with gay abandon. HANDMADE. SILK CHIFFON. c. EARLY 1930s.

2 & 5 Floral prints on velvet exhibit an old-fashioned charm that cannot be captured by a modern design, while the oriental scenic print on the jacket in **5** glows with a metallic finish that remains an expensive print today.

2 SILK VELVET. c. EARLY 1930s.

5 METALLIC PRINT ON SILK. c. 1930s.

3 A silk devoré has been printed to resemble an animal skin and is cleverly panelled to allow both the dress and its matching jacket to fall in a cascading 'waterfall' drape. HANDMADE. SILK DEVORÉ. c. 1930s.

4 Before fashion photography became the instant medium it is today, illustrations were used to relay the latest styles from couture houses. Early thirties spring fashions by British designers such as Norman Hartnell and Neil (Bunny) Roger show the era's coordinated look, with matching coats and dresses worn with hats and gloves. Prints and patterns were detailed so that dressmakers and manufacturers were able to interpret the latest styles.

3

4

Motley   Hartnell   Isobel   Neil Roger

5

1

2

3

4

5

1 The mid-thirties saw the revisiting of the milkmaid style of feminine crinolines and soft décolletages of the 19th century. HANDMADE. CREPE. c. 1930s.

2, 3, 5 The thirties enjoyed a grown-up femininity after the youthful flapper-led fashions of the twenties. Chiffon dresses worn for both day and evening wear can still be found, displaying a variety of interesting constructions. Ruffles, soft gathering, layering and tiers of fabric panels are all identifying looks from this romantic decade. The sheer fabrics are enhanced by the choice of a coloured underslip that makes their delicate coloration more pronounced. While original belts and slips have often disappeared over the years, buckles and ribbons can easily be found to replace them. HANDMADE. SILK CHIFFON. c. 1930s.

4 Hollywood actress Ginger Rogers poses in silk lounge pyjamas, the name given to wide-legged trousers worn for casual summer wear or relaxing at home. The all-in-one is given shape with the use of a long narrow scarf worn as a belt.

Gay Clothes For Out-of-Town Wear

Jaeger. Tailored, printed silk dress in shades of orange, pink, mauve, purple, worn with a mauve light wool jacket, straight hanging, purple flecked and purple braided round the collar and front edges

Derry and Toms. Worsted flannel shirty dress, apple green (other colours obtainable), buttoning down front with double pleats, one inverted pleat centre back. Stitched belt, cuffs and pocket edges. One dress of this type is almost a must in every woman's wardrobe

1

Derry and Toms

Jaeger

Burberry. Chestnut brown skirt with a belted top, belt chestnut and white checked jacket, its deep revers, pockets cuffs edged with braid. The one-button fastening is a smart this season

Jaeger. Dull hyacinth linen skirt over a shantung blouse tones of pink, the deeper making a centre panel back a Double-seamed box pleats with threaded-through belt Interesting tucking across the yolk and above the pockets

Jaeger

Burberry

VIA
TRAIN
PLANE
BUS
BOAT
CAR

6823   6806

• Travel decoratively when you can. If you go by plane you can dress up a bit, in 6823. It's a jacket dress, smart as a new penny with its Margot ruff neckline, full shoulders, bosom tucked bodice. For 36 (size 18), 5¼ yards 39-inch crêpe. Designed for sizes 12 to 20; 30 to 42.

• Board a bus in something comfortable and cool—it may be a warm ride. 6810 is the thing, tailored and trim. Under a fitted jacket the dress has cap sleeves, a yoke—for misses 5'4" or less. For 34 (size 16), 3¾ yards 30-inch printed silk. Designed for sizes 12 to 20; 30 to 40.

6825

• Board an air-conditioned train in 6806, a jacket-dress that is soft without being fussy. The dress is short-sleeved, round-collared, the jacket soft-shouldered. For 34 (size 16), 5 yards 39-inch spun rayon for frock and jacket. Designed for Junior Miss 12 to 20; 30 to 38.

• Coast-to-coast in a tailored suit, one of the smartest travelers. 6825 has a fitted single-breasted jacket, a slim skirt, and goes far without pressing. For 36 (size 18), 4⅜ yards 35-inch gabardine. Designed for sizes 12 to 20; 30 to 44. For other views, see page 55.

6810

6810

2

3

1, 2 This illustrated editorial demonstrating practical weekend clothes shows the rise of department stores, which began to excel in off-the-peg garments for busy women, who were filling the roles opened up by the First World War. Jaeger and Burberry, both still household names today, were just some of the British companies that began to cater for the new woman who worked, travelled and ran a home.

3 Thirties daywear was practical and frugally stylish. Belts and buttons were used to mark the return of the natural waistline. Accessories were a must.
HANDMADE. CREPE. c. 1930s.

4 The practice of utilizing scraps of material by cutting out floral patterns and appliquéing them onto contrasting backgrounds is highly attractive, and yet infrequently found, probably due to the technique being labour-intensive at a time when more women were undertaking war work. Here, the cut printed flowers are attached in a pattern of their own, adding emphasis to the puff sleeve. HANDMADE. CREPE. c. 1930s.

5 This late thirties dress features metal studwork in a modernist style that would not look out of place on the eighties catwalk. CREPE. c. LATE 1930s.

1 The jacket of the thirties played an important part in dressing up an otherwise simple skirt or dress. An elaborate jacket could transform an outfit. Finding a thirties jacket with exquisite embroidery, such as this one, does not necessarily mean it is missing its matching dress; it can be worn with the same style ethos as it would have been in the thirties. HANDMADE. EMBROIDERED CREPE. c. 1930s.

2 Dressmaking patterns were illustrated in the same highly detailed manner as magazine editorials. It was important to convey the colour palettes and suggest suitable fabric choices to achieve the right look. Patterns remain an important resource in conveying the mood of the time.

3 The favourite print of the decade was the floral. American fashions can easily be discerned from their advanced print styles and brighter colour palettes. SILK. c. 1930s.

4 A housecoat in a striking Art Deco print passes as a summer dress for today's vintage enthusiast. The heavy front-fastening zip and longer length is the only indication of its original purpose. HANDMADE. COTTON SEERSUCKER. c. 1930s.

5 Thirties dressing had a feminine elegance that is easily worn and is irresistible to today's vintage fashion collectors. HANDMADE. SILK AND VELVET. c. 1930s.

6 The relaxed casualwear that emerged in the twenties became widespread in the thirties and offered an alternative to busy feminine florals. Understated and kind on the eye, the silk and linen dresses are easy to wear today. HANDMADE. SILK. c. 1930s.

1 The 1939 film *Gone with the Wind* was set in the 1860s but the costumes, designed by Walter Plunkett (an authority on period dress), had a far-reaching influence on late thirties and early forties fashions. The green and white crinoline worn by Vivien Leigh for the picnic scene was adapted for dressmaking patterns and reportedly became one of the bestselling pattern designs of the era. This dress shows the influence of the crinoline combined with the tiered lace reveal. HANDMADE. SILK. c. LATE 1930s.

2 A classic thirties day dress: slim-line, mid-calf, button-fronted and belted, with a small puff sleeve. HANDMADE. CREPE. c. 1930s.

3 A 1934 cover of the British magazine *Radio Times* highlights the new role of working women. Broadcasting was one of the few areas where men and women were paid equally, although female voices were still not perceived to be as acceptable as male voices on the radio. The new woman's working wardrobe is reflected in the feminine but practical style of the era.

4 A design by Schiaparelli uses a scarf tied at the waist, apron-style, to give it shape. The dress and scarf set were designed to be versatile, offering a variety of ingenious ways they could be worn.

5 Plaids and checks were a popular print for day dresses. The dresses sat just above the ankle, with hems rising to a more practical length by the start of the Second World War. HANDMADE. COTTON. c. 1930s.

6 Thirties fashion for the beach evolved because the woollen swimwear of the time became shapeless after swimming. The new genre of fashion included playsuits, such as the one shown here, soft flowing trousers and kimonos. HANDMADE. COTTON. c. 1930s.

THE 1940s

FRUGAL FASHION

'FORTIES FASHIONS, WITH STRONG LINES, BEAUTIFUL TAILORING AND FABRICS, FLATTER MOST FIGURES. THE STYLES HAVE BEEN FREQUENTLY REINVENTED AND WE HAVE MORE AUDIENCE INTEREST WHEN WE USE FORTIES COSTUME ON SCREEN THAN ANY OTHER PERIOD.' SHEENA NAPIER, COSTUME DESIGNER, *POIROT AND MARPLE*

. . . .

Fashion from the forties, a favourite of many vintage lovers, is a distinctively chic, sharp silhouette that emerged in the midst of adversity. As wartime rationing throughout Europe and the United States limited the use of fabric and trimmings, and government regulations stipulated collar, pocket and belt sizes, a sophisticated and pared-down styling inadvertently became the look of the decade, and one that many find appealing today. '*Il faut skimp, pour etre chic,*' wrote *Vogue* as rationing was introduced in Britain. Forties style is sought after by those who also remain true to the revival of its spirit, replicating its style with an unyielding faithfulness not seen by those simply donning a seventies maxi or a little black sixties cocktail dress.

Garments from the wartime period conformed to a 'less is more' ethos, and, while many refrained from a glamorized appearance that seemed inappropriate during the horrors of war, it was regarded as a patriotic duty to maintain as attractive an elegance as possible. 'Every woman in Paris is a living propaganda poster,' wrote the editor of *Votre Beauté* on the eve of the German invasion in 1940.

Patriotic garments are some of the most prized by collectors of this decade. Predominantly seen in British and North American fashion, many of the Allied countries produced accessories depicting government slogans. In a continuing effort to boost morale, catchphrases such as 'V for Victory' and 'There will always be an England' were combined with imagery depicting soldiers, airplanes and the instruments of war on printed fabric. These textiles were handmade into dresses and shirts, as well as being used on customized bags and shoes; home-knitted garments incorporated the colours and flags of Allied countries; and ever-popular scarves made an ideal canvas for illustrative messages. These garments are attractive, rare and highly collectable, and therefore can command high prices. Fashion became

1 The practicality of this handmade wool suit has been given more aesthetic appeal with the addition of rouleau loop bows and covered buttons. HANDMADE. WOOL. c. 1940s.

2 Utility clothing in the United States was not as restrictive as that of Europe. A patriotic outfit glamorizes American savings bonds, introduced as a way of reducing inflation. The bonds were sold to finance military operations, yielding a small return after ten years to those who invested. After the bombing of Pearl Harbor in 1941 their name was changed to war bonds. Top agencies, as well as the War Advertising Council, created advertising campaigns to support the scheme.

3 A half-used British clothing coupon booklet. Rationing came into effect in Britain in 1941, when the allotted number of clothing stamps for each man, woman and child was sixty-six for one year. Some typical examples of a coupon's worth in 1941: a non-wool skirt could be bought with four coupons, trousers with eight, a dress with seven and a pair of stockings with three. Coupons were submitted as part-payment, along with cash. Items exempt from rationing were belts, hats, blackout fabric and lace.

1 A crepe dress bearing the common CC41 label of wartime Britain (see **2**). The government scheme was introduced as a way of controlling both price abuse and the amount of fabric used by manufacturers, although many women saw utility clothing as being substandard. The white rickrack trim on black here creates a cost- and material-efficient design statement, but the double collar is an unusual addition for a time of such strict control of fabric use. MOSS CREPE. c. 1941.

2 A collection of British CC41 labels from garments ranging from an apron to an evening dress. There is debate between fashion historians as to the correct terminology for these labels, whether Controlled Commodity 1941 or Civilian Clothing 1941, although advertising from the era suggests the former is correct. The first label to be introduced was a design by Reginald Shipp – an Art Deco crescent combined with the number 41. Much discussion also surrounds the later 'dinner plate' label – the full circle with two vertical lines either side. Some consider this to be a label used for utility clothing that was exported, although few garments bearing the label have been found outside of Britain. Others consider it the luxury label used to signify more costly garments, intended to remove the stigma attached to utility clothing. This had also been attempted when the British Board of Trade invited notable designers such as Norman Hartnell, Bianca Mosca and Hardy Amies to design a range of clothes within the government stipulations. These garments, bearing both the designer's name and the utility label, are highly sought after today.

a tool of propaganda, and fashion magazines even gave colours patriotic names such as French Soil Beige, Maginot Line Blue, Flag Red and Royal Air Force Blue.

Designers responded by creating a fashionable look in tune with the austere mood. Military chic became a recurring theme. Knife-edged pleated skirts (before pleating became restricted in the UK in 1942) were worn with both double- and single-breasted jackets. Soldier style was echoed with sharp tailoring and the use of buttons as a featuring trim (buttons were rationed and those used were frequently plastic or covered in the material of the garment, seldom in the metal or leather needed for wartime manufacture). The newly introduced metal zips that replaced the coloured Bakelite slide fastener of the thirties were short-lived, and rows of small buttons or hooks and eyes are the identifying fastening method for many garments of this time. In February 1942, the British government brought in a standard label for all civilian clothes that were made to the stipulated minimum requirements. This was an attempt to control escalating prices and restrict frivolous use of much-needed materials, while ensuring that manufactured garments were of a high quality and everyone, not just the wealthy, could wear clothes of a reasonable standard.

The label 'CC41' is generally believed to have stood for 'Controlled Commodity 1941' and, while the label can be an easy way to date clothing from the early forties today, it is thought that many people removed it in an attempt to hide the fact that their garment was not couture or even designer. A later label, the 'double elevens' (also referred to as the 'dinner plate' label because of the look of the design), is thought to have been used from around 1945, as rationing continued in Britain well after the end of the war. Some consider it to represent better quality, more expensive and slightly more elaborate utility garments, although this is the subject of debate between fashion historians and has never been proven.

While many theatres were forced to close, audiences rushed to the cinema for the pleasure offered by its escapist glamour and Hollywood became the source for many new styles. The cinema and its costumes were not exempt from rationing and, devoid of feminine frills and lace and superfluous embroidery, it required ingenuity to create new styles. Belted trench coats with oversized revered collars referencing army coats was a significant trend popularized by cinematic costume. First worn in 1928 by Greta Garbo

in *A Woman of Affairs*, they were subsequently seen on Marlene Dietrich, Lauren Bacall and Ingrid Bergman in the acclaimed film noir of forties cinema, each star giving a sensuality to the masculine garment.

'Fashions do not die because of wars... Many of the best of them are created by war's necessities,' said American *Vogue*'s editor Edna Woolman Chase in March 1942, and, despite the shortages and restrictions of wartime fashions, the forties saw key looks that transformed looks in the decades to follow. Although clothing made in the United States was subject to L-85 regulation, thanks to its broader manufacturing industry, the ready-to-wear market continued to grow and innovative designers such as Claire McCardell created chic and casual designs for everyday wear. Rationing and shortages affected designers in the United States less than their European counterparts, especially France where most of the Parisian couture houses closed during the war. In the forties, the sportswear and casual styles of American fashion began to take root – easy styling that eventually filtered through to Europe. McCardell's influence endured beyond the forties and after her early death in 1958.

In this period, the suit became a wardrobe staple transformed through innovative cutting, set-in panels and shapely, nipped-in silhouettes fashioned in alternative

2

1 Checks, in particular tartans and plaids, were used as an alternative to the busy florals and subdued colours of the forties. Checks of all types were especially favoured in the United States, commonly used for sportswear and even eveningwear. HANDMADE. SILK. c.1940s.

fabrics of rayon crepe, velvet and jersey. Such was the stylish result that the cuts became inspiration for seventies fashions. The shoulder pads of the era, already used in thirties fashion, grew to epic proportions, reflecting a decade that required confident, defiant style. Hollywood costume designer Adrian popularized the square shoulder, a result of his attempts to add definition to Joan Crawford's wardrobe, but Schiaparelli, who had been championing them since the early thirties, accused him of imitating her innovation. Whoever can claim their invention, shoulder pads retained their presence in following decades, returning with a vengeance in the eighties. Trousers as acceptable wear for women were arguably the true rule breaker to emerge from a decade of hardship. Australian, British and US government clothing consisted of durable material that needed styling and adapting to make it look attractive. Dungarees put on as protective wear for factory work, all-in-one siren suits (warm, zip-up overalls that could be hastily pulled on over clothes during an air raid) that were the forerunner of the seventies jumpsuit, or denim jeans adopted from cowboy westerns and championed by American college students are all style legacies from this decade.

Towards the end of the decade, rationing in Britain still hampered any real change in fashion. The United States, with an advanced manufacturing industry, was less affected by fabric shortages and debt, and became prominent in the ready-to-wear market, while Hollywood costume designers continued to perpetuate a glamour imitated among the glitterati of the big cities. Schiaparelli had fled to New York and American eveningwear designers such as Hattie Carnegie and Norman Norell began to have an international presence. 'For half a century, women have treasured their Norells as if they were emeralds or Renoirs. They wear them lovingly for years, content that they are dressed in the best money can buy. Then pack them away respectfully because they can't bear to part with them,' observed Bernadine Morris of the *New York Times*. But for the fashionable women of Europe, fashion had become stagnant and women were ready for the arrival of Christian Dior's triumphant New Look in 1947 that was to change the silhouette of the following decade.

Unlike vintage from other decades, where clothes are picked for the beauty of an individual piece, the forties is unique in how its striking styles only work as a complete look – a visual testament to the ingenuity of this era.

3

4

2 An emphasis on the shoulders is an identifying forties attribute. Buttons, embroidery, cuffed and puffed short sleeves were all common details. RAYON. c. 1940s.

3 Lauren Bacall wears a tailored suit from the late forties. The elaborate breast trim and double turned-back cuff are signifying details of post-utility design.

4 The bolero was a feature of both thirties and forties fashion, worn for evening ensembles and daytime jackets. A vintage bolero is frequently used as part of a contemporary ensemble, worn without its original dress. HANDMADE. CREPE. c. EARLY 1940s.

1

2

3

More smart women wear Gold (Red) Cross Shoes than any other brand of fine footwear in the world. Which doesn't surprise you. For what other shoe offers so much...in brilliant young styling...in beyond-its-price quality...in fit so "just for you" that it keeps the envied swing of youth in your step?"

GOLD RED CROSS SHOES

AMERICA'S UNCHALLENGED SHOE VALUE

*Each new style is Fit-Tested. Handmade originals are actually worn, walked in, checked, tested, Re-perfected before you can buy any new Gold Cross style. Shoes illustrated: A. The Cocktail Anklet; B. The Marquita; C. The Charm; on the girl—The Mantology.

The United States Shoe Corp., Cincinnati, O. Gold Cross Shoes are manufactured and distributed in England by Somervell Bros., Ltd., in Australia by "Gold Cross Shoes" Ltd., in South Africa by Edboth (S. A.), Ltd., in New Zealand by Duckworth, Turner and Co., Ltd.

4

1, 2 North American forties vintage fashion is always easy to identify by its vibrant colouring compared to the more sober tones of European countries. The peplum and hem length indicates early forties styling, while the interesting yoke, created by attaching narrow rolled strips of fabric to the netting with an overstitch, uses a technique found in both the thirties and forties. HANDMADE. RAYON. c. EARLY 1940s.

3 An American magazine advertisement for Red Cross shoes depicts an early forties dress with a layered skirt. This type of skirt shortened over the decade to become the popular peplum style.

4 Both the soft floral print and flowing cut of this day dress are indicative of transitional thirties to forties styling. The oversized shoulder pads were used in the late thirties although they are a feature most associated with forties sophistication. RAYON. c. 1940s.

5 An early forties dress by US label Cirilo uses a scarf to create the front detail. The mass-produced scarf is signed by Jean Peltier, a well-known French artist who also designed for scarf companies. The detail may have been added to the dress after purchase, as it would not have been economically viable for the manufacturer to use scarves to embellish a dress. CIRILO. RAYON. c. 1940s.

6 An advertisement for Forstmann, a United States fabric company that did not actually manufacture clothing although their label can often be found inside garments, alongside that of the designer.

3

4

1 The stripes of this jersey fabric from the United States have been placed to display the considered pattern cutting of the forties at its best. This detailed cutting was an inspiration for designers of the seventies. HANDMADE. SILK JERSEY. c. 1940s.

2, 3 The 'tea dress' of the forties remains one of the most popular garments of vintage fashion for its easy-to-wear, nostalgic style. HANDMADE. RAYON CREPE. c. 1940s.

4 The subtle hand-quilting stitch on this forties dress brings a plain tea dress to life. HANDMADE. CREPE. c. 1940s.

1 The elaborate ribbon embroidery indicates this garment comes from the United States. Such trimming would not have been allowed on a European garment of the time. MOSS CREPE. c. 1940s.

2 For lovers of vintage fashion one of the most interesting design attributes to emerge from the time of 'make do and mend' was an interesting combination of fabrics and patterns. A crepe top, probably the top half of a dress, has been joined to the bottom half of another dress to create a beautiful mix of floral and stripe. HANDMADE. RAYON AND CREPE. c. 1940s.

3 While zips were highlighted in thirties fashion, their use was restricted during wartime and buttons once again became used for trimmings. HANDMADE. COTTON. c. 1940s.

4 The blouses that became mainstays in an era of suits and trousers are sought after by today's fashionistas. This silk blouse with fine pin-tucking would create a statement when combined with contemporary fashion. VALERIE BLOUSE, STYLED BY MALCOLM ROWE. SILK. c. 1940s.

5 Placing elaborate pieces of embroidery on an otherwise plain dress was one of the many resourceful methods used to enhance an ensemble. HANDMADE. MOSS CREPE. c. 1940s.

1 This sophisticated hand-sewn evening dress has beaded shoulder straps that loop to catch the front bodice fabric. The dress displays transitional thirties to early forties characteristics, such as the embellished bodice and the use of the later, more sombre dyed crepes and rayons, such as this 'Air Force Blue'. HANDMADE. CREPE. c. EARLY 1940s.

2 A German evening jacket is paired with seventies Biba black trousers, identical in width and displaying the high waist styling of forties design. ELFRIEDE RUDIGER RAYON EVENING JACKET. c. 1940s. WORN WITH BIBA SYNTHETIC CREPE TROUSERS. c. 1970s.

3 Founded in the United States in the thirties, Lilli Ann made such elegantly cut suits and coats that their collections from the forties and fifties retain a fashionable presence still sought today.

4 The sunray pattern was seen in both embroidered and beaded embellishments throughout the twenties, thirties and forties. The label of this dress indicates the consortium of manufacturers and designers founded in 1940 with the aim of making New York the centre of fashion in the United States. NEW YORK CREATION, NEW YORK INSTITUTE. WOOL CREPE. c. 1940s.

5 This crepe evening blouse is embellished with floral sequin motifs that can also be seen on shoes and sometimes bags of the era. Before the war, Parisian couture unquestionably set the styles followed the world over. Under German occupation many fashion houses closed down and even French *Vogue* halted production. Hollywood began to generate its own styles during the thirties and, by the forties, American designers made an international impact with pared-down styling and mix-and-match separates, then a new fashion concept. SEQUINNED CREPE. c. 1940s.

3

4

5

VOGUE

Paris
Spring
Collections

Preview:
American
Summer Fashions

Dagmar

Incorporating Vanity Fair · April 1, 1947 Price 35 Cents   10 Cents In Canada

4 The April 1947 cover of American *Vogue* shows the immediate impact of Dior's 'New Look', introduced that season. It also highlights the continuing importance given to fashion illustrators and their role in conveying the style of a new fashion. By the forties *Vogue* covers were frequently photographic, yet Dior's trend-setting new silhouette was introduced with an illustration.

5 A 1947 advertisement for Swan & Edgar, a British department store dating back to the early 19th century. The advert illustrates the rationing regulations that remained in place after the Second World War ended.

1 Dior's 1947 'New Look' collection changed an austere, streamlined silhouette to the full-skirted fashion that continued to be popular throughout the fifties. COTTON. c. LATE 1940s.

2 The sailor collar has been borrowed by every decade. COTTON. c. 1940s.

3 This dress illustrates the transition from forties to fifties fashion. The full skirts of the fifties combine with the shoulder pads and the double collar associated with the forties. RHONA ROY. FLOCKED SYNTHETIC SATIN. c. LATE 1940s.

THE SKETCH, October 15, 1947

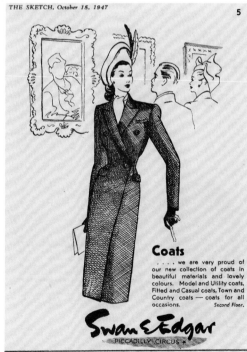

Coats
. . . . we are very proud of our new collection of coats in beautiful materials and lovely colours. Model and Utility coats, Fitted and Casual coats, Town and Country coats — coats for all occasions.   *Second Floor.*

Swan & Edgar
PICCADILLY CIRCUS

Swan & Edgar Ltd., Piccadilly Circus, London, W.1.   Regent 1616.

THE 1950s

LA DOLCE VITA

1

'IT WAS THE TIME OF LA DOLCE VITA. I THINK THIS ACTUALLY HELPED WITH THE AMERICAN MARKET, BECAUSE THE UNITED STATES AND ITALY HAD UNDERSTOOD EACH OTHER SINCE THE BEGINNING OF THEIR SHARED AFFINITY FOR THE CINEMA, THE SWEET THINGS AND THE COMFORT OF LIFE, THEIR TASTE FOR LUXURY AND MODERNITY.'

CHRISTIAN LACROIX

. . . .

The jubilance of post-war fashion was a well-documented sartorial response to a mood of international elation and, despite continued rationing, a gradual economic upturn allowed a stagnant fashion industry to once again follow the pace and direction set by the houses of French couture.

The celebrated 1947 'Corolle' collection ('corolle' meaning a circlet of flower petals in French) of Christian Dior was not dubbed the 'New Look' by American *Vogue* in vain. It dramatically changed the silhouette of fifties fashion and, after an initially mixed reaction from the public, Dior's extravagant designs were adopted by women the world over. After a decade of conservative frugal fashion, the fifties were ready for glamour. 'I have designed flower women,' said Dior of his soft, feminine forms.

The fifties was an era of print: the painterly florals, illustrative novelty designs and technology-inspired atomic geometrics make garments of this decade easily recognizable. Flowers bloomed on prints over silks and satins, cottons and even the new light wispy nylons that dried overnight, allowing women the freedom of affordable and washable clothes. With the continued post-war scarcity of silk, women welcomed the new printed nylons pioneered by Zika Ascher.

Dior himself believed that fashion should not stand still and introduced, in rapid succession, collections of contrasting proportions that challenged the preceding silhouettes. His autumn/winter 1951 collection, 'Longue', was followed in sequence by 'Sinueuse', 'Profilée', 'Tulipe', 'Vivante', 'Muguet', 'H-line', 'A-line', 'Y-line' and 'Flêche', each named after the shape inspiring the collection. It wasn't just Dior attracting attention. The Parisian collections of

1 Familiarization with the distinctive colour blends of each decade helps to identify a garment's age. Rich yellows and bottle greens are one combination frequently seen in fifties fashion fabrics. HANDMADE. COTTON. c. 1950s.

2, 3 Christian Dior's 'flower women' chimed perfectly with the mood of post-war fifties fashion. Floral fabrics were used everywhere and frills, flounces and petal-shaped details, such as the décolletage on dress **3**, unmistakably identify the era. Floral styling re-emerged during the eighties, with a full-skirted, fitted-bodice look that emulated the fifties original. The difference can be ascertained by looking for the shorter-length skirts, smoother finish to fabrics and 'tighter' print style of the floral textiles of the later decade. HANDMADE. SILK. c. EARLY 1950s.

2

3

1, 2 Two fifties silhouettes created in black and white broderie anglaise. Although both styles were fashionable in the early fifties, the pencil silhouette is a later design. HANDMADE. COTTON. c. 1950s.

3 Floral suits were the height of fifties fashion and are often worn separately by today's fashionista, as both jacket and skirt complement a modern ensemble. SILK. c. 1950s.

Jacques Fath, Givenchy, Balenciaga and Nina Ricci had international manufacturers rushing to Paris to observe their new look and invest in licensed patterns, sometimes even to smuggle home garments to copy.

At the same time, a new market that had been growing steadily since the late twenties blossomed in an affluent post-war United States. Focused on relaxed ready-to-wear separates for a younger market, it followed in the path of the already established Claire McCardell and placed an increasing importance on individual garments, blouses and tops, knitwear and jackets worn on their own, not as a coordinating part of an ensemble, in the so-called 'sweater dressing'. The new trend for casualwear became an alternative, internationally acceptable way to dress and provides many of the vintage garments worn from the fifties today. Couture designers responded with the creation of affordable diffusion lines not always sold under their own label. Shoes and bags were added to ready-to-wear collections and, by mid-decade, nearly every fashion house of note had marketed at least one perfume. Perfume became a marketing tool with considerable financial rewards that helped to sustain the expensive couture collections.

The decade is one of contrasts, whose modes suited both the curvaceous and the sinuous figure. The longer elegant 'pencil'-shaped skirt worn throughout the decade, an alternative to the full-circle skirts that required layers of petticoats, is often mistaken for the shorter cocktail length of the sixties. Full-circle skirts could be belted and sophisticated, or dressed down in the casual styling of the preppy trend that borrowed the 'boyfriend' college jumper and jacket, not just the prerogative of today's high street. Both the pencil and the full-circle skirt required a fashionably small waist, achieved with the foundation garments that women had been free of for three decades. The contrast applied to prints, too: polka dots were juxtaposed with sophisticated stripes; feminine florals contrasted with textural tweeds; while the chic black and white combinations of dog's-tooth, hound's-tooth and the Prince of Wales check were popularized by Dior.

This was an era of designs that have stood the test of time, including Capri pants, the elegant three-quarter-length trousers that earned their name from Emilio Pucci's Capri boutique patronized by the jet set, while ornate beaded cardigans worn for evening was a style brought to the forefront of fashion by American designer Mainbocher, who

3

used English cashmere as a base for his embellishments. It also saw the emergence of the 'prom' dress, an Americanism for the teenage evening dresses worn to high school balls; ballet flats, as designed by Salvatore Ferragamo for Audrey Hepburn to wear in the 1954 film *Sabrina* and a style also popularized by Brigitte Bardot in Roger Vadim's 1956 *Et Dieu … créa la femme*; and the notable mid-century classic, the Chanel 'box suit', designed in defiant reaction to the return of the corseted waistline. Even the decade's kitsch motifs such as poodle, automobile, ice cream and cocktail glass prints are constantly revisited by designers of the 21st century, such as in Prada's spring/summer 2012 collection.

It was in this decade that Italy began to exert a fashionable influence, enjoying its freedom from the fascist regime. With a heritage in luxury clothing and with a fabric industry that was unaffected by the war, the likes of Roberto Capucci, Contessa Simonetta Visconti (Simonetta) and Emilio Pucci paved the way for a successful ready-to-wear industry that is more often associated with Armani and Versace in the seventies. Italian cities and resorts became favoured holiday destinations, while films, such as 1953's *Roman Holiday,* were highly influential, not only in creating the stylish mood of the time but also in promoting new styles and emerging designers. Italian film director Federico Fellini was inspired to use Spanish designer Cristobel Balenciaga's 'Sack dress' in his 1960 film *La Dolce Vita*. This design was controversial because, unlike every other fifties silhouette, it did not celebrate the hourglass shape. Fellini felt this new silhouette made women look gorgeous, while hiding what might be 'squalor and solitude inside'.

The icons of fifties cinema, including Sophia Loren, Gina Lollobrigida, Marilyn Monroe, Elizabeth Taylor and Grace Kelly, radiated the glamour of the decade, utilizing its photogenic fashions to create their on- and off-screen persona. A flourishing women's magazine industry continued to report on 'Hollywood style' and the latest direction of Parisian couture. But, reflecting the shift in emphasis to a ready-to-wear market, even the elite of fashion journalism began to offer layouts of affordable and obtainable clothes that were also, most importantly, desirable. These international titles, many of which can still be found today, give an invaluable insight into the era's styling and, while they can command high prices, allow the reader to obtain a unique working knowledge of the era.

1 A tartan dress and jacket by Christian Dior. The label is numbered, marking it as a couture garment, although boutiques were also known to add their own numbers in a similar style, possibly to emulate the mark of couture. CHRISTIAN DIOR. SILK. c. 1950s.

2 The quality and cut of the US label Lilli Ann make their garments highly sought after, though they command high prices. Owner Adolph Shuman, who founded the company in San Francisco in 1933, sourced fabrics from French factories struggling after the Second World War. His action saved many of them from bankruptcy and he was given several international awards. LILLI ANN. WOOL. c. 1950s.

3 The start of the fifties saw two distinct silhouettes: the long, elegant pencil shape and the full-skirted style needing petticoats and corsetry to achieve the look. PRINTED SILK GROSGRAIN. c. 1950s.

4 Marilyn Monroe exhibits a rare informality on the set of *Niagara*, her first major role. The pale blue suit was one of a number of outfits shot as wardrobe tests and has a vulnerability not seen in the costumes she ultimately wore in the 1953 film. Although Monroe was known for her showstopping gowns, in reality she 'dressed for comfort', according to Jill Taylor, costume designer of *My Week with Marilyn*. Her breezy portrait has a contemporary quality, suggesting how easily fifties tailoring can be worn today.

1 An oriental influence on eveningwear and casual daywear became significant again during the fifties in a more refined style than in the decadent twenties. Shirts are easy to find today, an indication of their popularity at the time, but trousers that fit are more difficult to locate. The term 'dead stock' refers to old shop stock that remains unworn, as these trousers are, and will often carry the original label. RAYON BLOUSE AND SILK TROUSERS. c. 1950s.

2 Jonelle is the brand name for fashion and goods produced in-house by the British department store John Lewis from 1937. The watercolour floral on this dress and matching jacket was a highly fashionable print style for both day and evening wear. JONELLE. GLAZED COTTON. c. 1950s.

3 An illustration for mid-fifties summerwear shows the lingering formality of high-fashion holiday clothing, even when more relaxed, youthful styles of leisurewear were becoming fashionable.

4 A handmade cocktail dress is embellished with a piece of printed silk velvet probably dating to an earlier decade and showing the continued enterprise of the home dressmaker. The attached overhung bodice is a distinctive fifties look, used for both day and formal wear. HANDMADE. SILK AND VELVET. c. EARLY 1950s.

5 The blue plums on this fifties day dress are indicative of mid-fifties textile designs. The penchant for fruit and vegetable prints was never as pronounced in any other era; recent replicas have been seen in both high street collections and those of notable designers, such as the spring/summer 2012 collection from Dolce & Gabbana. 'MISS POLLY' BY POLLY PECK. COTTON. c. LATE 1950s/EARLY 1960s.

1 A cocktail dress by Carnegie of London – not to be confused with the renowned American designer, Hattie Carnegie. CARNEGIE OF LONDON. SILK GROSGRAIN. c. 1950s.

2 This cotton dress by British store Marks & Spencer, under their St Michael's label. They started introducing garments into their stores in 1928. ST. MICHAEL. COTTON. c. 1950s.

3 Italian chic – modern, understated elegance in a Mediterranean colour palette – was imitated from London to New York mid-decade. SATINIZED COTTON. c. 1950s.

4 An industrially knitted bolero with rounded front and three-quarter-length sleeves that was a fashionable look for both day and evening wear. SYNTHETIC YARN. c. MID-1950s.

5 Atomic prints (the geometric style influenced by atomic science) make for easy identification of fifties design. It was a style – introduced to furnishings and interiors in the 1951 Festival of Britain – that filtered through to fashion by mid-century. HANDMADE. COTTON. c. MID-1950s.

Horrockses Fashions
in Fine Cotton

1–6 Horrockses dresses were priced at the equivalent of some women's entire weekly wages, but the purchase was seen as an investment in a style that would last. Worn by everyone from the royal princesses to secretaries, the dresses were in their heyday in the fifties. Advertisements proclaimed 'the cotton gown which makes a girl feel like a queen', and the company received a royal warrant during the sixties. Some of the fabric designs are quite collectable, as the company commissioned well-known artists such as Henry Moore, Eduardo Paolozzi, Alastair Morton and Graham Sutherland. Illustrator Pat Albeck, who continues to work today, was one of their key textile designers. HORROCKSES FASHIONS. COTTON. c. 1950s.

1

2

*The season for DAKS**

3

4

This summer, when the occasion calls for the casual approach — make it in DAKS. More than mere comfort, DAKS offer superb man-tailoring; sleek slim lines — the famous sure-fit waist band. In worsteds, linens, pinpoints, tropicals, gaberdines, doeskins, corduroys in a wealth of colours — and black barathea. Waist sizes 24"–31". From £5.19.9

Worthy of DAKS — tailored blouse of finest poplin, in blue, green, yellow, white. 34", 36", 38". long sleeves from £4.2.6; short sleeves from £3.5.0

Simpson PICCADILLY

5

6

7

8

9

10

1, 4 The fifties is often referred to as the decade that 'invented' the teenager. Teen styles were adopted by working youth who rejected the formality of their elders' style. Consequently this era has an abundance of separates: blouses, jackets and skirts designed as stand-alone styles and remaining inexpensive pieces.

2 An illustration for Daks (which later became known as Simpsons of Piccadilly), a British label dating back to 1894. Established as a menswear tailor, they introduced womenswear in the mid-20th century and the masculine styling of their women's trousers is a throwback to practical wartime clothing.

3 A still from the 1958 film *Bonjour Tristesse* shows the relaxed informal fashions that had not really been apparent in previous decades. The style and cut of David Niven's trousers can be seen in the style of trousers adapted for feminine sportswear in the Daks advertisement (**2**).

5–8 The full-circle skirt, otherwise known as a dirndl, was internationally ubiquitous. Inspired by Dior's 1947 'New Look', the style was widely worn by teenagers, as its movement was particularly suited to the new rock 'n' roll dance craze. Cut from a full circle, the skirt used a wide volume of fabric and was as popular with home dressmakers as with manufacturers, including British high street store Marks & Spencer, as shown in **7** in winter tartans. Their international

popularity is seen in the three illustrated skirts that come from Britain (**5**), the USA (**6**) and Italy (**8**).

5 HANDMADE. COTTON WITH ENGLISH ROSE PRINT. c. 1950s.

6 COTTON WITH FRENCH NEWSPAPER PRINT. c. 1950s.

8 ANNA GIOVANNOZZI. APPLIQUÉD SILK RIBBON. c. 1950s.

9, 10 Two industrially knitted tops in fine double jersey illustrate the introduction of jacquard patterning that was to become such a trend during the sixties. SYNTHETIC. c. LATE 1950s.

1 Style icon of the forties and fifties Gene Tierney poses in a striped playsuit, a trend that has re-emerged on the contemporary high street.

2, 3 This plaid playsuit was designed to be worn with a skirt when more decorum was required. The chic French piece would be worn as Gene Tierney demonstrates after swimming or relaxing, part of the new leisurewear market. JACQUES HEIM. COTTON AND SATEEN. c. EARLY 1950s.

4 The British manufacturer Samuel Sherman produced under his own name as well as Dollyrockers (during the late sixties and seventies) and Sambo, which concentrated on cotton shirtwaisters in the successful style of Horrockses Fashions. SAMBO. COTTON. c. 1950s.

5, 6 Bottle green and black is a distinctive colour combination of the fifties, while dresses often feature oversized, round, centrally opening buttons and matching belts, many of which have been lost over time but can easily be replaced.

5 WOOL. c. 1950s.

6 HORROCKSES FASHIONS. TAFFETA. c. 1950s.

7 This dress uses Italian colours as inspired by the films of the era such as *La Dolce Vita* and *Roman Holiday*. HANDMADE. LINEN. c. 1950s.

The woman in jersey wears

JAEGER
JAEGER
JAEGER
JAEGER
JAEGER

Go to your nearest Jaeger or Jaeger · Jaeger House Regent Street W.1

FORSTMANN
100% VIRGIN WOOL

FORSTMANN WOOLEN COMPANY
PASSAIC, N.J.

1, 4 Knitwear became more sophisticated after the hand-knit kaleidoscopic patterning of forties 'make do and mend'. These two machine-knitted coats, beautiful in their simplicity, would blend easily with jeans and T-shirts of the 21st century.

1 MOHAIR. c. 1950s.

4 BOUCLÉ WOOL. c. 1950s.

2 This advertisement for Jaeger shows the emergence of the knitted 'sweater dress', a style that retained popularity during the early sixties.

3 A fifties advertisement for a wool 'swagger' coat, the full-backed style that was usually single-breasted. The fabric by American company Forstmann is dyed in one of the vibrant hues not uncommon in this era, particularly in mohair.

5 Simple, oversized buttons were a feature of many fifties coats and jackets. The neck bow indicates the coat dates from the cusp of the late fifties/early sixties. SILK. c. LATE 1950s.

4

5

THE 1960s

MINIS AND MAXIS

'WHAT WAS DIFFERENT … WAS THAT THE SIXTIES DIDN'T DO A REVIVAL OF ANYTHING; THAT WAS THE MAJOR DIFFERENCE. YOU FELT A FRESHNESS THAT WAS EXCITING… IT WAS AN ENERGY DRIVEN BY A BOHEMIAN WORLD.'

DAVID HOCKNEY

. . . .

The sixties was a rare moment of cultural history: an exciting collision of art, music, social revolution and fashion. A youthful workforce, wielding wage packets that were larger than those of the previous generation, created a new market of fashion-conscious buyers and a freedom of sartorial choice unseen before. The decade also saw the start of the phenomenon now a source of inspiration found in every city: streetwear. For the first time Parisian couture designers, hitherto the leaders of Western fashion, had to take note of individual style and fast-moving trends emerging from international fashion capitals. At the forefront was London, a melting pot of photographers, musicians and graduates of the British art school system unique in its teaching practices. Working class was seen as the new cool. Couture was worn by those who could afford it and imitated by those who couldn't. Aside from the well-paid stars of stage and screen, it was a system catering to wealthy older women and their daughters. Now their daughters had their own careers, the birth control pill and a mass production system that allowed fashions to respond to new ideas with a speed not been seen or needed before. Style was exploratory and a new discerning generation demanded forward-thinking fashions that were very different from the demure modes of their elegant elder peers.

Music, art and fashion interlinked to create a new culture, epitomized by the renowned informal boutique shopping experience, kick-started by independent designers such as Mary Quant in the fifties and Barbara Hulanicki, whose first Biba store opened in 1964 in a madeover chemist's shop. Individual taste was given scope to interpret trends and make unique style statements, giving real meaning to the term 'fashion stylist'. Boutiques stayed open ad hoc, a party atmosphere prevailing until the early hours, as consumers shopped listening to the newest music and the celebrities of art, pop and rock mingled with young

1, 3 Acid brights, along with monochrome black and white and sophisticated café au lait combinations, were the colour palette of the sixties. Jewelry-like embellishments were a common detail of evening and cocktail wear. CREPE. c. MID-1960s.

2 Lesley Hornby, commonly known as Twiggy, personified the elfin look of the sixties. The chic, understated pinafore, jumper and shirtdress were streamlined, childlike and sexless – everything that the fifties had

not been. The contrast between the two silhouettes of mid-fifties and mid-sixties could not have been more different, yet both are equally wearable today and both inspire contemporary designs. Note the scarf tied on the handbag, a trend that continues today, albeit with a vintage scarf.

3

4

4 Kaftans were introduced
as a bohemian fashion in the
later sixties and continued
in popularity well into the
seventies. The loud Pop Art-style
print helps to date this to the
sixties, as later kaftans used
more fluid, ethnic patterning in
keeping with the hippy spirit of
the end of the decade. SYNTHETIC.
c. 1960s.

1

shoppers all seeking forward-looking fashion that broke with convention. The independent shops of the King's Road and Carnaby Street, stocking designs inspired by the sophisticated Italian culture, sat side-by-side with emporiums full of antique, handmade and customized clothing. London's Antiquarius, I Was Lord Kitchener's Valet and Granny Takes a Trip were havens of new/old ideas. In New York's Paraphernalia, meanwhile, images of the garments were projected onto the minimalist walls of the interior. The designs by Betsey Johnson, Deanna Littell and Diana Dew fused Pop Art with fashion and were sold in the store among international imports including Quant, Foale & Tuffin and Paco Rabanne. Patronized by Andy Warhol and his muse, Edie Sedgwick, the boutique was the launchpad for fledgling designers such as Johnson who went on to create fashion empires. London's Quorum, owned by Alice Pollock, did the same for British style mavericks Ossie Clark, Celia Birtwell and Betty Jackson.

A new type of fashion show epitomized the new mood. Instead of what was previously a disciplined, sedate experience, designers such as Quant and Clark sent their models dancing down the catwalks in uncoordinated displays of beautiful clothes, movement and attitude. Clark, whose shows were frequented by David Hockney, the Beatles and the Rolling Stones, refused to let the press sit in his front row and was also the first designer to put black models on the runway.

While the energy of London boutiques caused worldwide ripples, the artisans of French fashion responded to the dramatic change by forging their own futurist innovations. Yves Saint Laurent was one of the first to respond to Parisian 'beatnik' street style. His last collection for Dior in 1960 elevated the black leather jackets, caps, berets and black turtleneck jumpers seen around the artistic quarters of the Left Bank to couture status, a move resulting in his dismissal. He continued to innovate under his own name and is credited as being the first to make high-end ready-to-wear available to a wider market, opening his Rive Gauche boutique (named after the Left Bank home of the store) in 1966, while his 'Le Smoking' suit was imitated the world over.

The pioneers of the minimal, modernist trend that typifies sixties style command huge sums in the contemporary market. The iconic designs of the decade by Mary Quant, Rudi Gernreich, André Courrèges, Pierre Cardin, Louis Féraud, Cristóbal Balenciaga and Paco Rabanne paved the way for a futuristic style emulated by designers everywhere. Box shapes, double-breasted pea jackets, short A-line skirts and dresses, geometric shapes and prints, colour-blocked fabrics and cut-out shapes define these looks, which concurred with the decade's space race and sci-fi films such as *Barbarella*. Many of the film's costumes were designed by Paco Rabanne, who shaped fashions in metal and plastic to create a sixties vision of the future.

Gradually the public figures frequently in the limelight for their designer wardrobes, notably Jackie Kennedy (Onassis) and Grace Kelly, began to wear less formal clothes in response to the prevailing mood of fashion. Kennedy, who was dressed by the eminent names of French and American fashion, is credited with helping to popularize the brightly patterned homemade shift dresses of Lilly Pulitzer. These designs, originating from the colourful dresses Pulitzer wore to hide spill stains from her Californian juice bar, became a huge success. Simultaneously, 'fruit' shades became an international trend for both fashion and make-up, with lime green, lemon yellow, mango and strawberry pink used

1 1968 ready-to-wear designs by André Courrèges. An engineer before he trained in fashion and textiles, Courrèges was determined to make his designs affordable and accessible. As well as being the first to make longer boots and trousers acceptable for feminine daywear he, along with Mary Quant and John Bates, is credited with promoting the mini skirt.

2 The 1967 film *Two for the Road* is a who's who of sixties fashion. Audrey Hepburn's wardrobe as a young wife with a troubled marriage was created by Mary Quant, Paco Rabanne, Ken Scott, André Courrèges, Foale & Tuffin and many others, all contained in Louis Vuitton luggage. Hepburn was advised

by the film's director to have a change from Givenchy, who normally designed her screen wardrobe. This dress is by Paco Rabanne and is made from plastic strung together with fine chains. It can be seen in the Riverside Museum in Glasgow.

3 Polly Peck was established in the forties by Raymond Zelker and his wife Sybil, who designed many of the lines, always at the forefront of youth-led fashion in the sixties. The company was bought out in the eighties. POLLY PECK. COTTON. c. 1960s.

3 Mansfield is a fashion label that can be found in tailored coats, suits and dresses from the late fifties and sixties. Its owner was Frank Russell, a tailor born in London's East End, whose nickname 'The King of Coats' signified the superior styling and finish associated with the company. The label 'Frank Russell' can occasionally be found in coats, suits and dresses of similar design, in addition to the label 'Cache-D'Or', marking the separates Russell designed in the seventies. MANSFIELD. WOOL. c. 1960s.

4, 5 These models for British high street store Marks & Spencer exude the carefree joy of sixties youth fashion. An illustrative advertisement shows the original prices.

1, 2 1961 saw the Russians win the race for the first man in space. Space travel helped shape a new design ethos that appealed to a generation wanting to look different from their parents. Clean shapes and minimal styling epitomized futuristic fashion.

1 WOOL. c. 1960s.

2 PETER MANSFIELD. WOOL. c. MID-1960s.

as typical colour combinations, making Pulitzer's designs very of the moment.

The world-famous mini has been attributed to a range of designers but was undoubtedly popularized by Mary Quant and rose to its shortest in 1967. The baby doll look that was at the forefront of mid-sixties fashion was inspired, in part, by a film of the same name made several years earlier, in 1956. The film caused outrage, starring Carroll Baker as a thumb-sucking, naïve, nineteen-year-old virgin who spends most of the film in girlish nightdresses detailed with puff sleeves and ruffles. It was a box-office success. The 'innocent' child theme continued in the 1962 film *Lolita*, presenting styles that inspired Youthquake sixties fashion: Peter Pan-collared, smocked and balloon-sleeved light cotton dresses so short they had to be worn with matching bloomer-style knickers. They were accessorized with lace tights or knee-high socks and Mary Jane bar shoes. It was a style famously embodied by the arrival of supermodel Twiggy. Her long, lean, tomboy silhouette clad in innocently girly clothes personified the ambiguous sexuality of the era.

Softer styles crept in towards the end of the decade. Ossie Clark and Alice Pollock designed the midi skirt in 1967, responding to the reworked thirties style as seen in one of the cult films of the decade, *Bonnie and Clyde*. Despite criticism of the costumes from Warren Beatty, who produced and starred in the film, and Faye Dunaway, who felt her thirties style was mundane, the film both introduced a stylish new way to wear the traditional beret and also a revamped skirt length that challenged the mini. Reactions to the midi

6 The circle is the identifying shape of the sixties. Metallic, plastic, PVC and easy-care synthetic fabrics were the basis of Space Age modernist designs of mid-sixties boutique culture. POLYESTER. c. MID-1960s.

Cotton safari dress, 59s. 11d.

Sundress in jersey Tricel, 49s. 11d.

Left: Beach dress with adjustable straps. Right: Semi-fitted sheath, both in cotton, 59s. 11d.

5

were as mixed as those given by the film's cast. The chic of its length depended on the height of its wearer (a criticism that continues today). Broadly accepted in Europe, many American women reacted to the 'instant age and instant dowdiness' of its 'ugly, ugly' length, even provoking street protests. However, by 1970, women were more ready for a new length and the trend became mainstream.

The 1966 film *Blow-Up*, inspired by the career of photographer David Bailey, is not only a who's who of the sixties but exhibits every fashion style from the modernist Space Age to the slinky maxi dresses that crept in with the anti-fashion hippy movement which became one of the most chronicled fashions of the era. The flower-wearing, peace-loving hippies that gathered in San Francisco were responsible for a fashion that continued well into the seventies. Embraced by fashionable names such as Laura Ashley, Thea Porter, Zandra Rhodes, Giorgio di Sant' Angelo and even Pucci and Chanel, the romance of all that was historical and natural inspired a fashion that – whether sophisticated or unstyled – is still wearable today.

The conglomerations of styles that emerged from an era beginning in the late fifties and ending in the early seventies exhibit a varied aesthetic that exploded the rigidity of mid-century fashion. The modernist simplicity of both mid-sixties boutique and couture continues to shape contemporary design, as seen in the winter 2012 collections that referenced the geometry of sixties design.

The diversity of the period ranges from seductive to mod, gamine to sophisticated and offers a wealth of styles reinterpreted so many times they remain familiar silhouettes today. Original minis, maxis, peasant blouses and skinny ribs slip seamlessly into a contemporary wardrobe.

1 The coatdress is a design so evocative of sixties fashion. Typically, the oversized yet simple gold buttons on this Christian Dior heavy wool dress are not functional and the dress fastens at the back with a zip. The camel colour is also typical of the streamlined and unfussy styles of the era, needing only accessories to complete the outfit. The gold-coloured belt buckle discreetly shapes a 'D', a contrast to the ostentatious logos of eighties fashion. Designed after Dior's death in 1958, the label is numbered, marking it as a couture piece that would have been created by Yves Saint Laurent or Marc Bohan. CHRISTIAN DIOR. WOOL. c. 1960s.

2 Even the traditional suit could be given a youthful makeover by covering it in a stylized, naïve, floral print. MANSFIELD. WOOL. c. 1960s.

3 Mary Quant became such a success she was able to bring out Ginger Group in 1963, a less expensive diffusion line. MARY QUANT. COTTON. c. 1963.

4 There was a grown-up sophisticated version of sixties style seen in the camels and creams, tweeds and linens worn by the 'beautiful people' of the decade. The First Lady of the United States Jacqueline Kennedy epitomized the look in suits by Oleg Cassini and dresses by European designers such as Givenchy, Balmain and Valentino. Her style was imitated by those wanting chic, not flower power, and continues to be influential. SILK JERSEY. c. MID-1960s.

1

2

3

EDDY
CHAMPS-ÉLYSÉES·LIDO·PARIS

4

5

1 The floral print of the sixties was often naïve and abstract, in tune with the streamlined silhouette of the time. Often printed in simple tones of black and white, or navy, white and red, it is typical of the era to find a design printed on transparent chiffon juxtaposed with opaque fabric of the same design. The effect is a distorted image in line with Op Art trends. SILK. c. 1960s.

2, 3 The coatdress typified the sixties simplicity of style. Made from heavyweight fabrics, it found a place in many wardrobes, as the high street imitated the craftsmanship of designs from the likes of Dior, Geoffrey Beene and Lanvin. Peter Collins was a London manufacturer of outsize womenswear and he rewarded his house mannequins with the clothes they modelled, as occurred with this garment. PETER COLLINS. WOOL. c. 1960s.

4, 5 The cape, both long and short, borrowed its style from the military. The British policeman was still wearing a long cape in the sixties and, for fashion, it was a look popularized by the Beatles, complete with frogging and velvet collar. WOOL. c. 1960s.

6 A 1966 promotion for Laura Ashley mini dresses. Ashley's popular feminine interpretations were in contrast to the slicker, modernist styles of youth-led fashion.

7 Classic tailoring was revamped by the use of colour: acid pinks, greens and yellows are identifying colours of the early to mid-decade. Their intensity has not been repeated in other decades, aside from the neon clubwear of the eighties. MARK RUSSELL. WOOL. c. 1960s.

8 After a short career in tennis, Teddy Tinling went on to design dresses for most of the leading female players at Wimbledon between 1959 and 1979. He specialized in sports and beach wear and this seemingly simple shift is made from elasticized cotton, making it ahead of its time but in keeping with Tinling's sporty style. TEDDY TINLING. COTTON. c. 1960s.

9 The far-reaching influence of Op Art can be found on prints, knitted and woven fabrics. It is the well-made, understated designs from this era that are wearable today, rather than the cheaper throwaway fashions. WOOL. c. 1960s.

1 This sixties dress indicates the arrival of polyester fibres, popular for their washable, drip-dry qualities and for making fashion affordable and widely available. Both British boutique culture and the American Youthquake movement of the sixties drove fashion faster than ever before. The three-dimensional stitch is created using elastic yarn against a space-dyed nylon to achieve the hallucinogenic effect so fashionable in this era. NYLON. c. 1960s.

2 The feminine printed floral, whether stylized or softly romantic, remained a constant of sixties fashion. Frills and flounces and girly styling were an alternative to the futuristic, streamlined silhouettes of Parisian-led couture. GLOBAL. SILK. c. 1960s.

3 Matching coats and dresses or coats and trousers in clean angular lines and bright colours were a forward style in the early part of the era. Wearing trousers as part of a suit helped to make them acceptable at a time when wearing trousers in the workplace or for an evening function was still not generally accepted. MARK RUSSELL. WOOL. c. 1960s.

4 The metallic studwork on this day dress complements the neat lines of modernist style. The style that first emerged from Parisian couture houses was emulated on every high street. WOOL. c. 1960s.

5 Nina Ricci was founded in 1932 by Maria (Nina) Ricci, with her son, Robert, running the financial side. This sixties suit would probably have been designed by Jules-François Crahay (before he took the helm at Lanvin). He was appointed head designer in 1954 when Maria was near to retiring. NINA RICCI. LINEN. c. 1960s.

1, 2 Louis Féraud became a well-known designer during the early fifties when he opened his first boutique in Cannes, France. Patronized by the jet set who visited Cannes for the film festival, he reached international acclaim for his on- and off-screen wardrobe for Brigitte Bardot. He created costumes for twenty of Bardot's films as well as designing for actresses Ingrid Bergman and Kim Novak. Both he and his wife, who worked alongside him, were known for their use of colour and Féraud also exhibited his painting work internationally. LOUIS FÉRAUD. SILK. c. 1960s.

3 Beaded sleeveless cocktail jumpers were a hugely popular look of the early sixties. Easily found today, they are often in very good condition, with little damage to the beading. Many were made in Hong Kong for British and US companies, using superior pastel-tinted yarns. Footage showing them being worn by singers such as the Supremes demonstrates their appeal. SEQUINNED NATURAL YARNS. c. EARLY 1960s.

4 By the late sixties the paisley with its Eastern associations had overtaken Space Age modernist themes. Hippy aesthetics were far-reaching and influenced even the most commercial of mainstream fashion. WOOL JERSEY. c. LATE 1960s.

7 Although Mary Quant has become synonymous with 'mod' style, her initial production was so homespun and work so of-the-minute (designs were made at home from fabric bought over the counter and delivered to her King's Road boutique in the evening) that her repertoire was far greater than many realize. MARY QUANT. COTTON c. 1960s.

5 The 'pussy bow' is the contemporary name given to the bow detail featured on many early sixties blouses and dresses. A vintage detail adopted by many contemporary designers, its use is more popular today than it was in the sixties. SUSAN SMALL. WOOL. c. LATE 1960s.

6 Home dressmaking was still prevalent, despite the efficiency of mass production that kept the high street shops stocked with up-to-the-minute fashions. Paper patterns remained an effective way to translate the latest trends. HANDMADE. WOOL. c. MID-1960s.

1, 2 The psychedelic swirls and explosions of flower power prints are a contrast to the clean block-colouring typifing the early to mid-decade. As Op Art patterns were softened with pastel colour palettes, a new mood was established that continued well into the seventies.

1 COTTON JERSEY. c. LATE 1960s.

2 COTTON SKIRT AND COTTON JERSEY T-SHIRT. c. LATE 1960s.

3 The distinctive textile designs of Italian designer Emilio Pucci were perfectly in tune with the sixties explosion of psychedelic patterns. Pucci's prints were so imitated he was forced to incorporate his signature into his textile designs. His sophisticated styling, using exquisite cottons, silk or silk jersey was popular with the jet set including Elizabeth Taylor, Marilyn Monroe and Twiggy. EMILIO PUCCI. SILK. c. 1960s.

4 Marilyn Monroe was a Pucci admirer, wearing his designs off-screen. She was buried in 1962 in a simple Pucci green dress with a slashed neckline but otherwise similar in styling to this tunic-shaped dress with no fastening. EMILIO PUCCI. SILK JERSEY. c. 1960s.

5 Throwaway paper fashions were a popular but short-lived concept. Surprisingly durable, the woven paper cloth was sold as packaged, ready-made designs or as fabric that could be bought by the yard. Among the most collectable are Andy Warhol's *Campbell's Soup Cans* and a series by Harry Gordon of blown-up photographic images such as a rose, an eye and a cat.

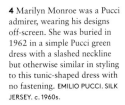

Hallmark
HOLLY
PAPER PARTY DRESS
SIZE: LARGE 16-18

*Ruffled Sleeves • A-Line Shift
Shorten with scissors
Press with cool iron*

*Disposable fashions for:
Entertaining • Lounging • Gifts*

Sizes Available:
Petite 4-6 Medium 12-14
Small 8-10 Large 16-18

80% Cellulose, 20% Cotton
Fire-resistant

This fabric is fire-resistant, however — fabric will be dangerously flammable if dry cleaned or washed.

Hallmark Cards Inc., Kansas City, Mo. Made in U.S.A.
390.CPD14-4

6 Susan Small, founded by Leslie Carr Jones, were known for their elegant cocktail and evening wear. Established in the early forties, their dresses were expensive and often advertised in *Vogue*. Labels of the late sixties are often printed with the wording 'Miss Susan Small'. SUSAN SMALL. SILK. c. EARLY 1960s.

1 Singer Sandy Shaw wears a chic black and white ensemble in 1967.

2 The skirts of the mid-sixties as interpreted for the British high street by Marks & Spencer. Traditional plaids have been reworked in the bright colours of the decade.

3 Much debate occurs over the invention of the mini skirt, seen at its shortest in 1966. Mary Quant is credited with popularizing a natural trend, but says herself that she observed what the youth of the sixties wanted to wear. Other designers who interpreted the fashion included Jean Varon, Pierre Cardin and André Courrèges. COTTON. c. 1960s.

4 'Stirrup pants' (so called because of the stretch fabric that went under the foot in a stirrup to hold the taut shape of the trousers) were an early sixties style revived in the eighties. STRETCH JERSEY. c. 1960s.

5 This advert for 'Mister Pants' shows how to achieve a glamorous look in ski-inspired clothing.

THE 1970s

MORE DASH THAN CASH

'YOU CAN FIND A WHOLE RANGE OF FASHION IN A STONE'S THROW – TWEEDY, ETHNIC, HOLLYWOOD, CLASSIC, GLAMOROUS, EXECUTIVE, NOSTALGIC, PRETTY OR INTERNATIONAL. FASHION HAS TURNED INTO A REPERTOIRE.'

GEORGINA HOWELL, *IN VOGUE*, 1975

....

The seventies saw a huge diversity in fashionable styles. The decade saw the first appearance of 'vintage' as everyday wear, as silhouettes of the past also influenced new designer fashions. The fifties silhouette resurfaced in glam rock fashions and the bias cut of the thirties inspired glamorous couture creations. Meanwhile, new fabrics and innovative cutting techniques encouraged experimental new styles. While fashion historians might argue that the decade was stylistically confused, the exciting array of clothes produced remain extremely wearable and continue to have a huge impact on contemporary fashions.

By the end of the sixties, ready-to-wear designs were referencing Pre-Raphaelite paintings and 19th-century romanticism. The seventies continued this nostalgic 'anything goes' approach, and second-hand and thrifted antique dresses were popularized as everyday wear alongside mainstream minis, maxis and midis. While the anti-establishment, anti-Vietnam War fashions worn at the end of the sixties included second-hand military jackets, distressed shirts and military-issue canvas bags, it was the early seventies that saw the first true appearance of 'vintage' clothing. Sometimes called 'the Granny look', the trend deliberately embraced historical fashion as a reaction to the sleek stylization of the early sixties. The first vintage shoppers snapped up turn-of-the-20th-century white lawn cotton dresses, pin-tucked blouses and intricate cutwork petticoats.

Books and magazines demonstrated ways of achieving high-fashion style on a limited budget. British *Vogue* introduced the 'More Dash than Cash' column, while Caterine Milinaire and Carol Troy's cult *Cheap Chic* book was published in 1975. Both encouraged the use of unique fashion sources such as catering suppliers, army surplus stores and traditional gentlemen's outfitters. It was now considered cool to dress alternatively, to interpret trends with personal style and to dare to be different.

1 The use of neon colours for fashion prints continued from the sixties to the early seventies. This mosaic geometric is typical of the psychedelic prints of the era and is given a further dimension by the pleating of the skirt. KATI BY LAURA PHILLIPS. SYNTHETIC. c. EARLY 1970s.

2 The knickerbocker fashion began in the late sixties, inspired by late 19th-century styles. Often manufactured in corduroy or velvet, the three-quarter-length trousers were cuffed below the knee and worn with long patterned socks or tights or tucked into 'Granny boots'. This pair by British designer Robert Dorland combines the traditional shape with a neon psychedelic print, typical of the patterns inspired by hallucinogenic LSD 'trips'. ROBERT DORLAND. COTTON. c. LATE 1960s/ EARLY 1970s.

3 These designs for the Italian fashion house Etro are by Walter Albini, who worked as both an illustrator and a designer.

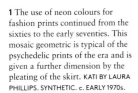

New fabrics became widely available for home dress-making, allowing high-end couture looks to be imitated for a fraction of the cost. Bold prints that echoed the styles of previous generations were used on inexpensive and durable synthetics. The naïve floral typical of the sixties was replaced with huge furnishing-scale botanicals and patterns deliberately imitating antique clothing. Aubrey Beardsley's late 19th-century illustrations were copied both small scale and as vast, one-off border prints, while the reinterpretations of Art Deco and Art Nouveau patterns in bright pastels or earthy colours by Bernard Nevill, a lecturer at London's Royal College of Art, also proved influential.

London's boutiques still enjoyed their prestigious reputation. The designers who had emerged in the later part of the sixties became household names. Also, as in the sixties, British music icons helped disseminate their style worldwide, relying on the new young breed of fashion designers to create their image. Shiny 'glam rock' outfits were a vital part of the personas of David Bowie, Bryan Ferry and even the Rolling Stones on occasion. Styles were explorative, playing with gender boundaries. For the vintage lover of today, the most wearable labels associated with this style include Mr Freedom and the Miss Mouse label from designer Rae Spencer-Cullen.

Ossie Clark was one of the most famous designers to emerge from the boutiques of the seventies. Clark and his wife, the textile designer Celia Birtwell, worked with Alice Pollock under the Quorum label (although from 1969 the boutique was under the helm of Alfred Radley, who saved it from bankruptcy). His work also displays an appreciation of past design. Clark trawled his local London market, Portobello, for inspiring antique garments. His designs in fluid crepes, chiffons and satins demonstrate the influence of the bias cut of the thirties and the sophistication of the forties. Often using the whimsical and feminine prints of Birtwell, his dresses confer a demure sexuality and celebrate the female form. As the fashion designer Anna Sui said of Clark, 'He dressed the woman we all wanted to be: the rock star's girlfriend.' The timeless wearability of his designs means they remain highly sought after today.

With up to 100,000 visitors a week, the Biba store, which opened on London's Kensington High Street in 1974, was another fashion phenomenon of the time. Like Ossie Clark, Biba designer Barbara Hulanicki's clothes – vampish recreations of forties film noir in what she called

1 Feathered marabou jackets – part of seventies nightclub fashion – have been adopted for boho-style contemporary wear. MARABOU FEATHERS. c. 1970s.

2, 3 Ossie Clark was saved from bankruptcy by Alfred Radley, a British manufacturer. Dresses labelled with Ossie Clark for Radley were the diffusion line designed by Clark for a larger production line distributed by Radley. The designs produced for Clark's own collection were in a more luxurious satin-backed moss crepe than the ordinary moss crepe of his Radley dresses. Highly sought after today, the designs still manage to look edgy, as seen on Sienna Miller. OSSIE CLARK FOR RADLEY. MOSS CREPE. c. 1970s.

4 Loulou de la Falaise, muse of Yves Saint Laurent, wears a peasant dress in 1970. The batik-printed chiffon and ethnic necklace were elements of a commercialized hippy style that appealed to the jet set.

5 Ossie Clark and his wife, Celia Birtwell, were a true design partnership, with Birtwell designing the prints Clark incorporated into his clothes. This is one of his more demure designs and evening dresses like this were often chosen by brides who wanted to look different. Designer Edina Ronay wore a Clark dress for her 1971 wedding. OSSIE CLARK. MOSS CREPE. c. 1970s.

1

2

'Auntie colours' of smoky mulberries, rusts and plums – are still very desirable. Her prices were more accessible than Clark's, meaning office girls could wear the same outfit as a celebrity, and often did. Their affordability meant many garments were disposed of over time and could, until recent years, be found easily, albeit not always in good order.

Awarded designer of the year by British *Vogue* in 1970, Bill Gibb was also inspired by historical fashion. Rather than look to more recent decades, his designs reinterpreted the ornateness of the Renaissance, and it was these fantastical garments that made fashion headlines. However, this much-loved designer also produced beautiful and simple, flowing garments – so wearable by contemporary standards – in Qiana nylon (popularly known as Qiana jersey), a superior fabric with a silky appearance.

Launched by DuPont in 1968, the fabric had a timely arrival in relation to the disco trend that emerged mid-decade. Disco was associated with the American sophistication of New York's Studio 54 nightclub, which opened in 1977. The club's entry policy only admitted the 'beautiful people' who dressed with serious style, whether they were famous, infamous or completely unknown. The scene is epitomized by the designer Halston, who worked incessantly with the glitterati of New York, including creating stagewear for his friend Liza Minnelli. 'You are only as good as the people you dress,' he claimed. His easy glamour relied on superior jersey, Ultrasuede and cashmere, and his garments from the seventies can fetch higher prices today than they did at the time.

Halston's influential style shifted the emphasis on fashion from London to New York, putting the spotlight on American designers Donna Karan and Calvin Klein. Ralph Lauren introduced masculine-styled womenswear to his previously all-male clothing range in 1971, after designing outfits for his wife. He went on to create the acclaimed *Annie Hall* look, influenced by Diane Keaton's personal style, for Woody Allen's 1977 film. And, in true testament to eternal vintage style, the 1974 wrap dress of Diane von Furstenberg is another simple sensation that embodied American easy femininity and is still worn today.

As with all bygone fashions there are elements that are unwearable today. While the infamous British Punk movement is documented in the many books concerning fashion history, its pioneering and irreverent street style was worn by a select following and is today collectable rather than

1 Walter Albini has been called 'the father of ready-to-wear' for his contribution to this emerging sector of the Italian fashion industry in the early seventies. He produced designs for several fashion lines, including the Milan-based 'Mister Fox' label.

2 Hippy fashions inspired designs that deliberately mixed and matched different textures and patterns. BUS STOP. COTTON. c. 1970s.

3 Seventies fashion became more sophisticated towards the end of the decade. This dress's rich earthy colours reference the thirties and forties, while the pattern recalls Art Deco geometrics. WOOL. c. MID-1970s.

4, 5 The blouse was a key item of seventies fashion. The bell sleeves are influenced by the cuts of the thirties and forties but given a modern twist with fresh patterns, colour combinations and oversized collars.

4 SILK. c. MID-1970s.

5 LANVIN. SILK. c. MID-1970s.

1 Janice Wainwright, a graduate of London's Royal College of Art, established her label in the seventies. She often decorated her garments with ribbon, embroidery and lace. The drawstring ribbon inserted through the neckline allows this dress to be worn high or off the shoulder 'gypsy' style, a trend seen in Yves Saint Laurent's Russian collection of autumn/winter 1976. JANICE WAINWRIGHT. SILK JERSEY AND LACE. c. LATE 1970s.

wearable. However, such was its impact that its inventors, Vivienne Westwood and Malcolm McLaren, influenced both high-end fashion as well as streetwear, and the artefacts of Punk fashion, such as chains, safety pins, rips and tears, have graced the collections of the likes of Versace, Zandra Rhodes and even Christian Dior.

It is arguably the fashion that straddled the end of the sixties and the beginning of the seventies that is the most wearable of vintage eras today. From this have emerged iconic looks with a perpetual presence in contemporary fashion. The many styles and shapes, in turn influenced by the thirties and forties, have a comfortable elegance and are successful on most body shapes – not always true of earlier decades. The original maxi dress and skirt have been so plundered for their patterns and details, it is sometimes hard for the novice to distinguish between the original and the contemporary interpretation. The trouser suit of the seventies has forties chic, as do the wedge- and platform-soled shoes of the period. The decade saw the introduction of shorts as fashionwear for both day and evening, and the decade's pinnacle trends of safari looks, bohemian style, ethnic influences and arts and crafts embellishments are epitomized in the era's couture collections from Yves Saint Laurent, Pierre Cardin and Zandra Rhodes.

2 The label Dollyrockers concentrated on a fast turnover of designs to reflect current trends. The simple woodcut style print and the high bodice-style waistband on this dress reference the fashion for medieval-influenced dresses. Often called the 'Princess' look, it was a style popularized by companies such as Laura Ashley. DOLLYROCKERS. COTTON. c. EARLY 1970s.

3 Laura Ashley typified the romantic, historical trend that utilized diminutive florals and an ultra-feminine design style.

4, 5 Medieval clothing was a huge influence on seventies design, as seen in the full balloon sleeves on these dresses. North American vintage collectors often refer to this style as 'prairie', referencing the sprigged cotton dresses worn by settlers during the 19th century.

4 SILK VELVET. c. EARLY 1970s.
5 HANDMADE. CREPE. c. EARLY 1970s.

6 Velvet was a fabric that suited the bohemian fashions of the late sixties and early seventies and, combined with brocades, lace and rich jewel-like colours, echoed the romance associated with historical dress. HANDMADE. VELVET. c. 1970s.

1 The kaftan dress was a popular style in the late sixties and early seventies, and illustrates the Eastern influence on Western fashions in this period. At its simplest, two hidden ribbons – placed inside the dress at the bust – were tied round the back of the waist, giving shape to the front and leaving the back to flow freely. This dress, from Zandra Rhodes's 1977 spring/ summer ready-to-wear collection, is constructed similarly with the addition of an interior elasticated belt that comes from the back and clips at the front to create further definition at the back of the dress. It is printed in one of Rhodes's 'wiggle' patterns on satin-backed rayon crepe. ZANDRA RHODES. SATIN RAYON. 1977.

2 The voluminous draped batwing sleeve works particularly well in Qiana jersey, a heavier synthetic than commonly used and a favourite of Bill Gibb's. BILL GIBB. QIANA JERSEY. c. 1973.

3 A customized Grecian-style Radley dress in layers of fine jersey. Radley are known for manufacturing clothes in simple fabrics and prints and the embroidery on this dress was probably added later. RADLEY. POLYESTER JERSEY. c. MID-1970s.

4 Gnyuki Torimaru is a Japanese designer who launched his Yuki label in 1972. He originally trained as an architect before retraining at the London College of Fashion in the sixties. Prior to setting up his own label, Torimaru worked for Louis Féraud, Norman Hartnell and Pierre Cardin. This cream silk jersey dress is indicative of his simple styling. YUKI. SILK JERSEY. c. 1970s.

3

4

5

5 The simplicity of this silk jersey dress reflects the seventies trend nicknamed the 'Goddess look', a fashion inspired by the clothes of ancient Greece. Alfred Radley was responsible for starting the careers of many designers, including Ossie Clark, Sheridan Barnett and Betty Jackson. Most Radley dresses bear the name of their designer as well as the Radley label. RADLEY. SILK JERSEY. 1970s.

1, 2, 3 One of London's most famous stores of the sixties and the seventies was Biba. Founded by Barbara Hulanicki and her husband, Biba sold glamorous styles to young women at relatively affordable prices. The dramatic interiors of their stores, influenced first by Art Nouveau and later by Art Deco, echoed the style of the clothes. Dress **1** was sold from Biba's huge store on London's Kensington High Street. Hulanicki was worried that it wouldn't be popular because of its then-high £50 price tag, with a £10 matching turban. The dress sold out and was one of the company's fastest-selling designs.

1 BIBA. JERSEY. 1974.

2 BIBA. JERSEY. c. 1970s.

3 BIBA. COTTON. c. 1970s.

4 This design, manufactured by British company Lewis Henry, combines the seventies fashion for Grecian drapery with the medieval princess style. The texture of the crochet bodice and cuffs offsets the simplicity of the silk jersey. LEWIS HENRY. SILK JERSEY. c. 1970s.

4

1 The jacket of the seventies was cut to look like a blouse, fitted and gamine. JEFF BANKS. COTTON. c. 1970s.

2 Italian-born Pierre Cardin worked for some of the most notable names in fashion before designing his first womenswear collection in 1953. He was famed for his sixties architectural tailoring, but the divergent style of this early seventies dress, with its soft drape and slashed sleeve, displays the dexterity of his designs. PIERRE CARDIN. SILK. c. 1970s.

3 A handmade top from the seventies utilizes jersey T-shirting for the body and a thirties Art Deco spotted crepe for the sleeves. HANDMADE. COTTON AND RAYON CREPE. c. 1970s.

4 This all-in-one 'hot pants' suit is from the cusp of late sixties/ early seventies fashion. *Women's Wear Daily* reported that hot pants – a style that was shorter than shorts – only earned their name if they 'left nothing to the imagination'. ALISTAIR COWIN. POLYESTER. c. EARLY 1970s.

5 A model in 1975 wears the style of trousers that became known as 'Oxford bags'. Borrowed, like the baker boy cap, from twenties menswear these wide, straight-cut trousers were worn with a small fitted shirt or a sleeveless tank top also reminiscent of twenties style.

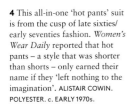

6 The partnership of Tommy Roberts and Trevor Miles under the Mr Freedom label turned the trend for what had become commercialized hippyism towards a kitsch and fun style. Inspired by Tommy Roberts's love of fifties Americana, the pair were the true pioneers of seventies novelty fashion and worked with many great names of pop, including David Bowie, Elton John and Mick Jagger. MR FREEDOM. VELVET. c. 1972.

1 Jean Muir is known for her refined simplicity and seldom created clothes using printed fabrics. Her fluid designs were instead decorated with topstitching, buttons and pin-tucks. The lack of ornamentation gives her garments a timeless appeal, as does her intransigent colour palette and her disregard for fashion trends. Muir designed for Liberty and Jaeger before establishing her own company with the financial backing of David Barnes, a jersey manufacturer. JEAN MUIR. SILK JERSEY. c. 1970s.

2 A Nina Ricci leather coat with matching sleeveless dress, bought from Harrods in 1970. The collarless neckline and three-quarter-length sleeves are indicative of late sixties styling. NINA RICCI. LEATHER. c. 1970.

3 One of Betty Jackson's first collections for Quorum was inspired by the Teddy Boys of the fifties. Many notable designers, including Ossie Clark and Wendy Dagworthy, began their careers under the Quorum label. BETTY JACKSON FOR QUORUM. WOOL AND VELVET. c. MID-1970s.

4 The vibrant red stripe of this Ossie Clark dress helps to emphasize the bias cut Clark so admired in the thirties work of the couturiers Vionnet, Schiaparelli and Molyneux. The dress is worn by Clark's wife, Celia Birtwell, in David Hockney's portrait *Mr and Mrs Clark and Percy* (**5**). Hockney was a close friend of the Clarks. OSSIE CLARK. MOSS CREPE. c. 1970.

5 David Hockney, *Mr and Mrs Clark and Percy*, 1970–71.

6 Gnyuki Torimaru's first collections were noted for their ingenious construction. They were all cut from full circles of fabric, as is particularly noticeable on the sleeve of this silk jersey dress. Thanks to their flattering drapery, his elegant designs remain as wearable as they were in the seventies. YUKI. SILK JERSEY. c. 1970s.

1 Much as today, maxi dresses were not reserved for eveningwear. Elaborate prints such as this mix of geometric shapes and florals were popular until mid-decade. POLYESTER JERSEY. c. EARLY 1970s.

2 Clothing inspired by many different cultures, particularly destinations on the hippy trail such as Morocco and India, inspired fashions from the sixties to the early seventies. Kaftans became very commercial, popularized by designer Thea Porter, who both imported and designed her own. Worn by the likes of Elizabeth Taylor and Barbra Streisand, the kaftan was adapted by high street companies such as John Neville. JOHN NEVILLE. POLYESTER JERSEY. c. LATE 1960s / EARLY 1970s.

3 Another dress by the British boutique label, Dollyrockers, whose forte was to quickly identify emerging street trends and reinterpret them for the commercial market. DOLLYROCKERS. POLYESTER. c. 1970s.

4 Frank Usher is now more often associated with cocktail dresses and wedding outfits than wearable vintage style. The company has been trading since 1944 and flourished even during wartime austerity because of its workmanship. This evening dress typifies the trend for prints inspired by the hallucinogenic effects of drug-taking. The silk jersey reflects the vibrancy of the print. FRANK USHER. SILK JERSEY. c. LATE 1960s/EARLY 1970s.

5 Quad was one of the boutiques that placed 'Swinging London' at the centre of fashion. They were known for their romantic, medieval-inspired dresses. Easily affordable, they helped British youth to keep up with the fast momentum of sixties and seventies fashion. QUAD. POLYESTER. c. EARLY 1970s.

1 Seventies suits were often cut from jersey to achieve a fitted silhouette with an exaggerated slender effect. The jersey on this Bus Stop suit is printed with a tweed check to resemble traditional woven suiting. BUS STOP. POLYESTER JERSEY. c. 1970s.

2 This black moss crepe dress combines ingenious cutting by Ossie Clark and the bold graphic floral print of Celia Birtwell. Many of Clark's designs incorporated bias cutting inspired by the thirties dresses he found in London's Portobello Market. His collections embraced a diversity of styles, from the most feminine to, as described by Birtwell, 'hard-looking rocky clothes'. OSSIE CLARK. MOSS CREPE AND CHIFFON. c. EARLY 1970s.

3 Gerald McCann studied at London's Royal College of Art during the fifties and began his career at high street store Marks & Spencer. After establishing his own business during the sixties, at a similar time to designers Jean Muir and Foale & Tuffin, he was spotted by a buyer from Bloomingdale's. He achieved huge sales in the United States and success in Britain continued with commissions for Harrods, Bazaar and Peter Robinson (now Topshop). He is known for the clean lines of his designs. GERALD McCANN. SILK JERSEY. c. EARLY 1970s.

4 Yves Saint Laurent created a selection of separates using this moon and stars print in the late 1970s. YVES SAINT LAURENT SILK CREPE DE CHINE SKIRT. c. LATE 1970s. WORN WITH CARVEN SILK BLOUSE. c. 1970s.

5 This rayon dress by designer Jeff Banks references the forties, using cuffed sleeves, a yoke, front-fastening buttons, fitted waist and even an inverted rear fishtail pleat. JEFF BANKS. RAYON. c. 1970s.

6 This is a rare design by Alice Pollock, the untrained designer who founded the British boutique Quorum in 1964. The dress closely resembles the chiffon dresses from the thirties that Pollock and Ossie Clark would search for in London's legendary Portobello market. The Radley label marks it as post-1969, the year Alfred Radley took over Quorum. ALICE POLLOCK FOR RADLEY. CHIFFON. c. 1970s.

THE 1980s

BODY LANGUAGE

'THE NEW MONEY ... WANTED TO DRESS UP. THE STYLISTS WANTED TO DRESS UP AND SO DID THE KIDS.' PETER YORK, *MODERN TIMES*, 1984

The eighties was a decade in which fashionable style emerged from both club and catwalk. While the overriding association with the era is one of excess and financial abundance, with 'power dressing' the dominant look of the period, it was also a time of great social divide. The young and the more economically disadvantaged were encouraged to be inventive, leading to exciting sub-cultural trends. Christian Lacroix, whose designs crystallized the time's mood of historical flamboyance and theatricality, remarked, 'It's terrible to say, very often the most exciting outfits are from the poorest people.'

The decade enjoyed a youth-led club culture that revelled in a creativity of dress as important as its music. From the clubs of Berlin, London, Paris and New York significant trends emerged that, in turn, influenced the leaders and creators in the business of fashion. Androgynous club costumes were generated with little money, a fearless exhibitionism and a desire to make a statement. The New Romantics, pirates, Goths and fetish fashions that rapidly became part of street style relied on ingenious styling that could never be bought over the counter. They staked their claim in the history of fashion by inspiring the collections of notable designers such as Jean Paul Gaultier and Vivienne Westwood and the infamous John Galliano who emerged from London's Saint Martins College in the midst of the club scene.

Mainstream fashion varied between the assertive femininity associated with the era – pencil skirts, puffballs and ra-ra skirts, cinched waists and shoulder pads – to the sophisticated, body-conscious and architectural styling of Tunisian Azzedine Alaïa. Referred to as 'The King of Cling', he was a devotee of Vionnet and used jersey to create designs that were both innovative and quietly provocative. Hervé Léger, Alaïa's former student, also successfully explored this look with his renowned 'Bandage' dress. It is a style that has seen many recent high-street interpretations. The influence of androgyny was also very evident on the high street, through the adoption of male garments and accessories, rather than displaying the sexually driven androgyny of

1 The illustrator Antonio Lopez was praised by Andy Warhol for his 'journalist's eye'. Lopez's kinetic style captured the spirit of an era, particularly reflecting the way fashion was worn in the seventies and eighties. His charismatic models were known as 'Antonio's girls' and he discovered and helped to launch the careers of many, including Pat Cleveland.

2, 3 Architectural pattern cutting, unique to this decade, could achieve spectacular results, as seen in these jersey jumpsuits. Cobalt blue was a key tone of a decade that embraced the use of primary colours and ice cream pastels in solid blocks. POLYESTER JERSEY. c. 1980s. WORN WITH EMANUELLE BUTTERFLY BELT.

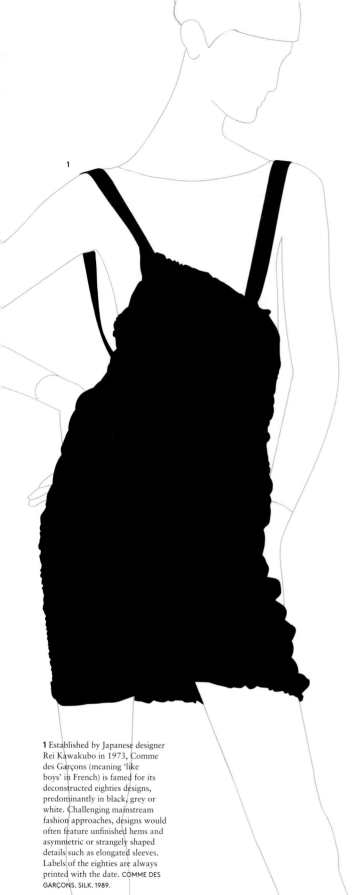

1 Established by Japanese designer
Rei Kawakubo in 1973, Comme
des Garçons (meaning 'like
boys' in French) is famed for its
deconstructed eighties designs,
predominantly in black, grey or
white. Challenging mainstream
fashion approaches, designs would
often feature unfinished hems and
asymmetric or strangely shaped
details such as elongated sleeves.
Labels of the eighties are always
printed with the date. COMME DES
GARÇONS. SILK. 1989.

the nightclub. Masculine pinstripe suits and textural tweed
jackets were worn with ties, cufflinks, visible braces and flat
caps, brogues and penny loafers. This style had been popularized by Marlene Dietrich in the thirties and re-emerged
in Woody Allen's 1977 cult film *Annie Hall*. Although some
cite the influence of Ralph Lauren's designs on *Annie Hall*'s
costumes, Allen is quoted as being so enamoured of lead
star Diane Keaton's personal style that he included her own
clothes in the character's on-screen wardrobe.

Thrown into the mix was a vintage look that also
explored masculinity of dress, although, at this time, the
term 'vintage' was not commonly applied to the second-
hand cult inner-city fashion in New York, Paris and London.
Original forties suits, collarless shirts, Fair Isle pullovers,
button braces and lace-up boots were worn by both sexes.
Eighties vintage fashion was worn as a considered and
deliberate mix of opposing trends – heavy Dr Marten boots
paired with Laura Ashley sprigged dresses; oversized men's
tweed jackets worn over feminine puffballs or flounced
ra-ra skirts; textured fifties overcoats and coloured mohair
scarves teamed with slinky slip dresses – while the oversized
Aran knit, still a vintage staple today, went with everything.
It was a selected mix of garments that created an offbeat
feel, worn by music and street style icons. The vintage shop
that consolidated this 'look' was US chain, Flick. Quietly,
from New York's Soho and Greenwich Village, the style
infiltrated areas of London such as the newly created shopping destination Covent Garden and design-orientated
Shoreditch. Their stock concentrated on military khakis
and, in particular, one-piece flying overalls (later copied in
parachute silk on the high street), coloured baseball boots,
checked lumberjack shirts and shrunken T-shirts carrying faded catchphrases, university emblems or images of
Mickey Mouse. This T-shirt style was not dissimilar to the
notorious over-sized slogan T-shirts designed by Katharine
Hamnett in this era, worn by anyone wanting to make a
political statement.

Also from American vintage came a street-style trend,
used in films such as *Desperately Seeking Susan*. Madonna's
look in the film was so influential it was manufactured
for the international high street, translated as coloured
tutus, biker jackets, lace hairbands and fingerless mittens.
Mainstream fashion identified the trend for second-hand
clothing and followed by recreating the tea dresses of the
thirties and forties, albeit with shorter hem lengths and

2 'The King of Cling' Azzedine Alaïa is famed for his body-conscious fashions which instigated a trend that spanned the eighties. AZZEDINE ALAÏA. STRETCH JERSEY. c. 1980s. WORN WITH ALAÏA LEATHER FRINGED BELT. c. 1980s.

3 Thierry Mugler's avant-garde, sculptural style was at its heyday in the eighties and nineties. These stretch fabric styles, featuring cut-aways, were popular with the stars of film and music. THIERRY MUGLER. STRETCH JERSEY. c. LATE 1980s/ EARLY 1990s.

4 Dorothée Bis has been at the forefront of high-fashion knitwear since its creation in 1962 as the ready-to-wear offshoot of the Parisian 'Dorothée' boutique. This one-piece is indicative of eighties styling, with oversized studded brass fastenings and enormous shoulder pads. DOROTHÉE BIS. WOOL. c. 1980s.

larger, furnishing-scale floral prints. Ironically, these are the very dresses that are sought after today by lovers of eighties vintage fashion.

The exaggerated silhouettes of mainstream fashion, the styles developed in a decade in thrall to the designer label, were created with a mastery of mathematical pattern cutting, using opposing fabrics, such as jersey with leather, to create a 'stress'. Velvet was combined with chiffon and satin used with lace inserts to create the identifying three-dimensional sleeves, collars and peplums of the decade. Acid neons and a vibrant colour palette depicted bold geometrics, lightning flashes, zigzags and asymmetrical detailing, from which the triangle emerged as shape of the decade. Identifying small triangles can be found decorating clothes, on buttons and especially on shoes. The ankles of stockings and tights were often embellished with a series of dots, triangles and squiggles.

At the beginning of the decade, a new architectural movement was founded in Italy. Memphis (named after a Johnny Cash lyric) was the brainchild of architect Ettore Sottsass. Its distinctive look was inspired by an unlikely combination of Art Deco and Pop Art and influenced both interior and fashion, particularly with its use of asymmetrical shapes and bright ice cream pastels, couched in black, the colour of the decade. Jewelry and accessories frequently display an obvious Memphis influence, particularly in the design of buckles on the many style-statement belts of the era. These are some of the most wearable and collectable items of fashionable eighties attire. Borrowing their style from the thirties, though with defining exaggeration, belt design explored every possible contortion and construction. Styles from the era have been so imitated in recent fashion that it is often impossible to ascertain the age of a design.

As well as the logo-adorned garments of luxury labels and the innovative styles coming from emerging young designers such as Body Map and English Eccentrics, a new phenomenon arrived that altered the perspective of fashion in this period. Spearheaded by John Galliano and Japanese designers Issey Miyake and Rei Kawakubo for Comme des Garçons, deconstructed designs challenged the perfection of the commercial and conventional eighties style. Their designs, using black, asymmetrical drapery, texturized stitchwork, ripping and ruching, are highly collectable, representing a pivotal moment in the history of fashion.

In the true incongruous spirit of the eighties, the two most photographed female icons of the decade were Madonna and Princess Diana, who both manipulated the fashions of the period to great effect. While Madonna personalized the cult trends of the club scene, Diana was dressed by notable names of fashion such as Bellville Sassoon, Versace, Zandra Rhodes, Catherine Walker and Bruce Oldfield, and her striking ensembles brought great attention to this era of authoritative design. From this spectrum of styles, all still relatively easily found, the contemporary vintage shopper can carefully curate a wardrobe of wearable classics that will defy dates.

1 Grace Jones carries off eighties sculptural shoulder pads and colour blocking with panache. Legendary for her androgynous style, Jones began her career as a model, becoming a muse for Thierry Mugler. 'I wasn't born this way. One creates oneself,' said Jones.

2 Colour blocks of black, white and primaries are an identifying eighties signature style. SYNTHETIC JERSEY. c. 1980s.

3 Leather was a fabric that suited the 'dress for success' ethos inspiring much of eighties mainstream fashion. Leather skirts, jackets and particularly trousers were pleated, studded and sculpted. Thierry Mugler and Claude Montana are particularly known for their creations in leather from this decade. EMBOSSED LEATHER. c. 1980s.

1, 2, 3 Power dressing was a tool of the working woman. It was associated with the suit, more often worn with a pencil skirt than shorts. Vibrant pastels and black accented with neons made up the colour palette. Details included contrasting collar and cuffs, with statement buttons (**1**) and oversized metal buttons and zips (**3**).

1 MANSFIELD. WOOL. c. 1980s.

2 UNIT 7. WOOL. c. 1980s.

3 VERSUS. WOOL. c. 1980s.

4 Princess Diana's outfit for a 1987 passing out parade at Sandhurst exhibited carefully chosen military overtones, a look prevalent among wearers of so-called 'yuppie' style. The princess used clothes to express the mood of her public appearances, wearing softer styles for her charity work. The suit was by Catherine Walker, who designed many of her outfits, and the hat was by Graham Smith at Kangol.

5 The powerful and authoritative little black dress was a staple in collections. YVES SAINT LAURENT. WOOL. c. 1980s.

6 English Eccentrics, founded in 1983, encompassed innovative print techniques in their clothing and accessories range. The baroque style seen on this blouse was a trend of the decade and was used by other British designers such as Sue Timney. ENGLISH ECCENTRICS. SILK. c. 1980s.

1 The pencil skirt was the most prevalent skirt shape of the decade. Flattering variations in leather and suede were made with a high waistline, as were jeans and trousers. The mandarin collar is also a signature style of the eighties. ESCADA. SILK BLOUSE AND SUEDE SKIRT. c. 1980s.

2 The 'body' was a fashionable staple of the period, a trend influenced by the fitness craze of the early part of the decade. This leather skirt echoes the 'U' shape of a horseshoe in studs. STRETCH POLYESTER BODY AND LEATHER SKIRT. c. 1980s.

3 This eighties jacket by Laurel takes inspiration from the insignia on a concierge's jacket. LAUREL. WOOL JACKET. c.1980s. WORN WITH VELVET AND METALLIC SYNTHETIC MOSCHINO TROUSERS. c.1990s.

4 Studwork was a typical eighties embellishment and can be found on every type of fashionable garment and accessory. LEATHER STUDDED JACKET. c.1980s. WORN WITH MOSCHINO DENIM TROUSERS. c.1990s.

5 An illustration by Antonio Lopez highlights the widespread masculine trend of the early eighties. Waistcoats, oversized jackets and Oxford bags were worn in tweeds and flannels. Accessories including both long and bow ties, cufflinks and braces accented the style.

1 The oversized sequin butterfly blouse needs no introduction for most vintage enthusiasts. These disco tops were a late seventies to early eighties garment, more popular for wear today than at the time. PHOOL. SEQUIN ON POLYESTER. c. 1980s.

1

2 The clean lines of nautical chic were conveyed in sailor collars, stripes and rows of gold buttons on many garments in this decade. The anchor was a common motif, although rarely depicted in sequin, as on this American club dress. SEQUIN ON SYNTHETIC. c. EARLY 1980s.

3 US television dramas had a big influence on eighties fashions. Shows like *Dallas*, *Dynasty* and *Miami Vice* ignited unisex trends such as pushed-back sleeves and penny loafers worn without socks. Designers such as Nolan Miller, responsible for the *Dynasty* wardrobe, did much to sophisticate eighties eveningwear that, at times, could be overstated. SEQUIN ON SYNTHETIC. c. 1980s.

1 Models applaud designer Azzedine Alaïa at a 1986 fashion show. His electric-coloured stretch bandage dresses have seen sightings in recent years.

2 The oversized satin bow on a stretch cocktail dress typifies the explosion of eveningwear during the boom years of the decade. Dresses were elaborately jewelled and creations used ruching and frills, and were generally coiffed while maintaining a figure-hugging body. STRETCH SATIN. c.1980s.

3–5 Body-conscious (body con) style is the name attributed to the stretch jersey shapes that clung to every curve. The Little Black Dress came into its own for eveningwear, embellished with gold accents. Studwork, sequins, frills and bows added definition.

3 WINDSMOOR. WOOL. c.1980s.

4 STRETCH VELVET AND LAMÉ. c.1980s.

5 SYNTHETIC STRETCH JERSEY. c.1980s.

3 Aside from the powerful statements associated with this decade of excess, subtler themes were also explored, as seen in this Valentino dress. Earth tones were inspired by a safari look, equestrian clothing and influential films such as 1985's *Out of Africa*. VALENTINO. LINEN. c. LATE 1980s.

4 British designer Bruce Oldfield is known for his bespoke evening and bridal wear as well as his occasion wear. He showed his first collection in 1975 and displays remarkable longevity, with designs from any decade remaining wearable today. He was closely associated with Princess Diana's wardrobe through the eighties. BRUCE OLDFIELD. WOOL. c. LATE 1980s/EARLY 1990s.

1 Although many eighties shoulder pads are too outrageous for contemporary taste, high-end names also offered pared-down versions suitable for today. MAX MARA. SILK. c. 1980.

2 Janice Wainwright was a name of the seventies who continued to enjoy success in the eighties, remaining true to her romantic style. JANICE WAINWRIGHT. SILK. c. 1980.

5 The Chanel tweed suit remains the much-aspired-to classic synonymous with the name of the fashion house. Heralding Chanel's return after the war, the tweed suit exhibited a chic presence against a backdrop of corsetry and full-skirted femininity. The beautiful tweed explored in the suit was a favourite fabric of Gabrielle Chanel and Chanel remains the only couture house to ensure verticality and hang by weighting the interior of the jackets with gold chain. CHANEL. TWEED AND SILK. c. LATE 1980s.

1 'Swagger' coats borrowed their cut from the fifties, with the addition of exaggerated shoulder pads and acid colours. LAUREL. WOOL. c. 1980s.

2 Black, the statement colour of the decade, was a natural foil for primary, acid and neon colour palettes. MARELLA. WOOL. c. 1980s.

3 The eighties was a heyday for Italian design. Gianni Versace, Giorgio Armani, Valentino, Gianfranco Ferré and Missoni created garments of enduring appeal in a decade that saw extremes of style. GIANNI VERSACE. SILK JERSEY. c. 1980s.

4 Charlotte Ford, daughter of Ford Motor magnate Henry Ford II, began designing fashion in 1977. The original label, Charlotte Ford Couture, folded but was replaced with Charlotte II and Charlotte Ford spanning the late seventies into the eighties. CHARLOTTE FORD. SILK. c. EARLY 1980s.

5 A printed velvet jumpsuit on the cusp of transitional seventies/ eighties design. A favourite for clubwear, the knickerbocker trousers are a hallmark of seventies design but the metallic gold print, cowl neck and shoulder pads date it to the start of the eighties. VELVET. c. EARLY 1980s.

Stiebel

Peter Russell

Worth

Tinling

popwath

Part Two

ELEMENTS

HATS SCULPTURAL STYLE

1 This turban from the United States would have been worn as glamorous eveningwear. Turbans were also worn as practical and popular daywear in wartime. MARY ELIZABETH. BROCADE. c.1940s.

2 Stephen Jones named this hat 'Pas des Deux'. The Juliet-style skullcap and veil typify eighties millinery design. STEPHEN JONES. VELVET AND BROCADE. 1982.

3 'The madder the hat ... the smarter the hat,' reported Elsa Schiaparelli on the design of her hats, popular with collectors for their quirky elegance. This is one of a series of hats designed for the collection christened 'Harlequin' by *Vogue*. ELSA SCHIAPARELLI. WOOL, FELT AND DIAMANTÉ. 1938.

Whether you consider a hat or a bag the ultimate fashion accessory, it's hard to dispute that, while a bag is expected, a hat will always be noticed. Wearing a hat, vintage or contemporary, is one of today's significant style statements. Millinery from the 20th century is an exploration in design and decoration, a story including some of the great international names of fashion who started their careers as designers of hats, as well as milliners whose names deserve to be more familiar today.

The term 'milliner' – maker of women's hats – originates from Milan and the surrounding northern regions of Italy notable for their haberdashery manufacturing trade, specifically the trimming used for hats. Milliners were both the exporters of haberdashery and the makers of 'straws', the basic straw block that was subsequently moulded and decorated to create the array of fashionable headwear worn throughout the 20th century, although it dates as far back as the 16th century.

Over the subsequent centuries, the hat has seen a seemingly infinite number of arrangements and ornamentations. It is arguable whether millinery styles affected hairstyles, or elaborate coiffures determined the stylization of hats in each era. Certainly the geometric bobbed haircut of the twenties sat perfectly under the hat of the decade, the cloche, and it is generally considered 'the bob' came first. A 1926 article in the *New York Times* confirms, 'Hats have never before been designed with such precise relation to the coiffure.'

Whatever her social status, the woman of the twenties was rarely seen out and about without gloves and a covered head. As in ancient times, etiquette demanded that a woman's head should be covered. Even in the forties, a decade whose dress code was challenged by the austerity of war,

'A HAT MAKES CLOTHING IDENTIFIABLE, DRAMATIC AND, MOST IMPORTANTLY, FASHION... IT'S THE ICING ON THE CAKE, THE DOT ON THE 'I', THE EXCLAMATION MARK, THE FASHION FOCUS. EVERYONE FROM SHOWGIRLS TO DICTATORS KNOWS THAT BY WEARING A HAT THEY WILL BECOME THE CENTRE OF ATTENTION.' STEPHEN JONES

sculptural headdresses drew inspiration from the Orient, Russia and the Egyptian artefacts from the recently discovered Tutankhamen's tomb. Despite frequently being associated with the era of the flapper, the cloche (whose name derived from the French word for 'bell') proved fashionable over several decades. The iconic shape was first created by one of the great names of millinery, Caroline Reboux. Reboux was a French designer of international repute, responsible for launching many careers in fashion, notably Lilly Daché's. The cloche had been worn as a deep-set helmet style since the early 20th century but became the height of popularity in the twenties and thirties. Inexpensive to make from felt blocks, they could be appliquéd and dyed in many colour variations, or they could be created from a variety of summer straws and painted each season to update them.

Like Daché, Chanel began as a milliner, setting up her salon in 1908 in the private Parisian apartment of her lover, Etienne Balsan, to great initial success. Two years later, with financial backing from the man who became her true love, Arthur 'Boy' Capel, she set up as a licensed milliner in a salon at 21 rue Cambon, launching 'Chanel Modes'. Reboux had designed hats for the great names of stage and screen (Marlene Dietrich being a loyal patron) and, likewise, Chanel's designs reached public acclaim after the actress Gabrielle Dorziat wore them in a 1912 stage production of *Bel Ami*. Chanel's hats became sought after by celebrities of the day and were the subject of many illustrative features in contemporary Parisian fashion magazines.

The thirties was a decade of daring and diversity. The sun-shielding parasols used in the twenties were no longer fashionable, and straw brims became wider and the crowns shallower to accommodate fuller, curly hairstyles. The masculine fedora was adapted for wear with the new trouser suit popularized by screen star Marlene Dietrich, and perky miniature fedoras are widely sought after today. Elsa Schiaparelli,

covering one's hair was not only a way of keeping safe and clean, but also a way of retaining a fashionable identity. A wide range of trimmings escaped rationing and many women went wild in their efforts to beautify their hats and brighten the frugal fashions of wartime. Elaborate concoctions of feathers and flowers, veiling and ribbon for day competed with beading and sequins for evening. During the German Occupation of France, hats became so decorative they were seen as beacons of fashionable defiance and were later dubbed 'les chapeaux de la Résistance'. This was in contrast to the First World War, when it was thought unpatriotic and frivolous to dress elaborately.

Although breathtaking examples can be found from all eras, perhaps the most interesting age of hat design is the era of sophisticated glamour dressing, a period when accessories were *de rigueur* and unashamedly creative – the twenties and thirties. Twenties hats echoed the trend for patriotically feminine and youthful fashion, with soft straw hats made with deep brims to keep the sun away from the face. Appliquéd felt cloches and

1 A twenties French fashion illustration beautifully depicts a woman wearing an ornate winter cloche and carrying her latest millinery purchase in a hat box that itself would be a worthy collector's item today.

2 Sally Victor was a millinery buyer for American department store chain, Macy's, during the twenties. She married the owner of a wholesale milliners and began her own line in 1934. SALLY VICTOR. VELVET AND SILK. c. 1930s.

3 The cloche hat was designed in a wide variety of fabrics. Wool, felt and velvet were the fabrics of winter, while simple deep-brimmed straws shielded eyes from the summer sun before sunglasses became a fashion.

4 The flattering cloche remained fashionable throughout the twenties and thirties. This design is enhanced with a side flourish of feathers. ELSA SCHIAPARELLI. BRUSHED FUR FELT. c. 1930s.

5 The decorative headpieces worn by the flappers of the twenties are widely sought after today for their elaborate yet wearable qualities. MARCELLE AGNELLET. MOTHER OF PEARL ON SILK. c. 1920s.

6 This cloche is by one of the most collectable names in American millinery, Jack McConnell. Pheasant feathers are a popular choice for hats due to their intricate colouring and availability. JACK MCCONNELL. PHEASANT FEATHERS AND VELVET. c. LATE 1950s/EARLY 1960s.

7 A mixture of seed pearls and flat sequins illuminates this Art Deco-influenced evening hat. SILK. c. 1920s/1930s.

8 The celebrated milliner Mr John created many hats for film, including Marilyn Monroe's showgirl headdress for *Gentlemen Prefer Blondes*, Greta Garbo's jewelled cloche in *Mata Hari* and several hats for Vivien Leigh in *Gone with the Wind*. MR JOHN. METALLIC. c. 1920s.

9 An enveloping straw cloche with an Art Deco jewel anchoring the turned-back brim. J. L. HUDSON. STRAW. c. 1920s.

4

5

6

7

8

9

who had already established an atelier, launched her first designs for headwear with the 'madcap', a fine knitted tube that could be arranged by its wearer into any shape. Worn by American actress Ina Claire, it was widely photographed for the fashion press and much copied. Tyrolean-inspired hats followed, and Schiaparelli's mid-thirties surrealist sensations created with artist Salvador Dalí culminated in her famous millinery line featuring surprisingly stylish upside-down shoes and lamb chops. Commercialized sculptural interpretations of her designs by other milliners form the basis of many of the interesting hats of the thirties and forties.

Schiaparelli is also associated with the snood and she often attached embellished versions to her miniature hats, fashionable in the late thirties. Despite conflicting opinions on its origins, the snood has survived many interpretations and has arrived in the 21st century with little alteration. A similar story surrounds another look adopted by many stylish vintage

fashionistas today, the turban. While the 'King of Fashion' Paul Poiret introduced the turban, both the turban and the snood were widely popularized by one of the most famous names in American millinery, Lilly Daché. Originally of French birth and training, Daché moved to New York, where she built her successful career. She created glamorous draped turbans for screen stars Carmen Miranda and Carole Lombard, for whom she also famously created a snood to keep her hair in place while filming a dancing scene. 'Glamour is what makes a man ask for your telephone number. But it is also what makes a woman ask for the name of your dressmaker,' wrote Daché.

Despite the elaborate creations worn by some, the formal requirement of wearing a hat was a natural casualty of wartime. However, the many utilitarian scarf-tied creations and draped turban ensembles of the era inspired fashionable wear in subsequent decades. The formality of the fifties produced small chic styles worn close to the head, and low 'wheels' and 'pancakes' that would mingle easily with the Ascot styles of today, while the array of designs of the post-war decades still inspire many contemporary interpretations, whether embroidered summer straws, one of the iconic 19th-century schoolboy caps or berets of the sixties, or the floppy wide-brimmed felts that lasted from the Summer of Love well into the sustainable seventies. These wearable styles have endured in contrast to avant-garde helmets and visors of 'space captains' André Courrèges, Pierre Cardin and Paco Rabanne, preserved in sixties sci-fi film *Barbarella* and immortalized in Audrey Hepburn's famed publicity shot for *How to Steal a Million*, a Givenchy-designed homage to Courrèges.

Undoubtedly, donning a hat of significant style affects the stature and poise of its wearer. Hats are grand statements that, according to Debrett's contemporary etiquette guide, are now 'compulsory at a diminishing number of British social occasions' and make it 'notoriously difficult to socially kiss'. It is certainly the braver fashionista who

1 The American millinery company Stetson has a history dating as far back as 1865. Although commonly associated with the hats worn by cowboys and herdsmen, they were also manufacturers of fashionable headwear for women. This advertisement dates to the forties.

2 The turban is a style that has been evident in every fashion era. Each decade has an identifiable style, and the high front drapery with jewelled paste brooch helps to establish this as a style from the thirties. VELVET. c. 1930s.

3 Feathers dressed either straight up or with a forward tilt were the height of French fashion in 1948. Many felt designs in this year were asymmetric, such as the upswept brim seen here. ROBERTS. FUR FELT. c. 1940s.

4 Early fifties hats were some of the most glamorous, covered in a fascinating variety of trimmings that varied from silk flowers to sequins and glass fruit. The natural vibrancy of bird feathers such as pheasant made them a popular decoration for elegant daywear. JILLIE ORIGINAL. PHEASANT FEATHER. c. 1950s.

5 FUR FELT. c. 1940s.

6 One of the influential films of the thirties was the 1938 swashbuckling spectacular, *Robin Hood*. The film's costume designer, Dwight Franklin, felt that the actors should bring their own 'modern' style to the historical fashions in the film, creating a contemporary feel that audiences could identify with. LILLY DACHÉ. FELT FEATHER. c. 1930s.

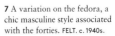

7 A variation on the fedora, a chic masculine style associated with the forties. FELT. c. 1940s.

8 Thirties illustration of a design by Jeanne Lanvin.

1, 2 Lilly Daché, a French milliner who settled in the United States, was the originator of many trends in millinery in the thirties, forties and fifties. As one of her many pithy quotes, she remarked, 'I truly believe that much of the joy would go out of men's lives if it were not for their wives' hats.'

1 LILLY DACHÉ. SILK AND VELVET. c. 1930s.

2 LILLY DACHÉ. SILK AND VELVET. c. 1950s.

3 A French fashion illustration depicting the profusion of trimmings used to decorate hats in the thirties, in keeping with the feminine fashions of the day.

4 Hat pins were treated as an item of jewelry and come in a multitude of styles, varying from practical wooden shapes and simple mother of pearl to elaborate semi-precious stones worn with evening creations.

'becomes the centre of attention' with a vintage sculptural headdress, yet many of the styles from past decades were designed to be worn on a daily basis and, as such, are not startling today. However, it is the adopted styles of masculine headwear that are most commonly worn. Fedoras, trilbies and fashionably faded straw panamas, many of which punctuated the eighties in vivid rainbow colours, as well as the tweed baker boys and gatsbys of twenties working-class men, can all be seen adorning the heads of stylish women today.

It seems appropriate to end on some advice on matching hat style to face shape for vintage millinery devotees happy to be noticed, taken from *Every Woman* magazine, March 1940:

Heart-shaped: When you're choosing hats, avoid anything large or heavily trimmed, hats with big bows in front or wide brims, or heavy folded crowns. You need witty, provocative little hats, tipped at a wicked angle on your curls. Your hat should be flat and round, with a rolled cuff brim.

Long and pointed: Your hats and hair style have to manage the job of making your face look shorter and probably fuller too. So your hats must be flat and wide. Avoid high crowns, tall brims, vertical trimmings and brimless hats, because they all add length... Choose sailor hats, bretons, broad-brimmed shapes.

Square outline: This type of face either has full cheeks or a strong well-marked jawline. You'll find that a flat hat or a broad-brimmed hat is apt to make your face look large by comparison... Look for high crowns, medium or turned-up brims, trailing ribbons or upstanding feathers, tricks that will give you length.

Oval type: You have the loveliest face type of all, the perfect shaped face that can wear any hair style that takes your fancy and any hat that suits your personality.

5 The shallow-brimmed platter, an elegant version of the earlier forties 'coolie', was a style much in evidence after the introduction of Dior's 'New Look' of 1947. VELVET. c. 1950s.

6 Sixties fashion adopted many styles from childrenswear to create youthful styles worn by young and old. Pinafore dresses, socks, shorts, baby-doll smocked dresses and schoolboy caps were all interpreted for the high street.

7,8 This Russian fashion catalogue from the seventies displays a Western fashion influence, including the soft, brimmed felt and cloche-like beret that saw a resurgence after thirties fashions were featured in the 1967 film *Bonnie and Clyde.*

9 Faded denim became the cult look of the late sixties, perfect for creating irreverent styles. What began as the fabric of workwear became high fashion, even used for accessories such as hats and handbags. MR DENIM. DENIM WITH ARTIFICIAL FLOWERS. c. 1970.

1 Simone Cange was an independent milliner who worked for Carven and also one of the leading names of Parisian millinery, Claude Saint-Cyr. This decorative cocktail hat, inspired by a Spanish matador's cap, is decorated with bullion tassels. SIMONE CANGE. METALLIC RIBBON AND BULLION. c. 1930s.

2 Caroline Reboux made a similar style of headdress to this to match Wallis Simpson's Mainbocher pale blue wedding dress. CAROLINE REBOUX. VELVET. c. 1930s.

3 As the wearing of hats dwindled, an element of playfulness can be seen in sixties designs, such as this Christmas tree-inspired hat. JACK MCCONNELL. FEATHER. c. 1960s.

Elsa Schiaparelli's hats often featured visual puns, such as the small bird used on the hat on the top right (**5**), whose tail feathers are placed to be the trailing coque feather decoration, but her designs were always intended to be flattering and sophisticated. She first gained widespread attention with her 'madcap', a fine knitted tube that could be worn in any shape chosen by its wearer. In the design shown right (**6**), the pert cashmere beret is decorated with faux pearls and features a 'chimneypot' tip.

4 ELSA SCHIAPARELLI. FUR FELT. c. 1930s.

5 ELSA SCHIAPARELLI. FELT. c. 1930s.

6 ELSA SCHIAPARELLI. CASHMERE. c. 1930s.

7 Illustration of a thirties hat design by Schiaparelli.

8,9 ELSA SCHIAPARELLI. SILK. c. 1930s.

THE GLAMOUR OF THE GLOVE

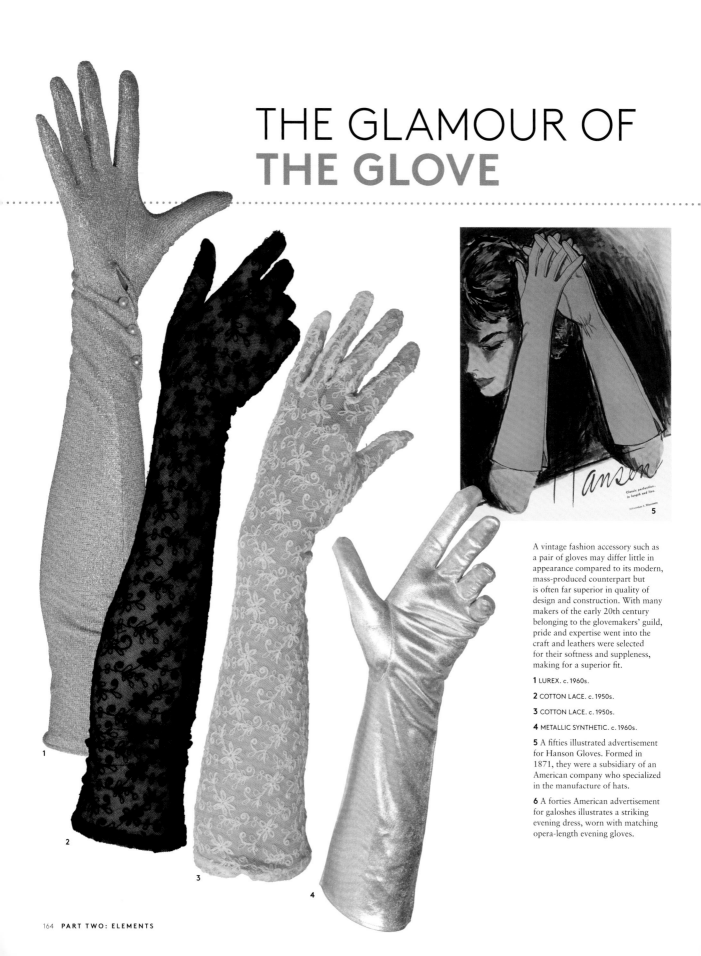

A vintage fashion accessory such as a pair of gloves may differ little in appearance compared to its modern, mass-produced counterpart but is often far superior in quality of design and construction. With many makers of the early 20th century belonging to the glovemakers' guild, pride and expertise went into the craft and leathers were selected for their softness and suppleness, making for a superior fit.

1 LUREX. c. 1960s.

2 COTTON LACE. c. 1950s.

3 COTTON LACE. c. 1950s.

4 METALLIC SYNTHETIC. c. 1960s.

5 A fifties illustrated advertisement for Hanson Gloves. Formed in 1871, they were a subsidiary of an American company who specialized in the manufacture of hats.

6 A forties American advertisement for galoshes illustrates a striking evening dress, worn with matching opera-length evening gloves.

'HANDBAGS, GLOVES AND SHOES ARE THE MARKS OF ELEGANCE IN ANY COSTUME.' EDITH HEAD, 1967

For centuries, gloves have held a formal place in fashionable etiquette. But they are also a purveyor of style, used on screen by starlets of mid-century cinema to project an erotic glamour, and they are still capable of adding drama to any contemporary ensemble.

Like Queen Elizabeth I, who reportedly distracted her councillors during meetings by removing her fabulously embellished gloves to reveal her elegant hands, the stars of forties and particularly fifties films were costumed in long satin opera-length gloves purely so the gloves could be seductively removed. Rita Hayworth caused scandal in the 1946 film noir, *Gilda*, when she performed what at the time was considered a striptease by removing her long black satin opera gloves while in full song. Marilyn Monroe, clad in fuchsia pink, performed a similarly

choreographed performance for the 1953 film *Gentlemen Prefer Blondes*. These pivotal moments transformed the modest glove into a fashion statement, a statement far removed from the practicality of the first gloves made of cloth bags tied to a wrist for warmth.

The earliest glovemakers were highly skilled artisans and formed one of the earliest guilds of tradesmen, with The Worshipful Company of Glovers of London formed in Britain in 1349 and evidence of the trade existing throughout Europe, with especially skilled examples coming from Italy. The technical craft of knitting gloves was passed down through generations, and gloves were knitted in silk thread to create elaborate patterns, personal initials or family crests. Leather gloves were made from soft perfumed chicken skin and were, for a short while, forbidden wear for women, as a gloved woman was seen as a threat to male authority.

As beautiful as many of these antique gloves are, particularly the jewel-encrusted and embroidered styles made in Venice, the majority are far too small for wear today. The fine leather shrinks with time and constant cleaning, and the modern hand is far bigger. Designs from the early decades of the 20th century are larger, with many constructed in an open stocking stitch that can stretch to accommodate a modern hand.

Leather gloves made in the thirties for the era of the open-topped car are particularly stylish. These sophisticated driving gauntlets are often cuffed and made in fine kid leather. It is the sixties driving glove, meanwhile, with its notched keyhole effect designed for ease of movement, that inspires the most reinterpretations today.

Couturiers experimented with glove design both as an essential part of an ensemble and a style statement in their own right. A 1933 edition of *Time* magazine notes that Chanel designed a pair of gloves in 18K spun gold, possibly created in response to her rival Schiaparelli's creations, which included several humorous pairs embellished with visual jokes such as musical notes, painted fingernails and gold frills.

The fifties and sixties were the heyday of glove fashion. Beautiful wrist styles can be found in coloured leathers, cuffed or discreetly ornamented, often designed to match handbags and shoes. Even easier to find today are the gauntlet styles of the eighties, an era when gloves saw a huge resurgence in popularity after being rejected as a sign of bourgeois fashion in the late sixties and seventies. Eighties power dressing borrowed the driving gauntlet from the thirties. The street style of the decade, meanwhile, was also enjoying a revival of 19th-century styles and the fingerless lace mittens, as seen on the hands of music industry icons such as Blondie, Madonna and Bananarama, continue to be worn as a decorative accessory.

If, like Grace Kelly who was dubbed 'the girl in white gloves' by *Time* magazine in 1955, gloves are your weakness, styles can be found from throughout the 20th century that have an elegance and originality not always seen today. The delicate wrist styles worn for daywear, the matinée style that barely reached the elbow, the opera style that stretched along three-quarters of the arm, or the sixties chic of a driving glove, can all still create a stylistic stir in the 21st century.

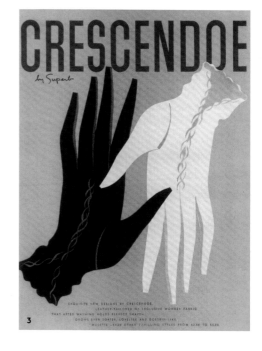

1, 2 These designs demonstrate the gauntleted glove of the thirties.

1 LEATHER. c. 1930s.

2 SUEDE AND FABRIC. c. 1930s.

3 Crescendoe was a glove manufacturer from the United States which created eye-catching illustrated promotions over several decades.

4 A twenties French advert for embroidered silk gloves. As etiquette meant gloves were meant to be worn as part of any outfit, there are many examples still to be found today.

5–16 While the old adage 'the shorter the sleeve, the longer the glove' no longer applies to contemporary fashion, the fascinating variety of 20th-century glove styles still creates stylish accessories today. Looking at vintage detailing, it is easy to see where current designers get their inspiration. Even gloves produced under the British government's utility CC41 label demonstrate attractive detailing, such as the leather trim used on this suede pair (**6**).

5 LEATHER. c. 1940s.

6 SUEDE. c. 1940s.

7 NYLON. c. 1950s.

8 LEATHER. c. 1960s.

9 STRETCH FABRIC. c. 1950s.

10 SUEDE. c. 1960s.

11 COTTON. c. 1960s.

12 COTTON LACE. c. 1920s.

13 LEATHER. c. 1950s.

14 NYLON. c. 1960s.

15 SYNTHETIC FABRIC. c. 1960s.

16 LEATHER. c. 1980s.

GANTS DE PEAU

Nos 3, 5, 6. — Modèles de la Maison Ch. PERRIN, de Grenoble
Nos 1, 2, 4. — Modèles de la Maison VILLARET, de Grenoble

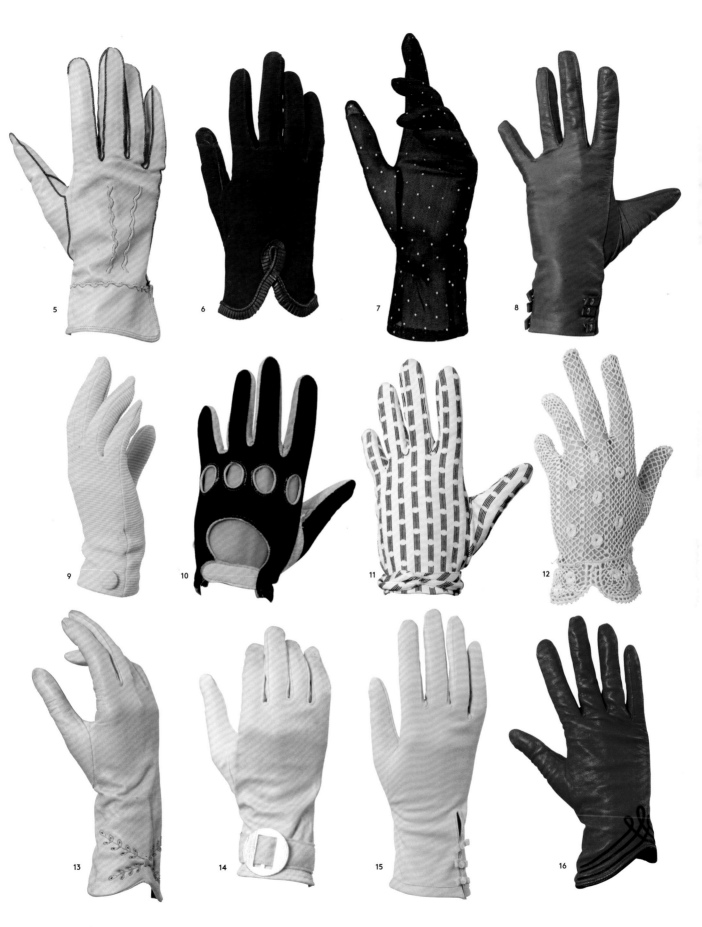

5

6

7

8

9

10

11

12

13

14

15

16

FOOTWEAR THE SOLES OF FASHION

1

Our obsession with shoes shows no signs of decline as surveys indicate that the average woman today owns more than twenty-five pairs, with many owning more than one hundred (compared with the pre-Second World War figure of eight). For the shoe-obsessed, the heritage of foot fashion offers a wealth of wearable and inspirational designs, with the number of shoe collectors and private archives of 20th-century footwear a testament to the diversity of designs that can be found from the twenties onwards, when rising skirt lengths exposed the foot as a new fashion focus.

Vintage footwear is a confident style choice that can accessorize a plethora of vintage or contemporary fashions. Beautiful vintage shoes in good condition are an inexpensive investment (although prices for archival designs of notable brands, such as Terry de Havilland, can realize far more than their modern creations). Unlike other vintage garments that can be easily cleaned to remove any trace of a previous owner, shoes suffer visibly from wear and tear and it is condition, as well as beauty and brand, which affects price.

Shoes from each era can be instantly dated from the simple point of a toe, the tilt of a heel, colour palette or ornamentation. Parallels are continually drawn between shoe styles of then and now, but, rather than being design plagiarism, this is in grateful reverence to past designs which remain beautiful.

1 These boots were a private order, handmade from an ocelot fur coat at a time when leather was required for the war effort. HANDMADE. OCELOT. c. 1940s.

2 The raised hemlines of the twenties put women's shoes on show for the first time and consequently they became dramatically modern. LARAND TENBY. LEATHER. c. 1920s.

3 Much of seventies shoe design took inspiration from both the material and styling of the forties. The platform sole and peep toe are details seen in shoes from the start of the decade, while cork was a wartime substitute that proved to be both comfortable and durable. MONDAIN. SUEDE, CORK AND SNAKESKIN. c. 1970s.

4 Stuart Weitzman, the designer behind the renowned company of the same name, was born into a shoe-manufacturing family. His signature style of incorporating unusual materials such as gold, Lucite or cork into his shoes is seen in this early eighties design that uses crystals to embellish the heels. STUART WEITZMAN. SUEDE AND CRYSTAL. c. EARLY 1980s.

2

3

4

Shoe trends have a longer cycle than the frequent fashion 'revisits' that occur on the catwalk. While fashion-forward footwear from four years ago may appear dated today, styles from forty years ago can feel surprisingly appropriate and right.

At the turn of the century, mid-calf, laced-front boots were prevalent for daywear. The low-heeled style that re-emerged as the 'granny boot' of the sixties and seventies then waned in popularity as skirt lengths rose and the ankle became a newly exposed erogenous zone. Their place was taken by the coloured leather- or suede-heeled pumps of the twenties. Colours varied from muted earth tones of easily dyed suede for daytime to surprisingly flamboyant hues that matched silk stockings and the 'savage skins' of crocodile, lizard and snakeskin – materials that blended with the rich exotica of flapper fashion. The prevailing shape of the era was the 'Mary Jane', named after the little sister of American cartoon character Buster Brown. The single one-button bar strap first worn by children was appropriated for flapper fashion and the many variations on the style included T-bars, cut-away loops and the addition of embellished shoe buckles and bows for evening. Just as the style is still appropriate for 21st-century fashion, it was revisited in the sixties by doyenne of youth fashion, Mary Quant.

The masculine two-tone flat brogues and lace-up oxfords, originally worn by women for sportswear and outdoor activity, are durable shoes from this era that remain sought after. They were colloquially named 'spectator' shoes because of their suitability for wear on the muddy sidelines of horseracing and other sports, and the craftsmanship behind their perforated leather, saddle stitching, fringed tongues and sturdy cream canvas has withheld the test of time. Perhaps more surprisingly, several of today's most popular sportswear brands also began in the early years of the 20th century. A classic of today, the Converse 'All Star', a high-topped trainer, is an American design with a blueprint dating to 1917, while the Superga lace-up began as an Italian tennis shoe even earlier, in 1911. Vintage sports shoes are a particularly collectable genre. Knowledgeable enthusiasts can date a pair of trainers by the width of an eyelet or depth of a sole. Manufacturers such as Nike and Adidas acknowledge the popularity for vintage style by re-crafting the features of iconic past designs. Weathered laces and suede inserts give seventies appeal to new designs.

It is interesting to see that by staying true to their original designs, the earliest sports shoe companies, such as Superga and Converse, still maintain a fashionable presence. On the high-end luxury side of shoe design, British brand Rayne, also founded in the twenties, maintains a shop on London's Bond Street today, as does F. Pinet, whose shoes from the twenties are displayed in museums around the world.

The name most associated with the thirties and shoe couture in general is unquestionably Italian designer Salvatore Ferragamo. Born in 1898, his passion for footwear was evident from a very early age and he opened his first boutique at only thirteen. He moved to California, where he described the shoes of a rival as having 'a toe like a potato and a heel like lead', and he succeeded in earning himself the accolade of 'shoemaker to the stars', with a client list that reads like a who's who of classic Hollywood.

A true innovator, Ferragamo introduced the reinforced steel rod to strengthen heels and many other inventions born out of wartime necessity, including replacing leather with Cellophane, felt or raffia, as well as using cork and wood for wedges and platform soles. While these substitutes were neglected as post-war life returned to normality, many of these styles, such as cork wedges, rope soles and espadrilles, have strongly influenced contemporary design. Whether introduced by Ferragamo, Pinet, Roger Vivier or André Perugia, the platform sole (a favourite of shorter stars such as Carmen Miranda) reached a zenith of popularity in the thirties, but their appeal lasted well into the forties. Shoes of the forties are differentiated by styles that exposed the foot and toes, strappy detailing, cut-away vamps or intercut sections of clear soft vinyl.

Very few people are unfamiliar with the shape of the stiletto, a form of the feminine fifties and another design with a much-disputed origin that has variously been attributed to Ferragamo, Perugia and Bruno Magli. This decade is characterized by innovation and patented designs from the stars of shoe couture. The heel was the focal point of early fifties shoe design, sculpted into dramatic spheres or contorted into high, fine needlepoints. Aside from the classic stiletto-heeled winkle picker, the decade saw heels manipulated into contortions of the cantilever, the spiralled corkscrew

'spring' heel and floating heels that appeared to defy gravity. Beth Levine patented the 'Spring-o-Lator', a device to help the new slip-on mule on the foot, subsequently incorporated by many shoe designers into their footwear.

The decade saw the emergence of sculptor-turned-shoe maverick, Roger Vivier. As shoe designer for Christian Dior, he is credited with refining the stiletto to become the 'needle heel' of 1954. He designed the jewel-encrusted shoes worn by Elizabeth II at her coronation and received the accolade of being invited to add his name to Christian Dior shoe labels, a public acknowledgment of their collaboration. His designs included exquisite examples of workmanship from embroidery experts Rébé, and the jewel-embellished evening shoes he created for Dior are true examples of couture: museum pieces rather than wearable fashions. His use of embellishment inspired mass-produced clip-on shoe jewelry that can still be found today, sold on small cards like the button cards of the thirties and often with matching earrings.

While the stiletto of the fifties retained a fashionable presence, heels became lower as hemlines got higher. Kitten heels, low square heels, chiselled toes and slingbacks epitomize the futuristic styling of the sixties that has had an enduring influence on fashion. With the focus moving to the toe, the iconic 'Pilgrim pump' accredited to Roger

1

1 Carved wooden shoes depicting holiday scenes of villages and palm trees were souvenirs of the Philippines and Hawaii in the forties. US soldiers brought many back as presents for girlfriends during the war. HANDMADE. WOOD AND LEATHER. c. 1940s.

2 Shells and seed pearls decorate the heel and toe of this evening shoe. Miniature shell trims seem to be a favourite of the fifties and can be found decorating bags, millinery and cardigans. HENRI FLATOU. SUEDE AND SHELL. 1950s.

3 The recent resurgence in Lucite shoes can be traced back to vintage examples, such as this evening sandal that uses a silk rose trapped within its heel. ANITA LAST FOR ENGEL FETZER. LUCITE. c. 1950s.

2

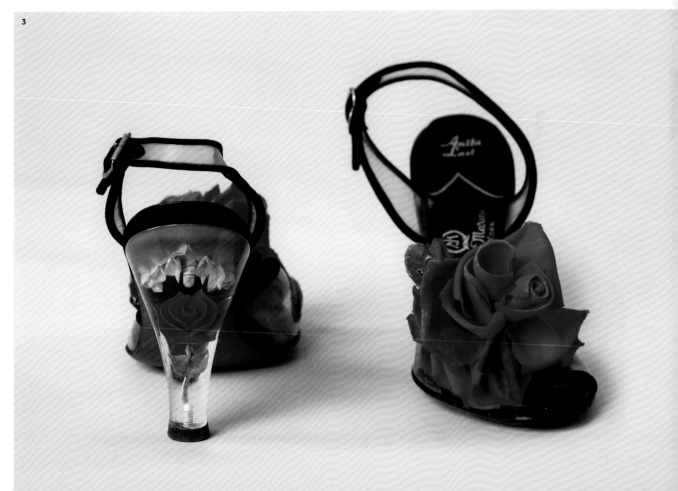

3

Vivier appeared with countless variations of toe and tongue embellishment. The decade's obsession with synthetics saw an influx of mass-produced designs in brightly coloured PVC and patent leathers. This culminated mid-decade, thanks to the influence of Space Age style, with the boot back at the forefront of fashion, available in a multitude of lengths from mid-calf to thigh-high.

Seventies shoe design readdressed archival styles in line with the varied dress silhouettes of the decade. The vintage emphasis is on the platform and the wedge reinterpreted from the fashions of the forties, but there is a vast array of styles available. The knee-high boot that typified sixties Space Age design adapted to a new bohemian era with lacing, fringing and embroidery inspired by both historical and ethnic decorative details. Long leather boots made by eminent names in the seventies (Kurt Geiger, Rayne, Sasha) were overlaid with intricate embroidery referencing motifs from the 19th century, just as contemporary footwear, such as Dolce & Gabbana's autumn/winter 2012 collection, references the tapestry and brocade styles of the seventies.

As the simplified shapes of twenties shoes often counterbalanced the exotica of its fashions, so the shoes of the eighties developed in contrast to the fashions of the decade. Sculptured, structural detailing was used to offset the simple colour blocking that defined the era. Scallops, appliquéd leathers, bows, arrows and geometric patterns, particularly the triangle, were used to emphasize the sides of shoes. Among the many eminent names in shoe design of this era, it is undoubtedly the creations of Manolo Blahnik and Charles Jourdan that continue to inspire contemporary designs.

The craftsmanship found in affordable shoes designed for everyday use from past decades can far surpass today's mass-produced shoes. While many were designed for the smaller foot of the past, with trial and effort it is possible to find unique designs that are wearable now and far into the future.

1 This 1960 photograph promotes Margaret Jerrold's line of 'matchless' shoes, identical in styling and fabric but in contrasting colours. It was a trend that did not catch on but one that was nevertheless beautiful.

2 The cantilever heel was first seen in the fifties and has made an appearance in each decade to varying degrees. CHRISTIAN DIOR. LEATHER. c.1960s.

3 A series of stylish illustrative advertisements ran in several periodicals during the early sixties to showcase Roger Vivier's designs for Christian Dior.

4 Like the mini skirt, the creation of the 'Spring-o-Lator' has been attributed to various designers. British designer Terry de Havilland certainly created a shoe that incorporated an elastic innersole and enabled mule-style shoes to fit snugly to the foot. Many manufacturers took out patents in America but the accreditation for its fashionable use is given to Beth Levine, wife of shoe manufacturer Herbert Levine. SPRING-O-LATOR. LEATHER. c. 1950s.

5 The fifties stiletto has a simple elegance still wearable today. The burnished metallic-coated leather of this American shoe has a modernity that makes the style relevant today. FRANK MORE. LEATHER. c. LATE 1950s/EARLY 1960s.

6 As well as being a feature of sixties design, contrasting black and white was also utilized by the refined end of eighties design and was often deployed as a backdrop for the decade's bright jewelled coloured suits and dresses. YVES SAINT LAURENT. SUEDE. c. 1980s.

Nous avons choisi pour vous
chez **A. GRÉSY** bottier

A) talon indépendant daim noir,
B) toile blanche, liège naturel,
C) plage ou piscine semelle bois,
D) toile blanche, gros bourrelets liège recouvert,
E) sport daim, semelle crêpe.

3

4

1 Italian-born Elio Fiorucci founded his company in the sixties and it became an international cult label. The wedge sole, ankle strap and peep toe of this shoe are all details borrowed from the forties, as can be seen in the almost identical styling on the forties shoe shown opposite (**4**). FIORUCCI. SUEDE. c. 1970s.

2 This wedge-heeled forties design uses layers of dyed snakeskin. Like fur, exotic skins were not restricted by the war and were utilized by those who could afford to have their shoes handmade. HANDMADE. SNAKESKIN. c. 1940s.

3 An advertisement for the French shoe company A. Grésy illustrates styles such as the rope-soled wedge, the studded clog and the wedged lace-up that are still regarded as high fashion in today's market.

4 The jewelled leaf embellishment on this shoe repeats the designs used on cocktail and evening dresses of the forties. HEIMELOCH. SUEDE. c. 1940s.

5 Seemingly a contradiction to the more restrained fashions manufactured under British government regulations, exotic skins were not useful for the war effort and therefore could be used in the manufacture of shoes and handbags, as in this pair stamped with the CC41 logo. Decorative highlights such as luxury skins were used sparingly, and mostly on eveningwear; over-decoration would have appeared frivolous in wartime. SUEDE AND SNAKESKIN. c. 1941.

6 This advertisement from the United States shows some of the styles of the thirties. The sandal became popular for both day and evening wear, while the sportier, two-tone 'spectator' style was worn during the summer. Slingbacks appeared for the first time in this decade.

7 Galoshes were the traditional over-boot used for protective wear during the thirties and forties. Deceptively, the attractive wrapover shape designed to be worn over delicate shoes and evening sandals is hollow in order to incorporate any heel height. RUBBERIZED CANVAS. c. 1940s.

8 Superga is an Italian sportswear brand, traditionally a manufacturer of tennis shoes, with a long history dating back to 1911. These rubber beach shoes are decorated with an imprinted starfish. SUPERGA. RUBBER. c. 1940s.

9 Patriotic fashions from the forties are rare and highly sought after, whether handmade or manufactured. While scarves, handbags and knitwear are relatively easy to find, shoes are rare. This pair is decorated with the Union Jack flag. HANDMADE. LEATHER. c. 1940s.

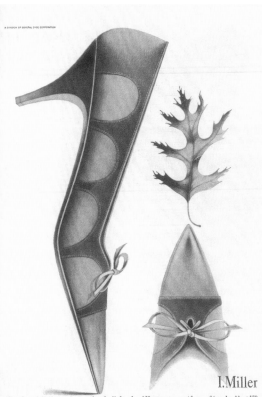

I.Miller

Shoe-Over- A double entendre in suede and calf, the color of Hue, our new go-with-everything color. About $30.

SEPTEMBER 1, 1958   169

1

2

4

3

1 Though popular, the fifties stiletto caused problems. The thin heel marked floors and often snapped or got stuck. By the sixties it had been scaled down to the kitten heel, as seen in this advertisement from the United States.

2 The heel became the focus of fifties shoe fashion: embroidered, embellished or sculpted. Like the evening dress of the decade, there was much focus on the back of the design. KAY SHOES. LEATHER. c. 1950s.

3 The popularity of lace cocktail dresses in the late fifties and early sixties inspired matching shoes. Care should be taken if wearing such shoes, as they can be fragile. FOOT DELIGHT. COTTON LACE. c. 1960s.

4 Eighties shoe styles referenced the Baroque and there was a trend for heavy metallic details, similar to the oversized belt buckles of the decade. GRANT OF KNIGHTSBRIDGE. SUEDE. c. 1980s.

5 Stockings worn in the twenties and thirties had unsightly reinforced toes and heels, so many shoes of the era had a closed toe and the slingback did not appear until towards the end of the decade when stockings had become more refined. SUEDE AND SNAKESKIN. c. 1930s.

6 Dip-dyed Lurex thread is used for the floral embroidery on this evening design by Barratts. The firm was founded in 1908 in Northampton, the traditional home of many British footwear companies. BARRATTS. SUEDE AND LUREX. c. 1950s.

7 Metallic finishes, geometric-shaped trims and electric colouring are all the hallmarks of late seventies disco style. DOUGLAS HAYWARD. LEATHER. c. 1970s.

8 Kurt Geiger was established in 1963 and remains an eminent name in British footwear fashion today. KURT GEIGER. SUEDE. c. 1980s.

9 An arrowhead is often indicative of eighties design, seen particularly on shoes, bags, rear ankles of stockings and tights as well as discreet garment placements. D'ANNA FRATELLI. PATENT LEATHER. c. 1980s.

10 One of the oldest shoe companies still in existence today, Bally was founded in Switzerland in 1850. BALLY. SILK. c. 1980s.

11 The shoe company Gina, founded in 1954 and still successful today, is inspired by the glamour of its actress namesake, Gina Lollobrigida. GINA. LEATHER. c. 1980s.

12 This shoe features overlapping snakeskin sections in the signature bright pastels of eighties design. ROLAND CARTIER. LEATHER AND SNAKESKIN. c. 1980s.

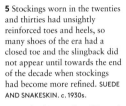

1 Many shoes and boots of the late sixties were made in suede dyed in the smoky colour palette of the early forties. Fashion was inspired by the historical, as seen in the open latticework of this design with strong medieval overtones. DANY. SUEDE. c. 1960s.

2 Space Age mod styling is reflected in these metallic leather slingback sixties shoes. DANILOW DI LUCA. LEATHER. c. 1960.

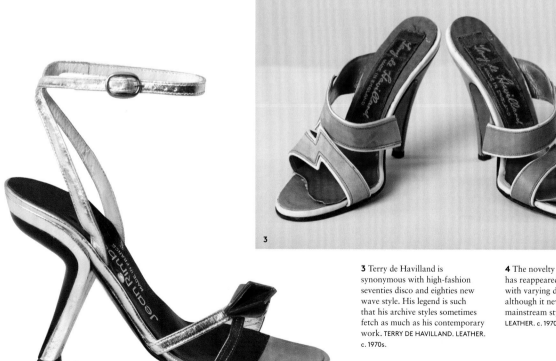

3 Terry de Havilland is synonymous with high-fashion seventies disco and eighties new wave style. His legend is such that his archive styles sometimes fetch as much as his contemporary work. TERRY DE HAVILLAND. LEATHER. c. 1970s.

4 The novelty 'cantilever' heel has reappeared over the decades with varying degrees of success, although it never became a mainstream style. JEAN RIMBAUD. LEATHER. c. 1970s.

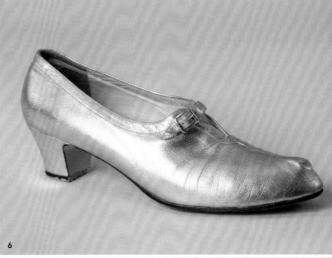

5 The seventies penchant for earthy two-tones and perforated leather was inspired by the traditional hardwearing 'spectator' shoes of twenties and thirties sportswear. PETER LORD. LEATHER. c. 1970s.

6 This is a rare metallic leather design that belies its age. Ferragamo is one of the most notable names in shoe fashion, leaving a legacy of design innovations. SALVATORE FERRAGAMO. LEATHER. 1951.

7 The daisy was the flower of the sixties, seen on everything including shoes. KEELING. LEATHER. c. 1960s.

8 The so-called 'Pilgrim Buckle' was a large square buckle used to decorate the fronts of many sixties shoes. The introduction of the style is generally attributed to Roger Vivier. BRUNO MAGLI. IMPRINTED LEATHER. c. 1960s.

9 As the sixties progressed the kitten heel became wider, with the square-toed, block heel becoming the look of the day. RIMMAL. SATIN. c. 1960s.

quant takes that brilliance to boots!

With quant afoot—boots with a difference in a sparkling first collection of shiny-bright boots by Mary Quant. In crystal clear plastic over colours that zoom into fashion's orbit, they're boots that shrug off wear and weather marks, come up shining. Five different styles, all with the uncluttered, unmistakable Quant touch, all in a choice of colours, all from sizes 3, 3½, right up to 7. The shiny red plastic bag is free—and, for the girl who likes things neat and tidy, there's a quant afoot cotton shoe bag in five different colours for 5/- each. Just watch quant afoot boots start walking, all over town.

1 ▲ 6 'Zip' 6 colours 49/11
2 'Porthole' 4 colours 49/11
3 'Cuff' 3 colours 49/11
4 'Chelsea' 4 colours 49/11
5 'Daddy Long Legs' 4 colours 79/11

quant afoot by mary quant

Mary Quant Footwear Ltd
3 Ives Street, Chelsea
London SW3

1, 2 Mary Quant introduced a highly polished rubber collection of shoes and interchangeable boots in vibrant colours into her design repertoire in the sixties. The identifiable Quant daisy is embossed into their heel. MARY QUANT. RUBBER. c. 1960s.

3 This is a refined, later version of the Mary Jane style, adopted from twenties footwear by Quant. MARY QUANT. LEATHER. c. 1960s.

4 The mirror-like surface of patent leather was a popular fabric for mid-sixties fashion accessories. Metallics and reflective surfaces went hand-in-hand with the Space Age look of the era. Early patent leathers have a tendency to peel and crack and are not a good investment unless they have been carefully stored. DANNEL. PATENT LEATHER. c. 1960s.

5 The fashionable introduction of the boot is generally credited to André Courrèges who included a low-heeled, mid-calf, pointed-toe design in his 1964 collection. The style grew in popularity in the seventies. SUEDE. c. 1970s.

6 Imitation snake, lizard and other animal skins were widely used in the late sixties and seventies as a celebration of all things natural. PLASTIC. c. LATE 1960s.

7 This early eighties photo shows Vivienne Westwood and Malcolm McLaren's 'Pirate' look. A pair of the boots was bought years later by Kate Moss from the London vintage store Rellik. Subsequent paparazzi shots created such frenzied internet auction activity that the design was reissued in 1999 and continues to be sold today.

8 Mid-sixties high street design took inspiration from the avant-garde styles of André Courrèges and Paco Rabanne. Primary colours and clean lines were combined with low heels to create futuristic looks. RIMMAL. SUEDE. c. MID-1960s.

9 Charles Jourdan designed under many labels, including Dior, Pierre Cardin and Hervé Léger. Here a version of the Louis heel supports an ankle boot. CHARLES JOURDAN. VELVET AND LEATHER. c. EARLY 1990s.

HANDBAGS
FUNCTIONAL FASHION

2

1

It is the fashionable heritage and inherent craftsmanship of the handbag that wins it 21st-century appreciation. Despite it being revered by many as the ultimate investable fashion accessory, there is no recognized seal of approval for handbag design, unlike the makers of shoes, millinery and even spectacles whose ancient skills are all recognized by a guild. Nonetheless vintage handbags are the work of craftsmen and are some of the most recognizable designs generated by fashion houses. Leathers, metals, luxurious fabrics, even Bakelite and plastics have been used to craft desirable and functional artefacts that display the zeitgeist of each era. Superior 20th-century artistry means that a vintage handbag does not have to be the product of a renowned brand or fashion house to be of commercial value. Many of the most desirable models bear no maker's name, and the waiting lists for each season's most desired offering has led to intense bidding on auction sites for their vintage equivalents.

Handbags originated as a simple hanging pocket hidden within women's skirts and, by the mid-1880s, developed into decorative hanging reticules, worn dangling from the wrists of upper-class women. Their decorative qualities were echoed in the homemade mesh bags of the twenties, a result of the fashionable pastime of knitting with beads and metallic threads.

The structured handbag as we know it today gradually developed from the array of luggage required to transport the array of elegant costumes worn by wealthy socialites for luncheons and dinners. As weekend sojourns became less formal and train travel more available, a need for 'hand' luggage developed. Louis Vuitton was one of the

earliest makers of luxury travel trunks and, in 1896, became the first company to establish a logo as a recognizable mark of their craftsmanship. Their early 'Keepall' bags were designed for twenties weekend travel and were renamed later, as they got smaller, as the 'Speedy'. Even smaller versions followed after Audrey Hepburn requested a handbag-sized version of the 'Speedy', which subsequently became one of the most photographed bags of the sixties.

The beautiful chainmail-inspired bags associated with flapper fashions of the twenties were the luxury products of jewellers and silversmiths and it was the technical advances of a company still in business today, Whiting & Davis, that made them more widely available. Early collaborations between the company and eminent names of fashion, such as Paul Poiret and Elsa Schiaparelli, and continual celebrity endorsement, placed these highly collectable bags at the forefront of fashion and helped establish a long, successful history.

By the turn of the century, women carried both framed bags with handles and '*pochettes*', the forerunner of the clutch bag for daytime. Initially carried by younger women, the *pochette*

1 The collectable metal mesh bags of American company Whiting & Davis can date back to the latter years of the 19th century, when the bags were still handmade. It is widely considered that their mechanically manufactured bags of the thirties are the most superior in quality.

2 The famous Hotel Meurice on the rue de Rivoli in Paris sold high-fashion accessories in their boutique in the years preceding and following the Second World War. These included Anne Marie's surrealist handbags. The bags are usually black and resemble the functional items that could be found around a hotel, such as a champagne bucket, a grand piano and, as seen here, a telephone. The bags are always labelled as Anne Marie of Paris, giving the Hotel Meurice as the address. ANNE MARIE OF PARIS. ANTELOPE. c. 1940s.

3, 4 Tartan in the fifties was used for a chic, high-end look and matching handbag, shoes and gloves were the height of fashionable elegance. These sets often become separated over time and can command high prices if complete today. WOOL. c. 1950s.

5 Later designs from the Chanel house have reworked the classic 2.55 design, including elements such as the distinctive metallic chain and quilted leather, making the brand's bags instantly recognizable.

1 A magazine editorial for a woven clutch bag by Josef of Gold Seal. Considered suitable for summerwear, the bag retailed at $4 in the forties and was manufactured in a variety of colourways.

2, 3 Two twenties beaded evening bags display the oriental influences that were so prevalent in this period. Bags like these were often handmade using patterns from women's periodicals. HANDMADE. BEADED. c. 1920s.

4 KID LEATHER. c. 1930s.

5 Little is known about the handcrafted bags that can be found by French designer Germaine Guérin dating back to the thirties. However, they command high prices in vintage shops and at auction today.

6 Like many shoe designers, Bruno Magli expanded his range during the eighties to include matching handbags. BRUNO MAGLI. LEATHER. c. 1980s.

7 The clutch bag of the seventies imitated the carpetbags of the 19th century. VELVET. c. 1970s.

5

8 Bag fashion in the sixties is more varied than in any other decade of vintage fashion, offering a plethora of choice for vintage enthusiasts today. SNAKESKIN. c. 1960s.

9 This casual bag was designed to be interchangeable with different outfits. The leopard-skin-patterned fabric unhooks from the main body of the bag so it can be changed for another pattern. PLASTIC AND COTTON. c. 1950s.

10 SNAKESKIN. c. 1930s.

11, 12 Leopard print was a favourite pattern of the fifties. At the start of the decade it was an expensive motif used by designers such as Dior, but it became so overused it appeared common within its own time.

11 PLASTIC. c. 1950s.

12 DESALE. PRINTED LEATHER. c. 1950s.

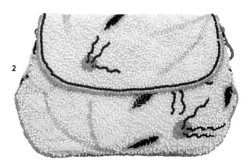

2

3

6

4

7

developed to become a 'clutch', the height of fashion, and by the thirties large streamlined envelope clutches echoing the fashionable silhouette of the era were the 'It' bags of the decade.

Like the fitted suits and feminine dresses of the thirties, the decade's bags were influenced by Art Deco style with oversized adorning buttons and buckles and, occasionally, defining sculpted handles. Evening bags are identifiable by features including jewelled Art Deco brooch-style fastenings, quilting and understated embroidery, or the rarer sighting of a hallmark or stamp from one of the jewellers of the decade such as Cartier or Asprey. Many day bags were made from exotic animal skins, such as snake, python, lizard or crocodile.

The functional shoulder bag of the early forties has a wartime chic in line with the practical clothing of the decade. Sturdy serviceable shoulder straps are reminiscent of satchels, with a military aesthetic. In surprising contrast, forties bags can be found made from fur skins, which were not rationed in wartime, especially in the United States. Raffia and wood were also used as alternatives to much-needed leather.

Guccio Gucci had established his Florentine company in 1921 on return from working at the Savoy Hotel in London. Inspired by the style of aristocratic luggage that passed through the hotel, he built up a notable leather manufacturing company. However, his first iconic bag, the Bamboo, came about as a result of wartime shortages. Designed in 1947, the bag had a handle made from burnished bamboo. Seen on the arm of Elizabeth Taylor in the fifties, it remains a celebrity must-have today. By the end of the forties, bag design became more structured and leathers were dyed in fashionable hues to tone with fashions of the period.

The fifties heralded the arrival of a bag copied since the date of its inception, February 1955. Also named after that date, the Chanel 2.55 was conceived by Coco Chanel to allow women to have their hands free at social functions. She explained, 'I was fed up

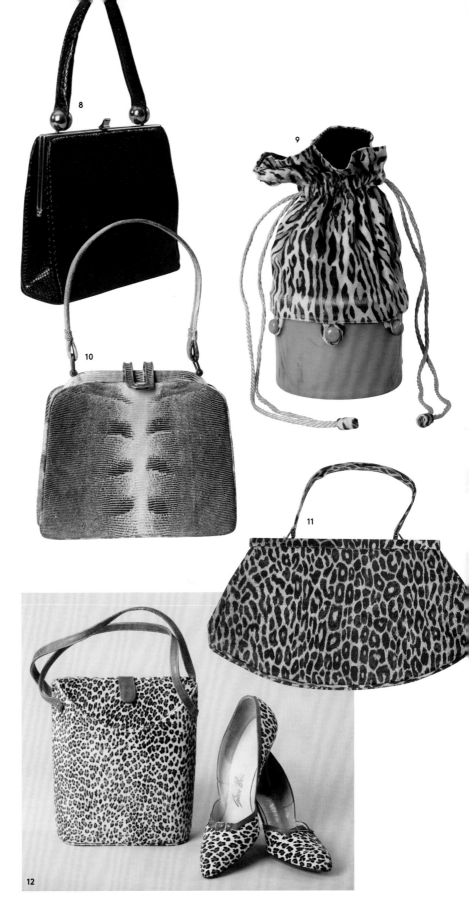

8

9

10

11

12

with holding my purses in my hands and losing them, so I added a strap.' As ever, its design attributes are thought to be found in Chanel's childhood roots: the quilting is like that of a stable boy's jacket and the metal and plaited leather straps have equestrian connotations reminiscent of Chanel's teenage riding days. She used the internal secret pocket to hide her love letters.

The equestrian heritage of Hermès has also proved influential on their bag design. This family firm was established in 1869 as a bespoke maker of equestrian equipment and began making their first handbags in 1922 at the request of the wife of a company director. Their famous bag, now known as the 'Kelly', was featured on the front cover of *Life* magazine in 1956, being used to shield signs of its namesake Grace Kelly's early pregnancy from the press. The photograph unintentionally led to huge sales for the bag. The company's iconic 'Birkin' bag was famously redesigned in 1984 to be big enough for the paraphernalia carried by actress Jane Birkin.

The innovations of the fifties also saw the introduction of the Lucite handbag in the United States. Lucite was a sophisticated plastic used by Will Hardy to design a series of tough, clear, boxlike bags. The Will Hardy 'Rocket' was handcrafted and embellished with semi-precious stones, but, like other iconic bags of the day, it was widely imitated when injection-moulded plastic took the world of accessories by storm. The visual appeal of these ornamental items means they are still high on collectors' lists today.

Sixties designs continued to use plastic, its qualities in tune with Op Art geometrics and Space Age sheen. Chainmail returned, not inspired by the small jewelled bags of the twenties, but with an industrial aesthetic and futuristic aspirations. In stark contrast, the latter part of the decade saw the first vintage bags, in the form of the well-worn traditional doctor's bag (the 'Gladstone') and the tapestry carpetbag of the 19th century (designed

from carpet leftovers to open out as a sleeping platform for travelling salesmen). These became 'It' bags of the decade, along with the fringed, macramé and beaded suede shoulder bags associated with hippy fashions.

The eighties love of brand awareness, power dressing and statement accessories needs no introduction. With architectural styling and fixtures and fittings designed to be noticed, these designs set a standard for the way bags are worn that is still with us today. Perhaps because the handbag has a job to do, the same design styles can be seen across each decade: the clutch, satchel, barrel, box and tote are traditional names for styles that are continually adapted to match the current fashion. A round wicker bag from the fifties may bear a strong resemblance to the 2013 Chanel 'Hula Hoop', but the pleasure comes in the fact that it is even more unique, a bespoke rarity that few others will own.

1 Beaded bags were among the most popular of sixties youth trends and varied enormously in quality. Plastic bangles, earrings and necklaces as well as bags were all manufactured in bubblegum colours. PLASTIC. c. 1960s.

2,3 The plastics industry in the United States was far more advanced than in Europe in the fifties. The result was some uniquely crafted fashion accessories. Lucite bags were the first of these plastic bags and are superior to the cheaper plastic versions that arrived towards the end of the decade.

2 PERSPEX. c. LATE 1950s.

3 GILLI ORIGINALS. LUCITE. c. LATE 1940s/EARLY 1950s.

6, 7 Often handcrafted or made at home, twenties tapestry bags frequently reference Art Deco chevrons, sunrays and abstracted geometrics. Embroidered styles often feature picturesque scenes or diminutive florals and were commonly used for daytime.

6 HANDMADE. WOOL. c.1920s.

7 HANDMADE. GROSGRAIN. c.1920s.

8 The fifties evening bag was also subject to novelty decoration, just like its daytime counterpart. On this evening bag a celluloid rose, the flower of the fifties, is used to form the clasp. VELVET. c.1950s.

9 The novelty theme continues with a lobster pot-shaped straw bag for holiday or seaside use. STRAW. c.1950s.

10 Woven raffia became a common fabric for inexpensive daytime bags. This spotted design is used in a typical fifties colour palette of emerald green, red and yellow on a black background. This coloration is evident on many printed dresses and upholstery fabrics of the decade. RAFFIA. c.1950s.

4 Novelty bags were very popular in the fifties in the United States, a light-hearted celebration at the end of wartime. PLASTIC. c.1950s.

5 Many bags from the twenties are typically made from fabric. The sliding buckle allows the contents to be anchored in place. COTTON. c. LATE 1920s/EARLY 1930s.

1

2

3

6

7

8

11

12

13

4

5

9

10

14

15

1 Small handled day bags with oversized clasps were typical of thirties design. SUEDE. c. 1930s.

2 By the forties clasps had become more discreet. SUEDE. c. EARLY 1930S/LATE 1940s.

3 Emilio Pucci, the 'Prince of Prints', designed bags in silks and velvets to match his distinctive fashions. EMILIO PUCCI. SILK. c. 1960s.

4 This envelope-style printed silk bag has an unusual opening for its handles. SILK. c. 1960s.

5 Tapestry effects that once signified an older generation have completely different style connotations in a contemporary market. WOOL. c. 1960s.

6 LEATHER. c. 1930s.

7 Jackie Onassis had a much-imitated style that utilized the clean lines and simple shapes that can be seen in this bag. FARFALLA. SILK. c. 1960s.

8 The wide soft handle on this bag marks it as a design from the early forties. SUEDE. c. 1940s.

9 Waldy bags were a popular wartime present of American soldiers who visited the UK. Their reasonable price meant they were frequently taken home as presents for girlfriends. WALDY. SUEDE. c. 1960s.

10 A bag made from wooden beads, one of the wartime substitutes for leather. WOOD. c. 1930s.

11 Moulded or imprinted leather is indicative of early to mid-thirties designs. LEATHER. c. 1930s.

12 The bag of the forties was distinctly utilitarian and sensible. LEATHER. c. 1940s.

13 The trend for bowling inspired a wide variety of bags for carrying the balls. SYNTHETIC. c. 1950s.

14 This rare design from the thirties features sleeping dog clasps made from Bakelite. LEATHER. c. 1930s.

15 The fifties are typified by their experimentation with different materials for bag construction. SILK AND LEATHER. c. 1950s.

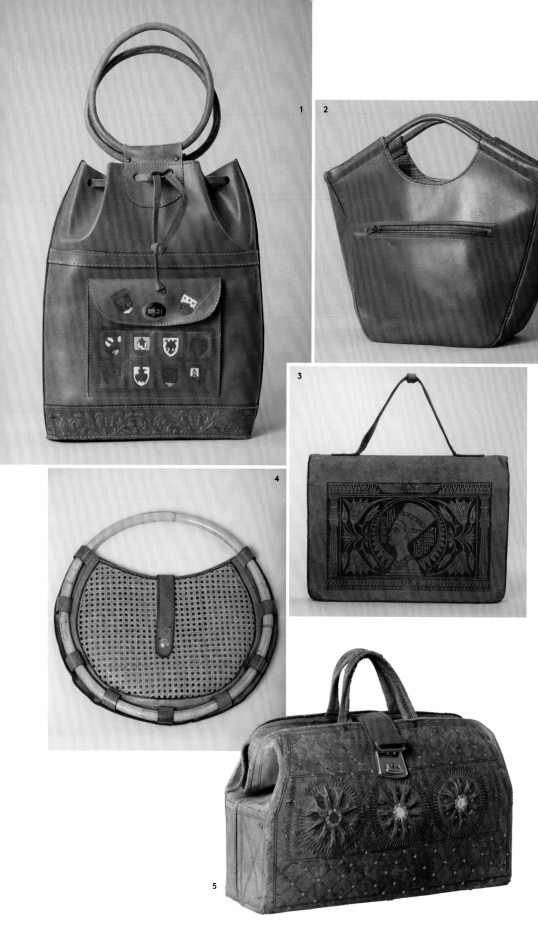

1, 6 Travel and all its ephemera had a big impact on the fashion industry. Flags, luggage stickers, stamps and train tickets were all used as design motifs on garments and accessories.

1 LEATHER. c. 1950s.

6 WICKER. c. 1950s.

2 The bucket bag was so-called because it resembled a bucket. It was traditionally oval in shape but there were many variations on the style. LEATHER. c. 1940s.

3 A rare tooled-leather bag from the late twenties illustrates the craze that followed the discovery of Tutankhamen's tomb. Nicknamed 'Egyptomania', Egyptian symbols were used to decorate almost everything. LEATHER. c. LATE 1920s.

4 This woven wicker and leather bag has a bamboo handle (a feature also used by Gucci because of the leather shortages during the Second World War). LEATHER, WICKER AND BAMBOO. c. 1970s.

5 As cheaper travel became available to many after the war, fashionable accessories displayed the influences of foreign travel. LEATHER. c. 1950s.

6

7

8

9

10

7 Parts of the United States had their own distinctive look, reflecting an outdoor lifestyle. North America helped establish a new relaxed dress code that, in turn, created a whole new genre of fashion: sportswear. New styles of bags were needed to complete the look. MIDAS OF MIAMI. WICKER. c. 1950s.

8 Simple leather strands provide the decoration on a casual 'weekend' bag. LEATHER. c. 1950s.

9 This fifties fashion editorial from *Vogue* illustrates a bold striped summer dress worn with a summer handbag in an eye-catching bull's-eye design of the same colours.

10 Seaside holidays and increased leisure time created a market for casual handbags. The fifties saw woven straw and raffia bags and printed plastics bearing seaside symbols. Real shells were inexpensive decorations often used to decorate the holiday handbag. PLASTIC. c. 1950s.

3

1

2

4

5

6

A FASHIONABLE EYE

1 The United States was far ahead of Europe in its development of the plastics industry, which had a profound impact on spectacle design. By the late forties, decorative techniques had become more elaborate and women's spectacle frames began to be treated like a piece of jewelry. PLASTIC. c.1940s.

2 Elsa Schiaparelli launched her debut accessories collection in June 1951. Her first commercial eyewear range for the company American Optical used platinum with diamanté embellishments and was one of the many fashion accessories Schiaparelli licensed her name to after the Second World War. Her fashion house was forced to close down in 1954 but auctions in recent years still record high prices for licensed fashion accessories manufactured after this date.

3 The elongated cat-eye was a development from the harlequin shape fashionable in the forties. Continued innovations in new plastics such as cellulose acetate allowed for exciting colour ranges and textured finishes. Fashion and eyewear became increasingly linked and frame colours matched vibrant new lipstick shades such as 'Fire and Ice' by Revlon and Avon's 'Congo Red', 'Blue Jewel' and 'Crimson Beauty'. PLASTIC. c.1950s.

4 An early example of the injection moulding that allowed the detailing finishes and dye techniques of glasses to become highly elaborate. TRANSLUCENT PLASTIC. c.1950s.

5 By the end of the fifties, the cat-eye developed into elaborate shapes resembling bird and butterfly wings. PLASTIC. c. LATE 1950s.

6 Fifties fashion was all about accessories. A hat, gloves, handbag, scarf and pair of sunglasses were integral to a fashionable ensemble. The delicate jewelled brows on this American frame were a popular trim that defined a well-shaped eyebrow and the fashionable make-up of the day. PLASTIC AND METAL. c. LATE 1950s.

'TO ME, EYEWEAR GOES WAY BEYOND BEING A PRESCRIPTION. IT'S LIKE MAKE-UP. IT'S THE MOST INCREDIBLE ACCESSORY. THE SHAPE OF A FRAME OR THE COLOUR OF A LENS CAN CHANGE YOUR WHOLE APPEARANCE.' VERA WANG

From their first conception, sunglasses have always been synonymous with glamour. The appeal of vintage sunglasses as the epitome of 'cool' reaches as far back as the twenties. It was a style that emerged amid the new-found popularity of foreign travel and the emerging starlets of a blossoming film industry.

Although tinted lenses had been invented as eyewear for those with perspective conditions as far back as the 18th century, it wasn't until the twenties that they were developed as a commercial venture. Sunglasses, or 'suncheaters' as they were known, really took off as a result of American company Foster Grant's efforts to avoid bankruptcy. Foster Grant was originally a manufacturer specializing in the production of colourful plastic haircombs, but, with the arrival of the flapper girl and her bobbed haircut, demand suddenly dropped for haircombs and pins, leaving manufacturers such as Foster Grant in financial trouble. In a resourceful move, the company used the easily dyed and moulded celluloid to make coloured frames with tinted lenses. These were sold for ten cents in the self-service section of Woolworths in the seaside town of Atlantic City, making Foster Grant the first company to market inexpensive sunglasses for fashionable wear.

Meanwhile, other companies including Bausch & Lomb developed a method of treating lenses to filter ultraviolet sunrays. The result was a mass of inexpensive and attractive sunglasses widely available in time for the post-First World War travel boom. Sophisticated travel on luxury yachts, cruise ships and steam trains took in the resorts of Lisbon, Paris, Monte Carlo, Nice and Deauville, and these playgrounds for the fashionable elite became catwalks for the latest styles.

In Hollywood, stars of the burgeoning and prosperous motion-picture industry readily adopted the innovative and attractive dark glasses on set to shield their eyes from the bright studio lights. Long hours under the harsh lighting caused unsightly redness. As stars were frequently spotted emerging from film studios, looking mysteriously alluring in their dark glasses, it was a look that gained popularity as it could easily be copied by their fans.

The endless variety of shapes and styles that emerged from the 20th century are echoed in contemporary designs, while some models have emerged as timeless classics whose design styles cannot be improved upon. Original aviators worn by pilots in the thirties have become expensive collectables, while the Wayfarer is a mid-century classic that enjoyed a huge resurgence in the eighties. From the round-rimmed 'tea shades' of John Lennon to the oversized 'O's' associated with Jackie Onassis, these legendary designs have enduring appeal amid a host of modern imitations.

Like the garments of each decade, each era of eyewear has its own distinctive shapes and styles meaning there is plenty of choice for each face shape. Frame sizes have grown steadily since the small 'round eyes' of the twenties, reaching dizzy proportions in the 'face framers' of the seventies. Frames from the twenties were typically round and made in fragile tortoiseshell or metal with the same shapes worn by both sexes. By the thirties, new manufacturing techniques and materials saw the introduction of angular and 'panto' styles in coloured celluloid, a form that became associated with styles issued by the National Health Service from 1948 onwards. The end of the thirties saw the introduction of the flimsy butterfly-shaped, rimless lenses of feminine sunglasses, a style that has been reinterpreted by almost every notable fashion house today.

Technology within the plastics industries in the United States in the forties was far more advanced than in Europe. American women were able to indulge in exciting ophthalmic frames stylistically in tune with all the trends of the era. Sunglasses frames displayed fabric-like patterns of checks and stripes; they could even be customized to match an outfit by trapping the chosen fabric within the plastic. As the decade progressed, decoration became even more elaborate, featuring diamanté, animal motifs, glitter effects and intricate engraving. Glasses were treated like a piece of jewelry and many women owned several pairs to accessorize individual ensembles. The end of the decade saw the introduction of the harlequin shape, forerunner of the distinctive cat-eye that followed in the fifties.

The pronounced shape of the elongated cat-eye is the definitive style of both sunglasses and prescriptive frames of the decade and a shape adopted by many present-day fashionistas. The fifties was an era that saw the first endorsements by several leading names of fashion. The American designer, Claire McCardell, created her own line of eyewear and each pair had her name printed on the arm, a forerunner of today's eyewear branding. Elsa Schiaparelli, meanwhile, who had

already explored the possibilities of artistic statement of eyewear having produced surreal blue-feathered eyelashes in the style of her friends and collaborators Jean Cocteau and Salvador Dalí, was invited to endorse a range for the company, American Optical.

As the feline cat-eye typifies eyewear shapes of the fifties, so the 'O' is present in every aspect of sixties fashion. A simplified modernism echoes through the designs of the Atomic Age, rejecting the fussiness of previous generations. Geometric shapes of circles, squares and even triangles can be found in many accessories of the time, not least spectacle frames whose designers were uninhibited in creating their futuristic fashions. Jacqueline Onassis popularized round frames and they became so associated with her elegance of dress that they were nicknamed 'Jackie Os'. Oliver Goldsmith, which had been founded in 1926, was one of the most iconic brands of the sixties. The frame shapes manufactured by the company at this time were at the cutting edge of design and marketed with great success using the power of celebrity endorsement. Audrey Hepburn, Britt Ekland and Princess Grace of Monaco were just some of the names who were seen wearing Goldsmith designs. Optical designers of this decade focused on function as well as aesthetics, and frames were solid and often handmade by companies such as Goldsmith, Persol,

1 A fifties advertisement for a French brand of eyewear, 'Amor'.

2 An early and unusual geometric version of the cat-eye with a plaid patterning inspired by a woven or printed check fabric. This was part of a trend to coordinate frames with fashion: occasionally actual fabric was trapped within the frame while in production to make for a truly coordinated outfit. PLASTIC. c.1940s.

3 A forties advertisement for harlequin frames, the shape that was the forerunner of the cat-eye. The harlequin shape was the brainchild of American entrepreneur Altina Schinasi Miranda, who, while working as a window dresser on New York's Fifth Avenue, was struck by the stylish frames on offer in a neighbouring optician. Taking inspiration from the theatrical harlequin mask, she designed a frame to flatter the contours of a feminine face.

4

5

6

4 A rare mirrored-lens pair of sunglasses with an Art Deco-inspired gold corner trim. PLASTIC. c. LATE 1940s.

5 A thirties moulded frame with a pressed cutwork design on the arm. The dye effects were created in the moulding stage. With the United States at the forefront of the plastics industry during the thirties, the decade also witnessed what was to become a design classic, the Ray-Ban Aviator, originally developed as an aid for airline pilots. PLASTIC. c. 1930s.

6 These glasses use an unusual combination of bronze metallic finish on transparent blue plastic in the harlequin shape. Women were encouraged to own several different frames to coordinate with different outfits. TRANSLUCENT PLASTIC AND METAL. c. 1950s.

7 The elaborate loop design on these fifties spectacles suggests this pair was probably reserved for eveningwear, with a plainer frame worn during the day. Magazine editorials discouraged the wearing of jewelry when wearing elaborate sunglasses or spectacle frames. PLASTIC AND DIAMANTÉ. c. 1950s.

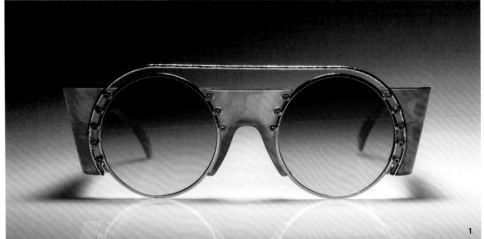

Relax, pretty one . . .

it's holiday time, and you have nothing in the world to do but laze and be your
charming self . . . and maybe to choose from the hearts that lie at your feet.
Homage will be yours wherever you go, for you have Yardley beauty-things
and skill in using them. And what man can resist loveliness so subtle that
it seems to have no need of art?

Complexion Milk 6/6
Lipstick : six shades 4/3
Refills 2/6   Skin Food 6/6
Sorry, no pots ordered!

Yardley
33 · OLD BOND STREET
LONDON

1 Towards the end of the eighties, eyewear became sculptural and sophisticated, and oversized style statements were the fashion of the era. PALOMA PICASSO. TORTOISESHELL AND GOLD-EFFECT PLASTIC. c. 1980s.

2, 3 The elaborate twist of these glasses highlights the effects that could be achieved with injection moulding.

2 HONEYSHELL. c. 1960s.

3 MOCK TORTOISESHELL. c. 1960s.

4 Seaside resorts were catwalks for the latest fashions. This thirties advertisement for Yardley promotes glamour on the beach.

5 These are a rare pair of wooden frames by Italian company Persol. It was founded by Giuseppe Ratti, who, as early as the thirties, introduced what was to become one of the most iconic insignias in eyewear design, the famous silver arrow. The arrow, which is also the hinge, is seen on all Persol frames and was inspired by the swords of ancient warriors. PERSOL. WOOD. c. 1960.

6 The sixties favoured unfussy geometric shapes for eyewear in tune with the modernist, Op Art-inspired fashion of the day. The most prevalent shape in fashionable sixties eyewear was the circle. Popularized by Jackie Onassis, round sunglasses were given the nickname 'Jackie Os'. PLASTIC. c. 1960s.

7 Fifties and sixties fashion took influence from the chic, understated appeal of Italian design. Manufacturers from the country, such as Persol, began to have a major fashionable presence thanks to product placement in films such as *La Dolce Vita* (1960) and *Divorce, Italian Style* (1961). PLASTIC AND METAL. c. 1960s.

8 Towards the end of the decade, the round frame that was so evident in sixties eyewear developed into the lozenge shape of this pair. The black and white optical effect is called a 'rising sun' motif. LAYERED PLASTIC. c. 1960s.

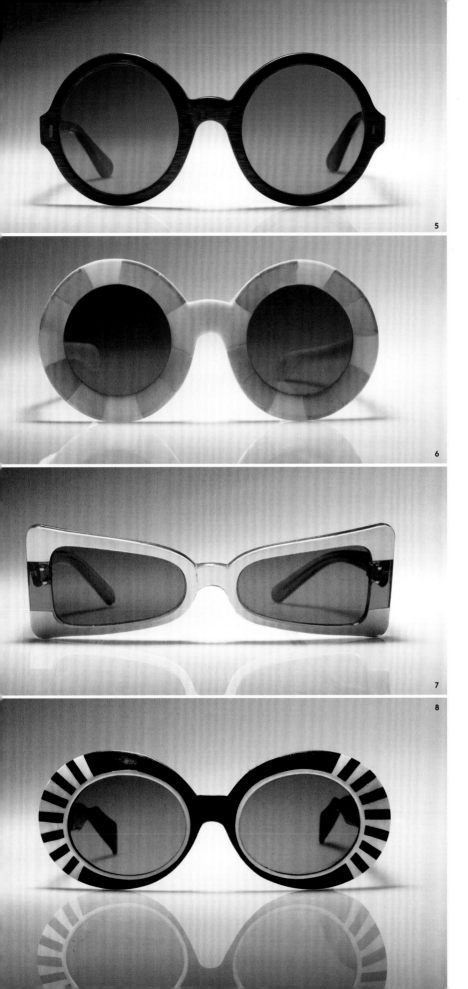

5

6

7

8

Neostyle, Ray-Ban and Anglo American. Eyewear of the sixties therefore remains eminently wearable today, although it is a little heavier and more fragile than designs from the following decades.

Seventies frame shapes are the most celebrated today and vintage samples mix happily with contemporary models that have been sourced from archival designs. Eyewear from this decade was revolutionized by the introduction of plastic lenses and, more importantly to frame design, a plastic known as Optyl. This exciting innovation was patented by Wilhelm Anger of Viennaline (later to become Carrera) and was valued for its lightness and durable elasticity, as well as being the first plastic that could be injection-moulded to allow experimental dye techniques. Names such as Yves Saint Laurent, Diane von Furstenberg, Pierre Cardin, Christian Dior, André Courrèges and Halston teamed with manufacturers to create desirable branded accessories, still highly collectable and one of the most in demand – and most expensive – areas of vintage eyewear.

While the epic proportions and electric colouring of eighties eyewear remain a staple of street culture, the sophisticated Ray-Ban Wayfarer also saw a resurgence in this decade prompted by product placement in cult films such as *The Blues Brothers* and *Risky Business*. Over forty variations of the style were manufactured at this time and remain highly sought after today.

Contemporary choices from the distinctive shapes and finishes that have emerged from a century of design may be governed by what best suits our facial features. But eyewear is an accessory that can add a unique touch to our chosen fashion. Be it sunglasses or prescriptive frames, vintage eyewear is a powerful accessory that can convey whatever image we desire.

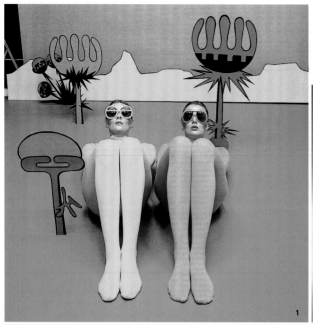

1 This 1974 advertisement is for Silhouette's Futura sunglasses, a limited-edition range of electric-coloured frames that became an international sensation. Established in 1964, the Austrian company quickly became the purveyor of cutting-edge style in eyewear. Their avant-garde frames were seen in the controversial 1974 film *Emmanuelle*, while 1972 saw the publication of the *Silhouette Journal*, 'the first magazine to showcase the very latest in all aspects of eyewear design', with covers often designed by René Gruau. The company even designed earrings to match their frames.

2 The frames of seventies glasses became so big that the term 'face framers' was coined. Colours were matched to the earthy make-up colours fashionable at the time. OPTYL. PLASTIC. c. 1970s.

3 Oliver Goldsmith was the first optical designer to appear in *Vogue*. Known for producing outrageous shapes, he continues to be at the forefront of design and his eyewear is seen on many famous faces. OLIVER GOLDSMITH. PLASTIC. c. 1960s.

4 Designed to be reversible, these frames by Jean Patou reflect the ethos of an era whose fashion was youth-led. JEAN PATOU FOR ZEISS. PLASTIC. c. 1960s.

5 Sophisticated novelty is a continuing theme of eyewear. The gold lettering effect on these Paloma Picasso glasses echo the street fashion for graffiti and the trend for 'message' fashion as

championed by Katharine Hamnett and Vivienne Westwood. PALOMA PICASSO. PLASTIC. c. EARLY 1990s.

6 The development of Optyl (not to be confused with the company of the same name) and the replacement of glass lenses with plastic meant that frames could reach almost epic proportions while remaining durable and light. PIERRE CARDIN. ACETATE. c. 1970s.

7 By the end of the 20th century, every frame shape had been explored and revisited. Even heart-shaped frames had been seen before during the sixties, popularized by the promotional poster for the 1962 cinematic version of *Lolita*. METAL. c. 1990s.

8 Advertising for the Silhouette brand of eyewear: colours became subtler as styles became larger.

9 Italy has always been a home for exciting eyewear designers, including Giuseppe Ratti of Persol and Leonardo Del Vecchio of Luxottica. These frames display the flair of Italian style but are by an unknown designer. PLASTIC AND METAL. c. 1960s.

10 By the seventies injection moulding had progressed to achieve sophisticated colour effects. Colours became subtle to blend with facial features. SILHOUETTE. PLASTIC. c. 1970s.

11 The novelty frames popular in the eighties featured in many fashion campaigns and editorials. High-quality designs took inspiration in everything from lips and cocktail glasses to the Eiffel Tower. LAWRENCE JENKIN FOR ANGLO AMERICAN. PLASTIC. c. 1980s.

ENJOY WEARING GLASSES

SILHOUETTE – internationally known for setting the trend in elegant eyewear. At registered opticians throughout the country.

Silhouette

BELTED AND BUCKLED

'WITH A STRETCH BELT ANYTHING CAN BE A DRESS – A DINNER NAPKIN, A TABLECLOTH, EVEN A TOWEL. JUST WRAP AND SNAP AND AWAY YOU GO IN AN INCREDIBLE OUTFIT.'

BETH DITTO

Used for both fashion and function, belts have changed shape and style along with the shifting fashionable silhouette. However, as a fashion accessory, belts were at their most prominent and decorative in the eighties. The body-conscious, curvaceous silhouette of the decade necessitated a defining feature and the oversized belt buckle became the focal point of an outfit. Dramatic belts were in keeping with the ostentatious tone of the time.

   Their opulence harks back to some of the very earliest examples of belts, when they were still an accessory of war. Often referred to as a girdle, a belt was a functional device used to carry a weapon. However, over time, it became a symbol of power, bejewelled with precious stones chosen for superstitious reasons. The embellishments were selected for their supposed powers to help their owner avert danger, avoid captivity and triumph over evil.

   Symbolic significance was also awarded to the feminine girdle. As well as giving shape to loosely structured garments, this ornament was believed to have the power to make suitors fall in love with its wearer. Although originally

1 LEATHER, REAR FASTENING. c.1930s.

2 HANDMADE. SUEDE. c.1920s.

3 MOSCHINO (REDWALL). LEATHER. c.1980s.

4 METALLIC-FINISH LEATHER. c.1980s.

5 METAL AND PLASTIC. c.1960s.

6 In this 1978 photograph by Terence Donovan, model Kristin Darnell wears a knitted cardigan coat with a metal belt and matching epaulettes by Chloé.

what was essentially a decorative status symbol, the girdle gradually gained more of a function, as purses, fans and even keys were attached around its body.

It was only much later when 19th-century fashions introduced 'separates' – the skirt and the blouse or matching jacket – that the waistline was highlighted and women began to wear what we know as belts today. Since then, the prevailing fashionable silhouette has dictated the fit and width of a belt. In the 19th century, metal was a precious rarity and belts of this period are commonly made of a narrow piece of elaborately embroidered cloth or coloured silk that fastened at the back with fine cord or hook and eye. This emphasized a fashionably small, corseted waistline.

The looser styles of the twenties, in contrast, suited softer sashes of coordinating fabric or plaited cord that were often worn low on the hip, the new focal point. While fashion plates showing the designs of couturiers Lanvin, Worth and Paquin do depict narrow belts on daywear, they are inconspicuous and delicate, usually in the same fabric as the dress.

Occasionally today rare examples of jewelled spider web-style constructions or narrow diamanté evening bands can be found. These would clip to the front of the dress under a bow or another small Art Deco ornamental motif. These fragile objects have often been backed onto a velvet ribbon for strength. By the thirties, the neat and streamlined profile, a shape aided by the introduction of the zip into fashionable clothing, once again emphasized the waistline. Belts of contrasting leather and suede began to appear in fashionable ensembles. Easy chic was the mood of the era and the inexpensive materials Bakelite and Lucite were used for the manufacture of buttons and buckles. These new plastics could be moulded and the clear resins dyed to create intricate designs that were frequently inspired by Art Deco motifs. Like buttons, buckles were sold separately as trimmings on cards. With fabric forming the body of the belt, a

6

favourite belt buckle could be changed and used to accessorize different outfits.

Another distinctive design dating to this decade are back-fastening belts. The front of these belts was often wider than the back or bore a 'V'-shaped centre-front dip. This design feature was revived and emphasized in the eighties.

In the forties, the closure of the couture houses in occupied Paris meant the centre of Western fashion shifted to the United States. American sportswear, with mix-and-match separates, championed by the likes of Claire McCardell and Norman Morell, used wide 'cinch' belts and laced 'waspies' as part of their new casual style.

In Europe, as the siren suit, overalls and trousers became standard wear for the new female workforce, wearing a belt became a necessity. In contrast to the ornate examples reserved for night-time soirées, bridal leather and brass buckles gave shapely definition to practical workwear. The forties leather belt has been reinterpreted on today's catwalk as a contrasting accessory worn over cardigans, coats and suits.

Belts were also important to the most influential style that came out of Paris in the post-war period, Christian Dior's 'New Look' of 1947. His designs, copied worldwide, placed even more emphasis on a tiny waist. Belts became wider to balance the full-skirted fashions and, as many women returned to corset and girdle foundation garments to obtain the svelte figure demanded by fashion, belts were an additional weapon in achieving the effect of a small waist. These wide belts used a variety of stretch elastics, leathers and plastics, and even woven raffia. The focus on the buckle was usurped by the use of decorative details, such as embroidery, studwork and print, on the belt itself.

While the multiplicity of widths and styles of belts of the fifties reflects the varied fashion silhouettes of the decade, the sixties saw some unique creations inspired by the avant-garde minimalism of the period. The metal chainmail and plastic discs of Paco Rabanne's architectural dresses were imitated in chain belts and dangling ropes of connected plastic discs that sat on the hip. (In fact, Rabanne had sold accessory designs to Courrèges and Balenciaga while still an architecture student.) Entire belts were sculpted from futuristic fabrics such as PVC and patent leather, while metallics were used for accessories and trimmings. But the simple shift and short tunic dresses of the early sixties did not need accessorizing in the same manner as the flowing garments influenced by hippy aesthetics that followed towards the end of the decade. Once again, the focal point moved from the waist to the hip and natural materials such as denim, leather, suede, rope and even wood were used to create low-slung belts for accessorizing androgynous looks. Punched, appliquéd and patchwork effects decorated leathers, lizard and snakeskins in fashions inspired by Native American designs, while buckles echoed the natural shapes of butterflies, bird wings and flowers.

The tailored, body-conscious and high-waisted silhouette of the eighties countered the free forms of the seventies. Accessories, in particular belts, became designer status symbols and were used to create a dramatic effect when paired with the oversized fashions of the decade. Branding, designer logos and bejewelled bling were used to amplify the glamour of the decade's cleverly constructed tailoring.

Belts of the seventies and eighties are among the most sought after today and are wearable with very different fashion styles from those first intended. No longer required to match shoes or the garment they circle, belts have become accessories enjoyed in their own right. With age, glossy buckles develop a softer glow, while superior leathers mature, not unlike aged wood, the marks of time adding to their charm. The seemingly unquenchable demand for pieces such as vintage Azzedine Alaïa leather corset designs or styles featuring Moschino logos has led to the revisiting and reproduction of these past styles in the 21st century.

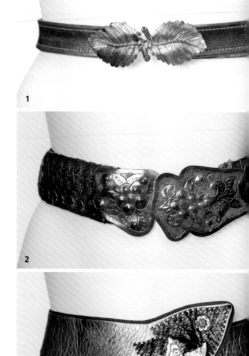

1 SYNTHETIC. c. 1980s.

2 METAL-PLATED WITH VELVET BACKING. 19TH CENTURY.

3 EMANUEL UNGARO. LEATHER AND METAL. c. 1980s.

4 In this fifties photograph, Lana Turner poses provocatively in a hooded jersey dress accessorized with an elaborately jewelled belt.

5 METAL. c. 1980s.

6 SYNTHETIC. c. 1980s.

7 ANTELOPE AND METAL. c. 1980s.

8 METAL SCALES. 1986.

9 YVES SAINT LAURENT, RIVE GAUCHE. LEATHER AND BRASS. c. 1970s.

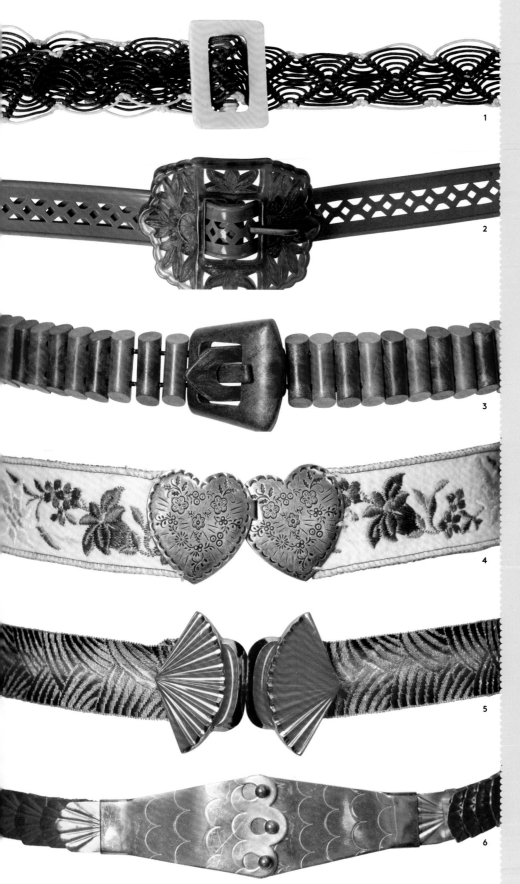

1 WOVEN PLASTIC. c. 1930s.

2 PLASTIC. c. 1930s.

3 WOOD. c. 1940s.

4 EMBROIDERED WITH METAL BUCKLE. c. 1940s.

5 BAKELITE ON WOVEN RIBBON. c. 1930s.

6 MOULDED METAL. c. 1930s.

7 A thirties Bloomingdale's advert for belts by leading designers of the day Edward Molyneux, Elsa Schiaparelli and Main Rousseau Bocher (Mainbocher). Many belts from this era were rear-fastening, with a decorative focus on the centre front – a design detail that influenced belts of the eighties.

8 METAL. c. 1930s.

9 Early buckles were commonly made from Bakelite and easily dyed resin that could be moulded into intricate shapes. BAKELITE. c. 1930s.

10 The buckle on a belt from a sixties Dior dress forms a subtle 'D'. CHRISTIAN DIOR. WOOL AND BRASS. FRANCE. c. 1960s.

11 BAKELITE BUCKLE ON PETERSHAM RIBBON. c. 1920s.

Mainbocher

The Mainbocher "bicycle" belt with adjustable back and 2 pockets. Black and saddle brown, adaptation **3.98**
Mainbocher daisies **59c**

Molyneux

Molyneux' "vest" belt with the new adjustable back buckle. Red, black, navy, kelly green or yellow patent leather.
BLOOMINGDALE adaptation . . . **3.98**
Molyneux tulips in pastels . . . **1.00**

Schiaparelli

Adaptation of Schiaparelli's "ruffle" belt in black or saddle brown **3.98**
Schiaparelli nosegay **1.00**

Bloomingdale
NEW YORK

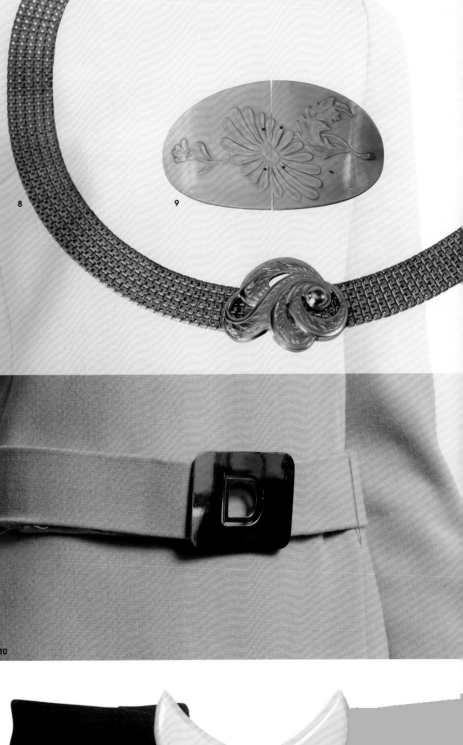

8

9

10

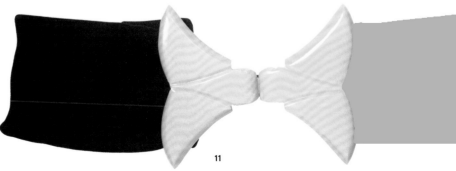

11

1

2

3

4

5

1228 1229

6

7

8

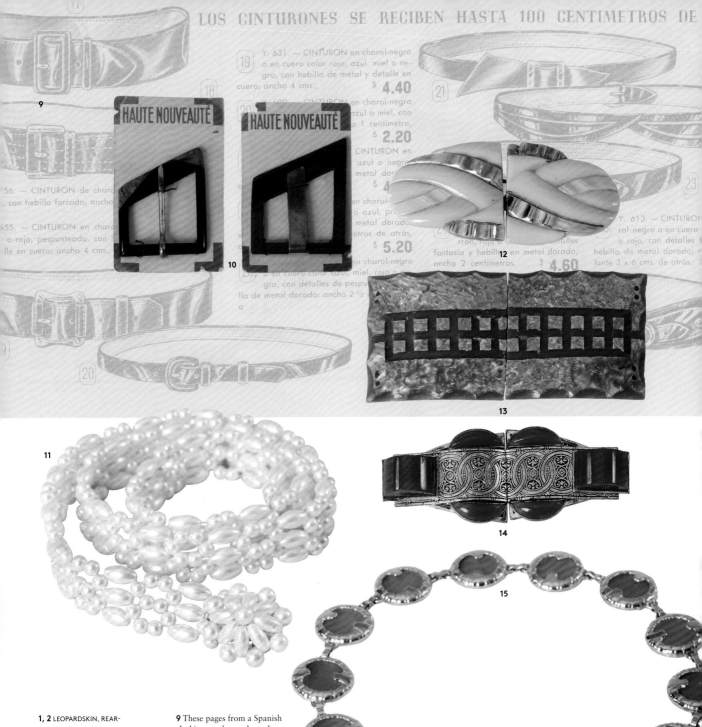

HAUTE NOUVEAUTÉ

HAUTE NOUVEAUTÉ

Y. 631. — CINTURON en charol-negro o en cuero color rojo, azul, miel o negro, con hebilla de metal y detalle en cuero; ancho 4 cms.,

$4.40

CINTURON azul o miel, con 1 centimetro,

$2.20

CINTURON en azul o negro metal dorad

$

en charol-negro

fantasia y hebilla ancho 2 centimetros, $4.60

Y. 613. — CINTUR rol-negro o en cuero o rojo, con detalles hebilla de metal dorado; lante 3 x 6 cms. de atrás,

56. — CINTURON de charol , con hebilla forrada; anch

55. — CINTURON en charo o rojo, pespunteado, con lle en cuero; ancho 4 cms.,

en charol-negro 2, o en cuero color azul, miel, rojo o n gro, con detalles de pespu lla de metal dorado; ancho 2 ½ a

1, 2 LEOPARDSKIN, REAR-FASTENING. c. 1930s.

3 SEQUIN ON ELASTIC. c. 1960s.

4 SUEDE, REAR-FASTENING. c. 1930s.

5 SUEDE, REAR-FASTENING. c. 1930s.

6 A twenties fashion illustration showing belts worn stylishly as a contrasting fashion accessory, not necessarily matched to blend with the outfit.

7 MOTHER OF PEARL BUCKLE AND LEATHER. c. 1940s.

8 SHELL. c. 1970s.

9 These pages from a Spanish clothing catalogue show the varied widths of belts offered in the fifties.

10–14 Twenties Bakelite and metal buckles were sold separately so they could be interchanged with different outfits.

15 METAL AND PLASTIC. c. 1980s.

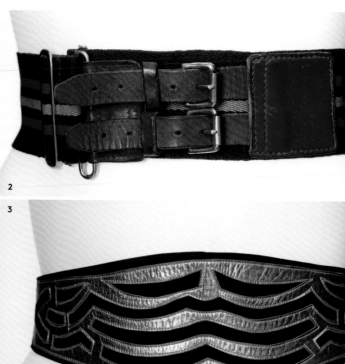

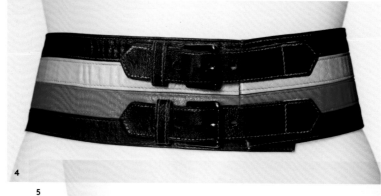

1 A leather belt from 1945 is worn over a dress by Lilly Daché, a designer mostly known for her millinery.

2 LEATHER/WEBBING. c. 1950s.

3 SUEDE WITH GOLD CUTWORK LEATHER. c. 1980s.

4 YVES SAINT LAURENT. LEATHER. c. 1980s.

5 LEATHER. c. 1980s.

6 LEATHER. c. 1940s.

7 WOVEN TAPESTRY-EFFECT. c. 1970s.

8 GUY LAROCHE. LEATHER. c. 1980s.

9 LEATHER. c. EARLY 20TH CENTURY.

10 LEATHER. c. 1980s.

11 BRIDLE LEATHER. c. 1950s.

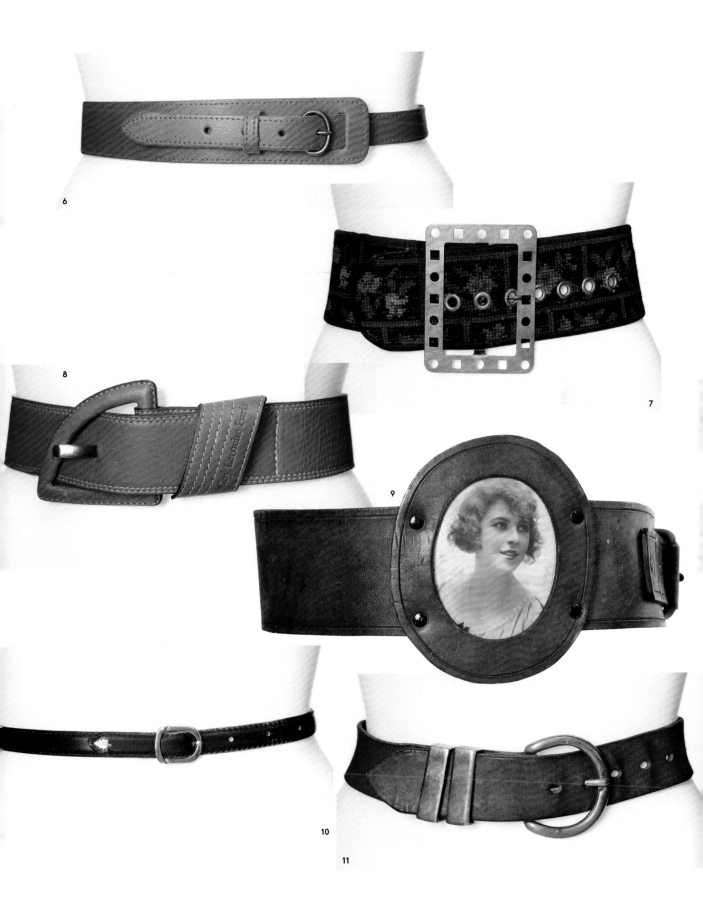

6

7

8

9

10

11

3 Illustrator Vittorio Accornero designed many of Gucci's most notable scarves, including the famous 'Flora' scarf for Princess Grace of Monaco. This scarf portrays the four seasons and, as with all his designs, his name has been incorporated into the pattern. GUCCI. SILK TWILL. c. 1970s.

4 Richard Allan was the former head designer for Jacqmar scarves. He bought the company in the late fifties and continued designing and manufacturing into the sixties and seventies. While Jacqmar was known for whimsical and pretty design, the Richard Allan style was chic and sophisticated. JACQMAR. SILK. c. 1960s.

1 The 'flower power' motifs used on this scarf are combined with psychedelic swirls that reflect the increased experimentation with hallucinogenic drugs in this era. RICHEL. SILK TWILL. c. EARLY 1970s.

2 This scarf is likely to have been given away as a promotional gift with a magazine. The magazine titles shown and the style of the fashions depicted date the scarf to the late fifties. SYNTHETIC. c. LATE 1950s.

5

SCARF STYLE

'A SCARF TO A WOMAN IS WHAT A NECK-TIE IS TO A MAN, AND THE WAY YOU TIE IT IS PART OF YOUR PERSONALITY.'
CHRISTIAN DIOR

5 Zika Ascher and his wife Lida worked for several years with artist Henry Moore to reproduce the artist's signature brush stroke through screenprinting on printed fabric. The Aschers approached many eminent artists to design a three-foot-square silk scarf, including Henri Matisse, Graham Sutherland, André Derain, Jean Cocteau and many more. Most of the scarves are machine-edged, instead of being hand-rolled, a sign of post-war economy. JEAN HUGO FOR ASCHER. SILK. 1947.

6 The rose became the flower of fifties design, whether full-blown or in rosebud form. Cecil Beaton was a celebrated photographer, costume designer and illustrative diarist who loved fashion. He was commissioned by Zika Ascher to interpret his sketches onto fabric and the 'Cecil Beaton Rose' is one of his most famous designs. CECIL BEATON FOR ASCHER. SILK. 1948.

7 PHILIPPE JULLIAN FOR ASCHER. SILK. 1947.

6

7

In recent years, the scarf has become one of the most desirable of vintage accessories. The appeal of what is essentially nothing more than a beautifully illustrated piece of fabric is rooted in the instant glamour a vintage scarf can add to an outfit.

A riot of colour and pattern, scarves can easily be incorporated into today's fashionable wardrobe. Styles from every fashion era find use today as part of creative outfits that would astonish their original designers. They also offer inspiration for the contemporary catwalk, as demonstrated by Dolce & Gabbana's memorable scarf print collection of spring/summer 2012. Scarves are put to sophisticated use in today's interiors as sumptuous cushions and upholstery covers, or simply framed as the rare artwork that many of them are. Whether it is the luxury of an eighties silk twill, the charm of a fifties floral or the long, narrow elegance of a twenties design, scarves are among the most versatile of vintage finds.

Etiquette of the early half of the 20th century required fashionable ensembles to be completed with coordinating accessories. A woman of the twenties, whatever her social class, would not leave home without her lace-edged handkerchief, neatly gloved hands and a covered head. The neck scarf completed the outfit. Scarves of the twenties are surprisingly easy to find today (an indication of their popularity at the time) and are very distinct. These scarves are usually no more than 15 cm (6 in.) wide but around 150 cm (60 in.) long, and they are always machine-made rather than hand-rolled. Their long, narrow contours are printed in designs

that reflect the artistic movements of the era, including Art Deco, Cubist, Fauvist and Futurist-inspired designs. The limited colour palette and elementary print techniques are part of their charm. Echoing the slim *garçonne* style of the time, the long scarf of the twenties is easily worn today, slipped through the denim waist-loops of jeans, twisted turban-style through hair or worn simply as they were first intended, coiled around the neck.

By the thirties, the neck scarf had become shorter, often oblong, and manufactured in softly printed floral chiffons displaying an intricacy that indicates improved printing techniques. The neck scarf of the forties, meanwhile, became the headscarf for many, a necessity of wartime frugality and urgency. The synthetic rayons and crepes that became the wartime alternative to silk provided comfort and protection against the debris of war and were an absolute must for women working in manual jobs. 'Cover your hair for safety – your Russian sister does!' read one British government poster, while the famous 'We Can Do It!' poster in the United States illustrates the utilitarian turban look that is emulated by those referencing a forties style today. The propaganda prints of wartime that used the headscarf as a canvas for their illustrative messages have become so valuable that many are exhibited in museums and are prized by collectors under glass as the valuable artwork they have become. Both Britain and the United States manufactured notable propaganda scarves displaying patriotic idioms, Churchill's speeches or illustrations by wartime artists such as Cecil Beaton and Feliks Topolski. Examples can also be found proclaiming the German/Italian alliance, although the imagery found on these is often more serious, depicting flags and wartime insignia, in contrast to the domestic pictorials produced to illustrate the Allied home front.

In a time of shortages, scarves supplied a touch of glamour. 'Scarves were never more brilliant and varied. Used with ingenuity and imagination they enrich our scanty wardrobes and bring individuality to uniform clothes,' run the opening lines of a 1945 *Harper's Bazaar* article. The popularity of scarves in the forties provided inspiration for Zika Ascher, the owner of a small but established textile production company in London's West End. In conjunction with his wife, Lida, he worked with the artist Henry Moore to replicate the effect of a brush stroke on canvas through screenprinting on fabric. Subsequently, other notable international artists were invited to create designs for the famous 'Ascher Squares'. Between 1945 and 1947 many of the most famous names in art, including Henri Matisse, Graham Sutherland, Jean Cocteau and many more, collaborated with the Aschers on a series of limited-edition scarves that, in part, initiated the trend for the painterly polychromatic style fashionable in textile design in the following fifties.

Post-war scarves displayed a real diversity of styles and trends, and the adaptable scarf replaced the now-seemingly frivolous hats. Hundreds of new designs flooded the market in inexpensive but appealing patterns. High-end fashion houses too seized the opportunity to create beautiful designs representative of their brand. Mid-century scarves from the most notable of fashion houses are fascinating, their signature styles often bearing a contrasting visual synchronicity to that of contemporary designs. Scarves by Balenciaga, Lanvin Castillo and Balmain all depict a painterly softness not seen today, the scarves of the now defunct Maggy Rouff exhibit delightful narrative intricacy, while those by Nina Ricci

resonate with the floral and cooing dove motifs still used by the fashion house.

The fashion house perhaps most associated with iconic scarf designs in this era was that of Emilio Pucci. Already established within the international jet set, Pucci began to include scarves in his collections from 1952. A sketch made on the island of Capri inspired his first design and his scarves went on to enjoy enormous commercial success, perhaps because he considered the printed configuration on his scarves to be of equal importance to that of his clothes. He did not outsource design work or simply adapt textiles designed for garments to work within a square. The movement within his colourful swirling designs, inspired by underwater photography and his love of travel, was particularly suited to the fluidity and folds of a draped scarf.

The nostalgic elegance of the fifties touring scarf – a method of tying a scarf over the head, wrapped under the chin but tied at the back of the neck – is evocative of open-topped sports cars and film star glamour and was one of the most significant styles to emerge from the mid-century. The look, frequently modelled by stars

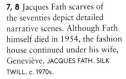

1 Marcel Vertes was a Hungarian painter and illustrator who established himself in Paris during the First World War. Some of his whimsical illustrations were produced as scarves, and interestingly he collaborated with Elsa Schiaparelli on the design of the 1952 film *Moulin Rouge*, for which they were jointly awarded a British Academy Film Award for Best Costume Design.

2, 3, 4 The craze for all things oriental saw imports from the Far East worn as items of fashion. These large, square, raw silk scarves from the twenties depict oriental scenes of birds and exotic flora, always using a rudimentary print style in delicate colour tones. Many scarves of this type produced in Japan were not technically scarves. Called *furoshiki*, they were cloths used to wrap and transport gifts and purchases. RAW SILK. c. 1920s.

5 Emilio Pucci was inspired by his travels as seen in the design of this scarf depicting the traditional 'Gombey' folk dance of Bermuda. EMILIO PUCCI. SILK TWILL. c. 1957.

6 This is unusually sombre colouring for a scarf by Emilio Pucci but a favourite palette of the seventies era in which it was designed. EMILIO PUCCI. SILK TWILL. c. 1970.

7, 8 Jacques Fath scarves of the seventies depict detailed narrative scenes. Although Fath himself died in 1954, the fashion house continued under his wife, Geneviève. JACQUES FATH. SILK TWILL. c. 1970s.

9 The fine parachute silk and the vibrancy of the printing dyes indicate this scarf is probably from the United States. Europe was subject to more restrictions at this time. SILK. c. 1940s.

10 Many scarves of the fifties resembled paintings, a style emulating the 'Ascher Squares' produced from 1947 onwards. JACQMAR. SILK. c. 1950s.

1

3–5 Narrative nautical motifs provided fashionable decoration for scarves and handkerchiefs in every decade. These 'kerchiefs show the influence of Art Deco in their decorative borders and stylized depictions of swimmers.

3 SILK. c. 1960s.

4 SILK. c. 1930s.

5 SILK. c. 1920s.

6 A printed paisley headscarf, designed by Hubert de Givenchy in 1952, is worn by a young French model in the style that evoked a glamorous image well into the sixties, until it became seen as the mark of an older generation.

4

5

3

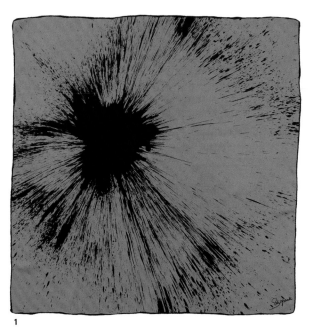

courrèges   paris

2

6

1 Elsa Schiaparelli designed to surprise, and, although she was forced to avoid bankruptcy by selling the name of her fashion house in 1954, the style of this sixties scarf remains ahead of its time and true to her legacy. ELSA SCHIAPARELLI. SILK. c. 1960s.

2 André Courrèges presented his renowned 'Moon Girl' collection in 1964, including futuristic and simplistic designs that electrified the mood of fashion at the time. ANDRÉ COURRÈGES. SILK TWILL. c. 1964.

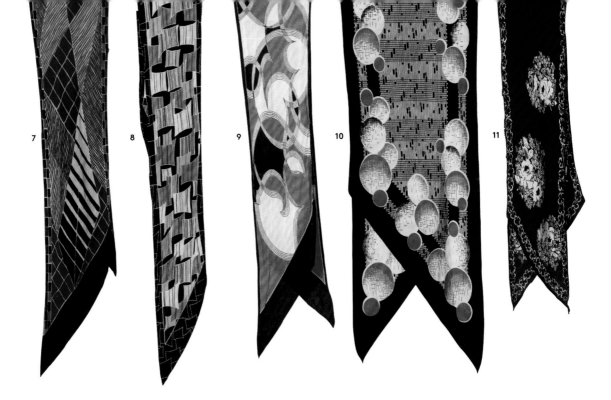

7   8   9   10   11

7–11 The long, narrow scarf of the twenties echoed the fashionable silhouette of the era. The ease with which such scarves can be found today is proof of their enormous popularity. Whether worn around the head in the bohemian lounge style sported by women of the twenties, coiled decoratively around the neck or pulled through the belt-loops of a pair of 21st-century jeans, scarves dating from this period are among the most versatile. SILK. c. 1920s/1930s.

12 The bold abstract patterns of the seventies work particularly well with contemporary fashions. SILK. c. 1970s.

12

such as Marilyn Monroe, Sophia Loren and Audrey Hepburn, is a brave style statement today, yet it is frequently used in contemporary advertising campaigns by fashion houses such as Dolce & Gabbana, often to reference the romance of the fifties.

Although the sixties Youthquake delighted in a rejection of mature etiquette, the scarf retained a fashionable presence manifested in the triangular head squares that were knotted under the chin and decorated with the simple geometrics and the abstracted florals popularized by Mary Quant's daisy. This decade also saw the artful knotting of scarves onto handbags, a trend that has recently resurfaced.

The end of the decade and the early seventies witnessed historically influenced fashion themes and a fondness for twenties fashion-plate novelty prints. There was a resurgence of the long, narrow scarves worn in the early twentieth century, which suited the ambience of seventies bohemian fashion and the layering of fabrics and jewelry with scarves, leather fringing and thongs. The difference between the long, narrow scarves of the two eras is easy to see – scarves in this style from the seventies were mostly manufactured in inexpensive polyesters and prints are

inferior to those of the twenties, even though the latter were restricted by elementary printing processes.

Scarves of the eighties became a billboard for couture houses and upscale department stores. Logos, initials and bold insignia decorated the heavy silk twill scarves, which became an accessory of fashionable power dressing. Their substance and size make them perfectly adaptable to interior projects, such as cushion covers and chair upholstery, or else to be draped as halterneck tops and blouses, as they are often worn today.

There are many notable names to look out for in the field of vintage scarves, whether high-end fashion houses, who branded their scarves, or the designers who specialized in designing beautiful signature styles for the simple square. Scarves from past decades can be endlessly reinterpreted within contemporary styles.

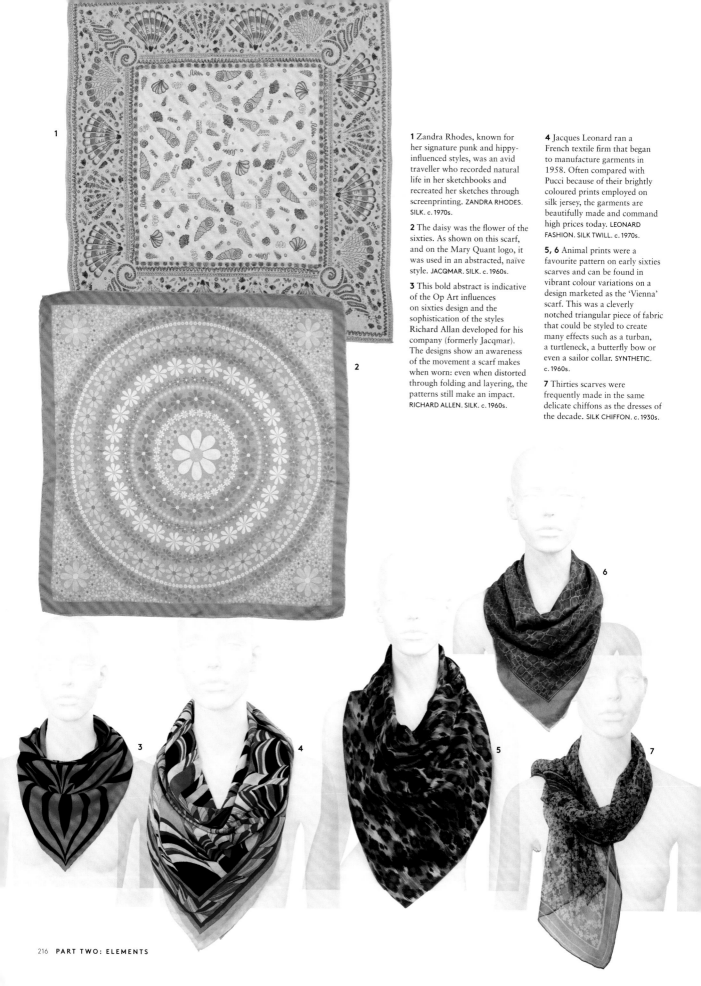

1 Zandra Rhodes, known for her signature punk and hippy-influenced styles, was an avid traveller who recorded natural life in her sketchbooks and recreated her sketches through screenprinting. ZANDRA RHODES. SILK. c. 1970s.

2 The daisy was the flower of the sixties. As shown on this scarf, and on the Mary Quant logo, it was used in an abstracted, naïve style. JACQMAR. SILK. c. 1960s.

3 This bold abstract is indicative of the Op Art influences on sixties design and the sophistication of the styles Richard Allan developed for his company (formerly Jacqmar). The designs show an awareness of the movement a scarf makes when worn: even when distorted through folding and layering, the patterns still make an impact. RICHARD ALLEN. SILK. c. 1960s.

4 Jacques Leonard ran a French textile firm that began to manufacture garments in 1958. Often compared with Pucci because of their brightly coloured prints employed on silk jersey, the garments are beautifully made and command high prices today. LEONARD FASHION. SILK TWILL. c. 1970s.

5, 6 Animal prints were a favourite pattern on early sixties scarves and can be found in vibrant colour variations on a design marketed as the 'Vienna' scarf. This was a cleverly notched triangular piece of fabric that could be styled to create many effects such as a turban, a turtleneck, a butterfly bow or even a sailor collar. SYNTHETIC. c. 1960s.

7 Thirties scarves were frequently made in the same delicate chiffons as the dresses of the decade. SILK CHIFFON. c. 1930s.

8

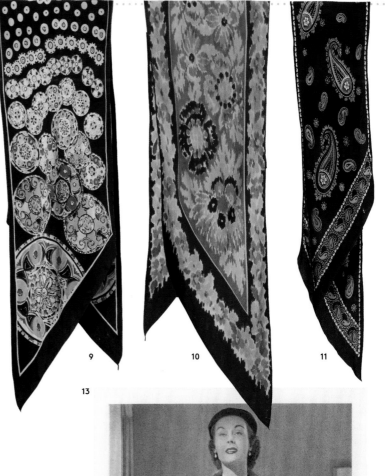

9 10 11

13

8–11 Designers of the twenties and thirties achieved astonishingly complex print effects, especially when one considers the elementary printing processes available at the time. Scarves, in particular, display their designers' obvious enjoyment of their art, with the confines of a square or a narrow oblong becoming an explosion of colour and pattern. Printing defects and occasional overlaps of colour only add to the charm of these scarves. Whether printed on silk or rayon (the cheaper alternative to silk, which first started being used for scarves in the early thirties), the designs are effective and vibrant, with the designs on rayon often being the more durable of the two.

8 SILK. c. 1920s.

9 RAYON. c. 1930s.

10 WOOL. c. 1920s.

11 SILK. c. 1930s.

12, 13 The use of glorious coloured mohairs was pioneered by Zika Ascher and made Ascher Studio a household name in the fifties. Zika persuaded the Scottish mills to dye their woven mohairs (particularly suited to absorbing pigment dyes) in vibrant hues that were more appropriate for high fashion than their traditional heathery palette. Mohair became highly sought after by the couture houses of Dior, Balenciaga, Cardin, Capucci, Dessès, Givenchy and Lanvin Castillo as well as companies such as Jaeger who were at the forefront of fashion. In this fifties illustration, Scottish department store Jenners demonstrates how to wear a mohair scarf. ASSORTED SCOTTISH MILLS. MOHAIR. c. LATE 1950s.

12

'GLEN CREE' MOHAIR SCARVES

These lovely 'Glen Cree' scarves and wraps are available for personal shoppers or by post from . . . . .

JENNERS
PRINCES STREET EDINBURGH
LIMITED

UNDERWEAR AS OUTERWEAR

'LOVELY LINGERIE IS THE BASIS OF GOOD DRESSING.' CHRISTIAN DIOR

1

The phrase 'underwear as outerwear' has been used for fashion headlines ever since Madonna wore a conical satin corset for her sensual performance on her 1990 *Blonde Ambition* tour. While this design by Jean Paul Gaultier boldly reinterpreted the sculptural lines of fifties corsetry, the deliberate display of underwear as a fashion statement was not a new phenomenon. Only a few years earlier, in the 1985 film *Desperately Seeking Susan*, Madonna had appeared as a streetwise girl from downtown New York, wearing frothy fifties petticoats and black bras exposed through lace shirts and string vests. Even earlier during the seventies, Vivienne Westwood, still then an emerging designer, experimented with provocative and fetish clothing, sold in the King's Road shop, 'Sex' (founded with Malcolm McLaren), and adopted by followers of the punk street culture. Later in the eighties, when Westwood's collections were at the forefront of mainstream fashion, her designs referenced historical corsetry and crinoline structures.

Even during the seventies and eighties exposing undergarments to make a style statement was not a new concept. Since the early 16th and 17th centuries, when the elaborate dress of the Tudor and Stuart elite revealed fanciful lace and embroidered underclothes, the custom of displaying glimpses of beautiful underwear has waxed and waned throughout the fashion eras. The many layers of petticoats, chemises and smocks that formed the foundation garments for this silhouette were so lavishly decorated with embroidery that outer garments were designed with cuts and slashes to reveal the exquisite embellishment below.

While the tantalizing glimpses of beautiful underwear of the Tudor and Stuart aristocracy sent messages of wealth and power, the 21st-century trend is one that refuses to hide away clothes suffused with nostalgic detailing. Truly beautiful vintage underwear is such a rarity that gorgeous pyjama suits, petticoats, dressing gowns and corset covers make unique outerwear, in contrast to their mass-produced contemporary equivalents.

Designers of the 21st century take inspiration from the intricate embroideries and appliqués that were painstakingly applied by hand to pastel silks and satins. Recent collections from Dior, Fendi, Marc Jacobs and Antonio Berardi have all referenced the styling, construction and stitchwork that are distinctive of twenties, thirties and fifties lingerie. Model and underwear designer Rosie Huntington-Whiteley expresses her love of vintage design, finding inspiration in the Art Deco embroidery of the twenties for her highly successful Marks & Spencer collaboration: 'British girls love a good vintage find... You look at these exquisite pieces like art and wonder where this was or who was in this fifty, sixty years ago. It's very romantic.'

The evolution of underwear through the 20th century follows a natural progression, led not only by the developing style of the outer garments for which it creates the foundation, but also by the increase in physical activity that saw the emancipated woman cycling, enjoying sports and generally becoming more active. While there had been many attempts to design garments resembling a bra, its first appearance is generally placed around the late 19th and early 20th century. However, the first recorded commercially

1, 2 'Lingerie is part of my DNA and my heritage,' said Jean Paul Gaultier, whose designs for Madonna's nineties world tour were inspired by watching his grandmother, a corsetier, at work while he was a child. Madonna's conical bra plays on the circular stitchwork of fifties 'bullet' bras, while the pink satin corsetry references the girdles worn by women between the thirties and the early fifties. The illustration used for the forties advertisement for the Diana corset (**2**) already plays with the underwear as outerwear theme, suggesting the corset is too nice to be hidden.

3 A rare hand-printed silk slip from the twenties. Thanks to the slip having been carefully stored in the dark for many years, the floral print has not faded and shows a strong Art Deco influence. HANDMADE. SILK. c. 1920s.

3

4

DIANA

The Daintiness Girdle with detachable, washable crotch

The slim-waisted, round-hipped loveliness of the ideal Diana figure! . The matchless comfort of a panty girdle! . . .The assurance of complete personal daintiness always!

These virtues will make you thank your lucky stars for DIANA. The new lastex up-and-down stretch in back gives freedom of action. The crotch can be whisked out and washed after every wearing! See the beautiful new Diana made of gleaming rayon satin with satin lastex panels, at these and other fine stores. There is a DIANA for every figure type — regular girdle, panty girdle or Diana's famous Daintiness Girdle. From $5.95 to $10. For free illustrated booklet V-9 write

THE DIANA CORSET CO., INC.

1 EAST 33rd STREET, NEW YORK 16, N.Y.

4 The chemise, teddy, camisole and envelope chemise are variations on the style that replaced the corset and petticoat during the twenties. Soft all-in-one slips joined at the crotch created a feminine undergarment suited to the fashionable *garçonne* style. HANDMADE. SILK. c. LATE 1920s/EARLY 1930s.

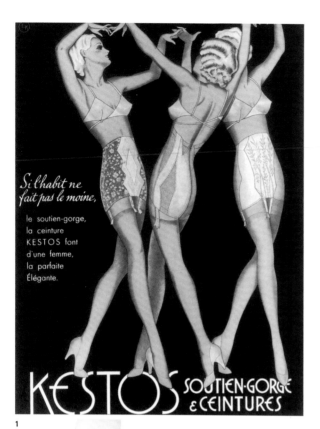

2

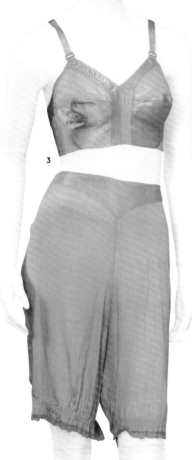

3

4

5

6

7

1, 10 These French adverts for Kestos underwear from the thirties (**1**) and early sixties (**10**) show the international success of this British company, widely credited with designing the first commercial bra with separate cups.

2 Artificial silk flowers were used to decorate these specially designed bras by Lilly Daché and were intended to be worn as interchangeable accessories over evening dresses. Daché, famous for her millinery, was accustomed to using extravagant trimmings on hats and it is a shame this beautiful new accessory didn't have more impact on fifties fashion.

3 Underwear of the twenties and thirties was commonly made of rayon or silk for those who could afford it. While the underwear of the twenties was demure and hidden, thirties manufacturers ran advertising campaigns establishing underwear as desirable, highly fashionable garments. SILK SATIN. c.1920s.

4 Intricately embroidered lace underwear such as this would have been made as part of a wedding trousseau. HANDMADE. COTTON. c.1930s.

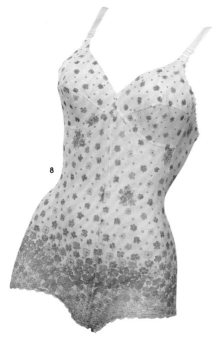

8

5 The cone-shaped bra, colloquially known as the 'bullet' bra, helped create the curvaceous bust line of the late forties. Circular stitching reinforced cups to create the desired effect. COTTON. c.1950s.

6, 7 Girdles were also topstitched and reinforced with steel boning before Lycra was introduced.

6 SATIN. c.1950s.

7 SATIN. c.1940s.

8 British company Marks & Spencer only introduced underwear to their stock in the twenties under the St Michael brand, although they had been trading as a store since 1894. In the sixties, they were one of the first companies to experiment with Lycra for corsetry. ST MICHAEL FOR MARKS & SPENCER. NYLON. c.1960s.

9 Many of the bras worn by Marilyn Monroe were handmade, incorporating features to enhance her famous 'Sweater Girl' figure. Extra straps were added to lift and separate, while, on this bra, the lace cups could be removed (as seen in the second image) to create a risqué 'no bra' appearance and large pockets could be padded to enhance her 36D cup to a 38. HANDMADE. SATIN, VELVET AND LACE. c. LATE 1950s.

successful attempt was by an American publisher, Mary Phelps Jacob. Originally for her own needs, she combined two handkerchiefs with pink ribbon and cord to create a garment that retained her modesty underneath an evening dress so sheer that her corset would have been exposed. Eventually patented in 1914 as a 'brassiere', a term derived from the French word for the upper arm, the new bra was a commercial success, coinciding with the *garçonne* silhouette of the twenties. Not only did the fresh style of eveningwear demand a new style of modesty but in addition metal was in scant supply, desperately needed for the First World War. Women were asked to abandon their corsets containing metal stays or boning (the name derived from the constraining lengths of whalebone once inserted into the corset) and, as they took up positions in factories and in the services, they required practical and comfortable undergarments that allowed freedom of movement.

It was only during the thirties that manufacturers effectively began to design bras with different cup sizes and therefore bring about the demise of the intricately embroidered corset covers and chemises worn as blouses by vintage lovers today. The all-elastic bra arrived in this era, developed to flatter the feminine figure into the more curvaceous form again favoured as the fashionable shape of the day. Even Schiaparelli designed a pointed bra for her swimsuits of the thirties to emphasize the feminine shape while on the beach.

The heyday of the 'pin-up girl' arrived post-twenties when the sensual bias cut, which required womanly curves to wear

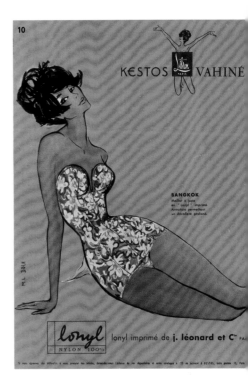

it at its best, had replaced the gamine, flat-chested, *garçonne*-style fashions. The pin-up girl sensation encouraged an erogenous silhouette, augmented by Hollywood's desperate desire to flout the strict morals of the Hays code. This Motion Picture Production Code – popularly known after the name of its chief censor, William H. Hays – restricted nudity and the wearing of lingerie on screen. Starlets such as Lana Turner and Carole Landis were costumed in tight, fitted clothing that hinted at their womanly curves, rather than flouting bare flesh on screen, as had become the style of earlier twenties sensationalist films. Manufacturers began to experiment with using lines of machine-stitch work to strengthen bra cups and these eventually became the distinctive cone-shaped, spiral-stitched 'bullet' bra of the late forties.

Stars of the screen had custom-made bras to enhance their assets: the pictured bra belonging to Marilyn Monroe was designed to give the appearance she was not wearing a bra at all. Even millionaire aviator Howard Hughes attempted to design a push-up bra based on the principles used for suspension bridges in order to show off Jane Russell's famous 38D-sized

9

bust in his 1943 film *Outlaw*. (Although her revealing costumes in the film did attract the attention of the board of censors, she refused to wear the bra due to its mediocre fit!)

The 'slip', the name given to the all-in-one, dress-style, synthetic or silk petticoat, inspired the nineties fashion for slip dresses – simple, fitted, strappy dresses designed in sheeny fabrics to resemble lingerie. The first interpretation to be featured in *Vogue* was that of Courrèges, but its emergence is most identified with Calvin Klein, whose notable advertising campaigns featured a young, sultry Brooke Shields. The slip dress was cited by *Vogue* to be as enduring as the T-shirt, the bikini and the jean jacket in their 'turning point' list of 20th-century fashion. Original slips from the fifties and sixties are often bold in colour and can, very occasionally, be found in exciting and evocative animal or oriental prints. Styles from earlier decades were made in silk or silk-like rayon and are rarely found in anything but creams and pastel shades of pink and peach. Elizabeth Taylor provides a memorable silhouette in the lace-edged, white slip she wears in the 1958 film *Cat on a Hot Tin Roof*.

The group of lingerie encompassing teddies, chemises, camisoles and slips is worn as blouses today for their delicate beauty. Always in soft pastels, the price they command is determined by the amount of decoration and embroidery. The 19th-century chemise was worn next to the skin, underneath a corset, and grew shorter alongside fashionable hem lengths. By the twenties it became known as an 'envelope chemise' (or teddy), joined at the crotch and replacing the corset for wear under the fashionable boyish silhouette of twenties flapper fashions. The 'French knickers' or slimmer-style 'directoire knickers', created in this decade as a natural development of pantaloons and combinations, are worn as shorts by brave fashionistas today.

Harder to wear as contemporary outerwear are the nightgowns and dressing gowns that were often made

1 The manufactured forties nightdress typically features the V-shaped midriff panel and a rear tie belt to allow one size to fit all. RAYON. c. 1940s.

2 Nightdresses of the twenties were simple and unstructured and reflected the rejection of 19th-century fussiness in fashionable daywear of the period. The delicate embroidery, scalloped edges and faggotted neckline of this nightdress belie its original use, making it perfect for contemporary wear. HANDMADE. SILK. c. 1920s.

3 The nightdresses and dressing gowns of the thirties in particular have a refined glamour that makes them highly sought after today. HANDMADE. SILK SATIN. c. 1930s.

4 Silk stockings of the twenties can be found in surprisingly vibrant colours, dyed to match fashionable dresses and shoes, or in natural flesh tones. SILK. c. 1920s.

5 Founded in the United States in 1910, Holeproof Hosiery amalgamated with other companies during the fifties and sixties. This advertisement dates to the twenties.

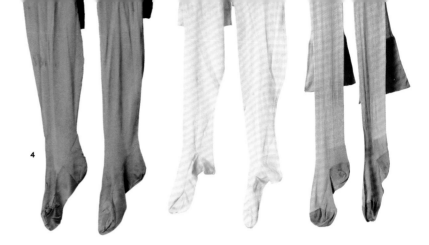

4

3

as matching sets. Nightgowns made before the mid-20th century are similar in appearance to their sheeny counterparts, the teddy and the chemise. Beautiful handmade versions in satin and silk can be found made for the wedding trousseaus that were commonplace until the mid-20th century. Nightgowns dating to the thirties and forties are often cut on the bias, as were evening dresses from that decade and, as such, can be worn as partywear by braver dressers.

Glamorous lounge or beach pyjamas incorporate loose kimono-style jackets with wide palazzo trousers, a style with Indian origins. 'The Parisienne's latest whim is to wear tea-gowns that are pyjamas,' informed a twenties issue of British *Vogue*. Designed to be worn as sensuous daytime loungewear at home or for a fashionable beach parade, they too have inspired contemporary design. Interpretations can be seen from the seventies designs of Ossie Clark through to the spring/summer 2011 collection from Marc Jacobs. Sadly, original pyjama sets are often separated and finding a complete outfit is a rare occurrence.

Tights were patented as 'Panti-Legs' by French scientist Allen Gant in 1958 and first appeared, photographed by Irving Penn, in American *Vogue* in 1964. Initially expensive and therefore not commercially viable, tights became successful with the phenomenon of the mini skirt, in tune with the 'streamlined simplicity' of the era. Mary Quant struggled to find the right sort of colour and finish so initially had to look to companies that manufactured tights for theatre and dance productions to complete her mini-skirted ensembles. However, while tights played a key

role in sixties youth fashion, it is their precursors, the silk stockings and hose, that are most sought after today. Silk stockings from as early as the twenties can be found in an astonishing array of colours as, like tights, they have always been manufactured to co-ordinate an outfit. They were dyed to match evening 'slippers' or blended with flesh tones and even, on occasion, matched the vibrancy of lipsticks. In 1948, New York department store Bonwit Teller promoted a pair of tights named 'Stunning', coloured to match a racy red lipstick of the same name.

The most recent in the history of underwear as outerwear reinterpretations is the vintage bed jacket. As the name suggests, they were designed to wear for extra warmth in bed, in the days before central heating. Beautiful examples can be found, knitted

5

1, 2, 3 Nightdresses from the early decades of the 20th century are some of the most sought after vintage garments today. Pastel-coloured fabrics were embroidered, trimmed in lace and sometimes beaded.

1 SILK. c. 1930s.

2 RAYON. c. 1930s.

3 SILK. c. 1930s.

4 Katy Perry chose a vintage evening slip dress by Nolan Miller – best known for his work as costume designer for the eighties television series *Dynasty* – to wear to a benefit event in Los Angeles in 2012. Slip dresses inspired by silk or synthetic underwear became everyday wear in the nineties. Their influence on fashion continues today, such as in the Louis Vuitton autumn/winter 2013 collection.

5, 6 One-piece slips dating from the twenties through to the sixties are often worn as summer dresses by vintage enthusiasts today. Slips were often made in silk in the twenties and into the thirties, when rayon also began to be used. By the sixties, nylon was a popular fabric.

5 NYLON. c. 1960s.

6 HANDMADE SILK. c. 1930s.

7 The influence of vintage underwear on today's fashions is very evident on the contemporary catwalk. *Vogue* reported how the spring/summer 2010 collections took inspiration from the pastel tones and detailed styling of 20th-century underwear. SILK SATIN. c. 1930s.

8 Even underwear was subject to government control during the Second World War. The CC41 label on this nightdress indicates it was of a standard approved by the British government. SATIN RAYON. c. 1942.

9 Before the 20th century, underwear and nightwear were traditionally made from white cotton. Adopted as daywear during the seventies by bohemian dressers, the styles have enjoyed a revival in recent years, inspiring many contemporary designers. Modern copies are so similar in style it is often only the thickness of rough 19th-century cotton that indicates an original piece. HANDMADE. COTTON. c. 1900s.

in spider or sea foam stitch in gentle pastel tones and often decorated with satin ribbons and embroideries. Even more sought after are silk and lace jackets sometimes printed or quilted and appliquéd with delicate patterns of butterflies and florals. Loosely styled for comfort, these can date back to the pre-twenties and were worn up until the sixties, although later examples tend to be manufactured in less attractive nylons and other synthetics welcomed at the time as new and exciting, easy-care fabrics. Easily worn today as outer jackets, they have inspired the modern 'shacket', a colloquial fashion term given to a lightweight, unstructured jacket that is neither shirt nor tailored jacket.

It is underwear of the fifties that contributed the most defined fashion silhouette of the 20th century. 'Without foundations there can be no fashion,' said Christian Dior in reference to his dramatic 'New Look' of 1947. He reintroduced corsetry to create a sylph-like, cinched waistline in contrast to his opulent full skirts. A couture garment of this time often incorporates a built-in corset and petticoats to create the desired, curvaceous effect. Women of lesser means wore girdles to recreate the look, which could be pulled on without help from a maid, with attached suspenders to hold up the stockings. Layers of frothy net petticoats were added to finish the full-skirted, feminine silhouette of couture-led fashion.

Both corsetry and petticoats returned as part of eighties fashions. While the sixties and seventies rejected the corset and the girdle in favour of a more relaxed silhouette, the restrictive corset returned as part of eighties power dressing, to help shape the look of figure-hugging fashion. In contrast, deliberate displays of underwear became a statement of street style, as vintage 'Victoriana' corsetry demanded attention when mixed with tulle and net petticoats inspired by the fifties. These petticoats have been adopted as a perennial favourite of youth fashion, initiated by Madonna's eighties appearance in *Desperately Seeking*

Susan, and featuring in the opening credits for *Sex and the City* as the tutu style worn by Carrie Bradshaw, a celebrated $5 bargain-bucket find.

As the trend for combining vintage clothing with contemporary dress has increased, mixing in selected vintage underwear has a sophistication that far surpasses the raw street style of the eighties. By their nature, vintage undergarments from the early decades of the 20th century are both nostalgic and charming in appearance, attributes enhanced when worn with modern utilitarian fabrics such as denim. Success relies on the edit, adding a hand-embroidered camisole into an otherwise contemporary outfit, the exchange of a cardigan for an ornately stitched bed jacket, or the exquisitely embroidered dressing gown worn as a summer coat.

1, 2 Petticoats worn during the fifties have such wearability that they have been employed as outerwear ever since Madonna portrayed the street chic of eighties New York in *Desperately Seeking Susan*.

1 COTTON AND NYLON. c. 1950s.

2 NYLON. c. 1950s.

3 The love and care that went into making a bed jacket is always evident in its embellishment and embroidered decoration, making the jackets eminently wearable when mixed with a modern ensemble. While the knitted bed jacket was worn for warmth, the lighterweight silk, rayon or cotton bed jacket was worn decorously while sitting in bed. SILK. c. 1915.

4 Far Eastern imagery – the snakes, serpents and dragons that carry sexual connotations – was a popular embellishment for the kimono-style dressing gowns worn during the bohemian twenties and thirties. SILK. c. EARLY 1930s.

3

4

1 A silk dressing gown printed with delicate rocking horse imagery could pass as an evening dress today. SILK. c. 1940s.

2 By the forties, Hollywood film was exploiting the use of underwear on screen as a way to bypass the Hays Code. The femme fatale was a popular character in forties film noir, inspiring a less innocent style of lingerie. SILK SATIN. c. 1940s.

3 The fifties dressing gown is distinguished by its large-scale floral prints and was often made with a matching nightdress. HARRODS. COTTON. c. 1950s.

4 Oriental themes were a favourite, particularly for twenties underwear and nightwear. Original jackets and long housecoats can be hard to distinguish from their modern counterparts, which have changed very little in design, but modern silks do not have the textured feel of early fabric and labels are an easy clue. Most garments from the twenties were imported from Japan rather than China, and a Hong Kong label obviously indicates a later issue. SILK. c.1940s.

5, 6 Dressing gowns from the twenties and thirties can often be found in stunning printed designs. Often in the kimono style borrowed from the Far East, these dressing gowns are sometimes worn as dramatic coats by vintage enthusiasts. HANDMADE. SILK. c.1930s.

SWIMWEAR
BEAUTY ON THE BEACH

'NOTHING INSPIRES MY CREATIVITY MORE THAN VINTAGE CLOTHING. ALL OF MY SWIM PRINTS ARE FROM VINTAGE ARCHIVES – IT'S THE BEST RESOURCE FOR DESIGNERS AND TRULY INSPIRATIONAL.'

MELISSA ODABASH

Contemporary swimwear pays homage to vintage inspiration more than any other genre of fashion. Our love affair with nostalgic 20th-century 'fashion for the beach' is displayed in the revisiting and reinventing of the frills and flounces of past swimwear for today's wearer. The curvaceous swimsuits and statuesque bikinis of the celebrated pin-up girls of the past have been shaped to combine the best of both sportswear and lingerie to create garments that truly flatter the wide variety of female figures.

The mono-swimsuit of the twenties arrived as a garment that was both fashionable and functional, replacing the cumbersome costumes worn by long-suffering bathing beauties of the late 19th and early 20th centuries. A growing demand for comfortable, flattering and stylish swimwear led to rapid changes within the textile industry, as manufacturers competed to be at the forefront of a newly emerging fashion genus that was both stylishly provocative and exciting.

But the one-piece swimming costume for women of the twenties did not arrive without causing uproar, particularly in Britain, where beach fashion lagged behind places with sunnier climes and where society still considered the exposure of whole legs and arms to be scandalous. Prior to this, many women had been drowned by their elaborate and cumbersome swimwear and it was only the bravery of a few loudly protesting the restraints of women's swimwear that created awareness of the need for practical and safe swimwear for

female bathers. Professional swimmer Annette Kellerman, an Australian who refused to be bound by the rules of etiquette, made front-page news for her repeated public appearances in a homemade one-piece costume, culminating in her arrest in 1910. Her sentence was lenient and she went on to showcase her swimming abilities in early silent films, convincing authorities of the need for safe, streamlined swimwear. She was later immortalized by Olympic swimmer-turned-actress Esther Williams in the 1952 film *Million Dollar Mermaid*. Williams also starred in many aqua-musicals, including *Bathing Beauty* (1944), *Neptune's Daughter* (1949) and notably *Ziegfeld Follies* (1945), and, as she became a legend of synchronized swimming, her statuesque figure became a familiar sight in many advertising campaigns. Like many other stars of the screen, Williams was dressed by leading swimwear companies. Cole of California created an 'Esther Williams' swimsuit and Williams gave her name to many associated swimming products,

Basket weave suit. Straps crossing over at back and tying at front, giving instant adjustability. Designed to give you sun, more sun and still more sun.   4/11

In contrast to the "all one colour" styles now so fashionable, this costume strikes a different note in its striped coloured top.   3/11

Basket weave spring knit costume, perfect slim-fitting skirt attached, the unique weave makes this model distinctive.   4/11

A regulation one-piece style, with low sun back.

A costume which essentially spells Swimming.   3/11

MARKS AND SPENCER LTD.

4/11   3/11   4/11   3/11

1 A promotional leaflet for British high-street store Marks & Spencer from around the late twenties/ early thirties illustrates the new swimsuits with 'low sun backs' so no unsightly tan lines would be revealed when wearing the low-backed evening dresses fashionable at the time.

2 By the twenties the one-piece swimsuit was a common sight on the beaches of the French Riviera and the West coast of the United States, usually made from wool or even heavier cotton and serge fabrics. Swimsuits made on industrial machines, such as this one, had a more flattering stretchy fit than home-knitted versions. The Art Deco chevron and the crossover straps, a new fashion detail of the twenties, indicate it was an expensive design. The modest square-cut legs remained a feature of swimwear well into the fifties. AQUASIA. WOOL. c. LATE 1920s/ EARLY 1930s.

3 A twenties illustration from the risqué French publication *La Vie Parisienne* depicts the then-new fashion genre of beachwear. The soft, flowing garments designed for *après*-swim are highly sought after by today's fashionistas.

4 The decorative faggotting on the side of this rare swimsuit by Schiaparelli gives a corsetry effect. ELSA SCHIAPARELLI. STRETCH RAYON. c. LATE 1930s.

N° 451   *le sourire*   22 Juillet 1926

Les belles et la bête

Aquarelle de Jacques Leclerc

2 The two-piece swimsuit arrived during the thirties but strict modesty requirements meant that the navel was never revealed. Wartime rationing really established the style: with governments asking for a ten per cent reduction in the amount of fabric used, designers had no choice but to remove fabric from the only part of the swimsuit modesty allowed – the midriff. WOOL. c. LATE 1930s.

3 This French illustration shows the high-waisted two-piece swimsuit of the thirties that was not referred to as a 'bikini' until its later 'invention' in 1946.

4 A hand-tinted postcard showing the fashionable beach parade that was the Côte d'Azur in the thirties.

1 This swimsuit indicates the link between lingerie manufacturers and swimwear. Made by Brettles, who have been manufacturing underwear in Derbyshire in the UK for more than 200 years, the swimsuit has a flattering fit formed by the stretch satin rayon. The skirted front demonstrates thirties decorum but the daring cutaway back is a very modern detail for the time. The suit is printed in an unusually sophisticated design for swimwear of the era. BRETTLES. STRETCH SATIN RAYON. c. 1930s.

including a brand of swimwear that still sells retro Hollywood-inspired styles.

Without doubt, the two biggest influences on the revolution of 20th-century swimwear were the growing popularity for seaside holidays and, as with many other fashion genres, the impact of the film industry. The United States led the stylistic revolution in swimwear, ahead of Europe in its technological developments within the textile industry and with a climate that allowed the West Coast beaches to be filled with bathers determined to be fashionably bronzed, enjoying new sporty pursuits and the advocated healthy outdoor lifestyle of the time. European resorts, particularly those of the French Riviera, became a playground for the rich and famous and a catwalk parade for the latest fashions. 'Le Train Bleu', the midnight express that ran along the Riviera coastline dropping society's select at their holiday destinations, inspired the story of a ballet created by Serge Diaghilev and performed by his Ballets Russes in 1924. The elite of twenties modernism, Jean Cocteau, Pablo

Picasso and Coco Chanel, collaborated on the design of the ballet, which told the stories of seaside holiday-makers on the French Riviera. Chanel designed a series of knitted, striped, all-in-one sports costumes for the ballet, unusually inspired by everyday modern clothes. A pioneer in the use of fine jersey fabric, she began to explore the use of this material, previously solely employed for underwear and stockings, for sportswear and menswear.

Independently, Chanel's contemporaries Jean Patou and Jeanne Lanvin began similar experimentations. Patou is credited with perfecting the fabric for swimwear and was the first to brand his designs with an initialled logo. Many women sought out his sleek sportswear, which was displayed within its own section in his boutiques – the first time daywear was grouped and separated into categories and an acknowledgment of the emerging leisure and sportswear industry. His swimming costumes used straight-fronted modesty skirts and were defined with narrow waist-belts to create an elegant and sporty appearance. He was also the first to brand and market a formula of suntan oil, 'Huile de Chaldée', a refined version of the homemade sun oils used to aid tanning.

As the beaches, public swimming baths and fashionable open-air lidos of Europe and the United States evolved to become glamorous new gathering points, a whole new genre of fashion was created. Resortwear became the new all-important must-have. As the knitted one-piece swimming costume, the 'maillot', sagged and pulled when wet, bathers needed to be able to change into dry, less revealing clothes. Lightweight 'beach pyjamas', wide-legged palazzo trousers worn with loose tops, kimono-style wraps, robes and short jackets were fashionable essentials.

Stars of the silver screen upped the style stakes as producers sidestepped the rules of the Hays Code. Swimwear was not subject to the same rules and was written into as many scripts as possible to replace lingerie. This resulted

in a series of aqua-films that gave Hollywood the quota of titillating flesh required to draw cinema-goers. An early form of product placement took place as the burgeoning new swimwear companies signed film stars to model their costumes and herald the arrival of innovative designs, waterproof fabrics and figure-enhancing improvements.

The resulting promotional material is some of the most enticing imagery found in fashion archives, combining fashionable images with scenic nautical backgrounds showing stylized waves, seagulls and beach frolics. Each decade delights in its own distinctive style, and early photography and illustrative artwork of the twenties and thirties are as appealing as the fashion plates of pin-up girls and screen sirens of the forties and fifties. The artwork is echoed in many contemporary fashion campaigns – confirmation of a fashionable blueprint as successful in bygone eras as today.

As the thirties dawned, many manufacturers of lingerie and knitwear furiously adapted machinery to compete in this rapidly evolving new area of

fashion, and such was their technical prowess that many of them are still producing swimwear today. Fred Cole, an American twenties star of silent movies, experienced the increased prominence of swimwear with the film industry first-hand and gave up his acting career to return to his parents' West Coast knitting mill. Cole's parents manufactured long socks and long johns but were persuaded to start a swimwear line under their son's direction. The company, later to be known as 'Cole of California', brought in Margit Fellegi, who was already designing for Hollywood, as head designer. Together they utilized the plentiful glamorous fabrics and embellishments not needed for the war effort, such as velvet and rhinestones, as well as leftover parachute silk. They invented techniques to combine elasticized rubber threads, such as Matlex, with fabrics such as cotton, to create a shirred effect. Focus was always on glamour and, in 1943, they were the first to use side-lacing. This had the controlling effect of a corset and the design was dubbed the 'swoon suit'.

Other American companies such as Jantzen, initially the manufacturers of rowing suits, simultaneously began to experiment with elasticized and rubberized yarn, combining latex rubber with rayon to create a breakthrough fabric that was not only elastic and waterproof, but could also be printed on and dyed in exotic colours. Jantzen marketed themselves as a company that took swimwear seriously. Using the tagline 'the suit that changed bathing to swimming', they introduced their famous logo, a red swimming-costumed diving girl, in 1923. Husband and wife Frank and Florenz Clark were commissioned to devise a memorable logo for the brand and the design duo sketched divers as they practised for the twenties Olympics to create the template for the logo still seen on costumes today. In their efforts to establish an image as a serious swimwear label, Jantzen dressed Olympic swimmers as well as the Hollywood stars Loretta Young, Joan Blondell and Ginger Rogers.

1

European technology lagged behind America's and it wasn't until the end of the thirties, when revolutionary fabrics such as Latex were imported, that European beaches witnessed the stylish sophistication of American swimwear. Elsa Schiaparelli designed a backless swimsuit in 1930 to aid suntanning for those partaking in the vogue for backless evening dresses, while the mid-thirties saw the introduction of a two-piece swimming costume that was not, as is commonly mistaken, a bikini. Always covering the navel and finishing level with the thigh, this fashion did not really take off until the forties. Further design details that help to identify swimwear from this period are waist belts, halternecks, adjustable shoulder straps and early internal bra constructions.

Early forties rationing stagnated swimwear design, which was far down the list of fashion priorities. Hollywood continued to inspire with blockbuster films like *The Ziegfeld Follies*, but

1 Comfortable, artificial fabrics for swimwear really developed in the thirties. This swimsuit is not at all waterproof, but it has a flattering cling due to the stretch of Celanese jersey. 'Celanese' was the trade name given to synthetic fabrics experimented with as a cheaper and hardier replacement for silk. Although many fashion historians regard Celanese as an American invention, there is plenty of evidence to show 'British Celanese' was in great demand in the early thirties, particularly for eveningwear. Catalina (named after the island on the coast of Los Angeles) is a swimwear label synonymous with the glamour of early film, as many starlets such as Joan Blondell, Olivia de Havilland and Bette Davis were used to promote its designs. CATALINA. BRITISH CELANESE JERSEY. c. 1930s.

2 Jantzen marketed itself with the slogan 'the suit that changed bathing to swimming' and their famous logo, showing a girl diving in a red hat and one-piece swimsuit, has remained on all their designs to date (see **4**). Their swimwear can be dated by the changing style of the logo over the decades.

3 The curvaceous swimwear of the forties owed much to the corsets and girdles worn to create the hourglass figure of the era. The feminine figure was actively promoted on-screen and in advertising to appeal to a male audience wanting distraction from the horrors of war. The pin-up girl of the forties posed coquettishly in tightly fitted swimsuits with heart-shaped necklines accessorized with perfectly coiffured hair and make-up in an effort to boost morale. ORHIDE. COTTON. c. 1940s.

4 JANTZEN. COTTON. c. 1960s.

5 NELBARDEN. RAYON. c. 1940s.

6 HANDMADE. COTTON. c. 1940s.

7 The influence of Hawaii, a favourite post-war holiday destination, can be seen in American forties fashion on everything from cocktail dresses to swimwear. Tropical prints and sarong styles were hugely successful in both American and European markets. The figure-enhancing drape of the sarong was particularly suited to swimwear and was incorporated by designers such as Carolyn Schnurer. WALTAH CLARKES. COTTON. c. 1940s.

3

4

5

6

7

American rationing demanded a ten per cent reduction in the amount of fabric used in swimwear. The only place it could be lost was the middle of the swimsuit, which resulted in much experimentation with cut-outs and variations in front-fastening ties and straps in attempts to cover the banned navel and lower the waistline. All superfluous decorative details, such as belts, frills and above all the modesty skirts that had prevailed since the initiation of 20th-century swimsuits, were removed.

1946 saw the arrival of the true bikini, a natural development of the two-piece swimsuit and wartime rationing. Both couturier Jacques Heim, who was based in the glamorous French resort of Cannes, and car engineer Louis Réard, who ran his mother's Parisian lingerie boutique, claimed to be its inventor. Heim launched his 'atome' by hiring a plane to skywrite 'the world's smallest bathing suit' above the beaches of Cannes. Three weeks later, Réard designed his bikini bottoms to be even smaller, thereby revealing the navel, and advertised his 'bikini atoll' as 'smaller than the smallest swimsuit'. The name was taken from the South Pacific beach where the Japanese had tested an atomic bomb the previous year. Banned by the Miss World pageant in 1951, it took the bikini a while to become established and it wasn't until 1953, when a bikini-clad Brigitte Bardot in Cannes made headlines, that it started to become universally accepted.

The late forties also saw the arrival of the 'playsuit', the one-piece shorts and top combination that still holds a fashionable place today. They were pioneered by American designer Claire McCardell, whose 'diaper' swimsuits were created in jersey and towelling. These unusual fabrics for water were perfect for after-swim beach wear, and helped popularize this look.

It is perhaps the swim silhouette of the fifties that is most popular today, with its curvaceous, hourglass outline that benefitted from boning and general corsetry to create the womanly figure fashionable in the era. It was a style inspired, in part, by Dior's 1947 'New Look'. Dior created only one swimwear line, in collaboration with Cole of California in 1955. On invitation, he claimed to know nothing about swimwear design, but complied when Cole reportedly retorted, 'You're a designer, aren't you? So design.' Fifties swimsuits remained glamorous throughout the decade. Givenchy designed for Jantzen, while animal prints, particularly leopard, were a signature print of the decade. Decorative rubber swim hats completed the look.

As with mainstream fashion of the day, the revolutionary sixties swept away all traces of retrospective glamour. Helped by the introduction of a range of inexpensive, durable nylons, swimwear diversified to resemble the range of styles on offer today. A streamlined and sportive modernism prevailed post-fifties and swimwear styles were increasingly governed by the image of the fashion houses. Emilio Pucci, Paco Rabanne, Pierre Cardin and André Courrèges all stamped their individual style on fashion for the beach, but the design that created the biggest sartorial impact on the latter half of the 20th century was Rudi Gernreich's 'monokini'. Believing that all beaches of the future would be covered with topless women bathers, innovative Gernreich revealed his one-piece topless swimsuit in 1968 to a shocked audience. While the beaches of St Tropez already witnessed topless sunbathers, the one-piece, high-waisted monokini featured two straps that crossed between the breasts, reaching over the shoulder to fasten at the back of the bottoms. Although the design had little commercial success, it had an undeniably huge impact on swimwear design of the following decades.

For the vintage collector, it is the swimwear produced up until the sixties that holds the most aesthetic interest and, perhaps surprisingly, that is the most wearable today. The early cottons, seersuckers, grosgrains and sateens are often more durable than the post-fifties assortment of nylons. Early swim fashion was designed for gentle bathing and fashionable parade, and, over time, its natural fibres have been less corroded by saltwater and chlorine than the synthetic sensations of the sixties, seventies and eighties. Some of the most successful and wearable swimwear designs are those produced by the early underwear manufacturers, who had an understanding of the cut and fit required to create a swimsuit that flattered the female form.

1 This image by Venice Beach photographer Mimi Haddon styles a contemporary model in a fifties swimsuit.

2, 3 Swimsuits of the forties and fifties were often double-fronted, with a top layer of fabric that skimmed across the thighs for modesty. In tune with fifties fashion, styles of the decade were overtly feminine and used elasticated ruching, smocking and pin-tucks to create costumes used both as swimsuits and as fashionable sunsuits, for posing rather than swimming. The scalloped dipped front on the costume on the left was known as an 'apron' front and protected the wearer's modesty, making the sunsuit acceptable for socializing around lidos or on the beach.

2 COTTON. c. EARLY 1950s.

3 NELBARDEN. COTTON. c. EARLY 1950s.

4 This 'sunsuit' or 'playsuit' has elasticated smocking at the back and an attached bra inside to create a flattering silhouette for socializing in the sun. Bright colourful prints were a reaction to the austerity of wartime fabrics when printing dyes were restricted. HANDMADE. COTTON. c. 1950s.

5 The use of stripes helps to create the illusion of a flattering silhouette. HANDMADE. COTTON. c. 1950s.

6 SILHOUETTE. SYNTHETIC. c. 1950s.

7 Although the relaxed style of American dressing led the way in swimwear, France was still regarded as the centre of fashion, and even the successful Cole of California invited Christian Dior to design a swimwear collection in 1955. Manufacturers gave themselves names with a French association to be seen at the forefront of fashion, like this British 'French Pin-Up' label. FRENCH PIN-UP. COTTON. c. LATE 1950s.

4 The vibrant print on this swimsuit reflects the sixties obsession with psychedelic Pucci-esque pattern, while the metal hoop also appeared everywhere from belts to dresses, inspired by the French couturiers Pierre Cardin and André Courrèges. Thighs were not high-cut until the end of the decade. POLYESTER. c. EARLY 1960s.

5 The swimsuit of the seventies experimented with new 'second skin' stretch fabrics for a natural freeform silhouette and 'tan through' swimsuits for more modest sunbathers who still wanted to replicate the results of topless sunbathing. This Lycra swimsuit uses an elaborate jersey stitch to create a see-through appearance, but includes sewn-in, flesh-coloured, second-skin underwear for mainstream appeal. TRIUMPH INTERNATIONAL. LYCRA. c. 1970s.

1 The sixties vogue for all things denim is seen in this one-piece swimsuit manufactured from imitation denim stretch nylon. The clean and understated chic of the decade was a reaction against the frilliness and over-decoration of earlier fashions. ST MICHAEL. NYLON. c. 1960s.

2 Vibrant prints continued throughout the seventies as swimwear became more streamlined and revealing in order to maximize the must-have suntans of the decade. The swimwear line Nelbarden had its own boutique in London's Regent Street. NELBARDEN. POLYESTER. c. 1970s.

3 By the sixties swimwear designs became more demure, ladylike, streamlined items of sportswear that radiated less glamour than the 'pin-up' styles of the fifties. JANTZEN. SYNTHETIC. c. 1960s.

6 Cole of California dates back to the twenties but the company is still at the forefront of swimwear today. This sundress from the sixties is made from the same water-resistant Spandex used for many swimsuits of the era, with an attached bra to give uplift. The sundress illustrates the emergence of resortwear as a new trend in the decade. COLE OF CALIFORNIA. SPANDEX. c. 1960s.

7 The playsuit of the fifties and sixties has seen a recent high-street revival, with original vintage prototypes worn as well as the mass-produced styles they inspired. HANDMADE. COTTON. c. 1960s.

8 Although the sixties saw the bikini become an established swimwear style, astonishingly, bottoms were still large, barely exposing the navel. Meanwhile, the new inventions in Bri-Nylon and other synthetic fabrics were not strong enough to give a good bust shape so many bikini tops from this era can be found with built-in bras. ORHIDE. POLYESTER. c. 1960s.

9 The fashionable body of the eighties was athletic and toned. Cutaway styling in block primary colours or sophisticated black and white revealed a body sculpted from hours at the gym or aerobic classes. The television series *Baywatch* and Jane Fonda's bestselling Workout video helped to promote a swimwear style closely resembling the dancercise leotards worn in the gym. LYCRA. c. 1980s.

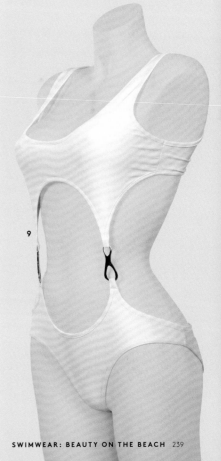

APRONS SARTORIAL DOMESTICITY

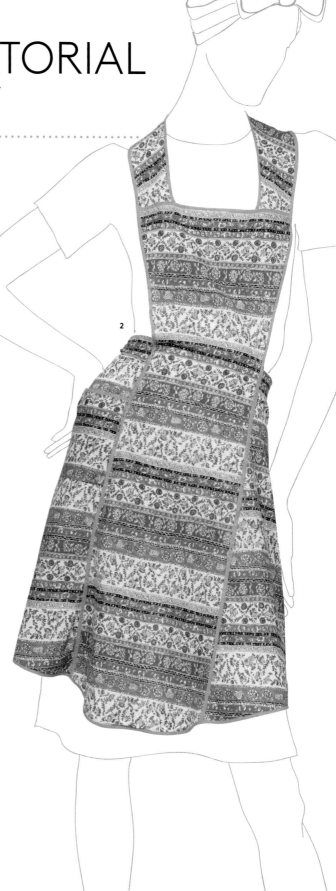

1 This illustration from a forties dressmaking pattern gives the wartime apron a glamorous appeal. Home sewing was both a necessity and a pastime.

2 Because home sewers in the forties utilized every scrap of material, aprons can often be found made from good quality dress fabrics. COTTON. c. 1940s.

3-5 While the aprons of the forties were generally made with clean lines and no trimmings, fifties aprons used a multitude of flounces and frills. These three half-aprons also demonstrate the fifties fondness for novelty patterns, particularly fruit and vegetables or kitchen ephemera such as teacups. HANDMADE. COTTON. c. 1950s.

'I'M INTERESTED IN THE LIVES OF WOMEN IN GENERAL, WHICH IS WHY
I LOVE APRONS. THE APRON IS A RECURRING THEME IN MY WORK
BECAUSE IT IS SYMBOLIC OF WOMEN'S SUFFERANCE. IT IS AN EMBLEM
OF WOMEN'S DESPAIR, THEIR POVERTY, THEIR PASSIONS.' MIUCCIA PRADA

As Miuccia Prada's quote reveals, aprons appeal to collectors of vintage fashion on many different levels. As a visual document of female subservience, or a display of artisan skills or coquettish domesticity, vintage aprons may be humble or ostentatious but their appeal is undeniable and their wearability for today is surprising.

It was historically a garment with a job to do, and references to the protective apron can be found in biblical scripture. For many centuries, it remained an item of practicality for both sexes and something for which decoration would have been considered frivolous and unnecessary. By the 16th century, it denoted the profession of its wearer: butchers, barbers and servants, for example, wore differentiating checks and colours.

This remained a pattern for domestic service well into the 20th century. Laura Ashley, who began her fashion empire by making aprons and oven gloves with her own fabrics on her kitchen table, remembered her grandmother's 'array' of aprons: 'When I was a child in Wales, there were different aprons for different tasks: a black one for cleaning the grates; a green apron for washing and scrubbing; and then best of all the white starched ones (with matching caps) for cooking.'

A 'working' woman's apron worn before the 20th century was traditionally white and completely covered the full-skirted fashion of the day and often the upper torso too. Valuable aids to domestic duties, apron pockets held eggs or vegetables, and the coarse, thick fabric provided protection from hot pots and pans. But, as the intricacies of class

distinction blurred in female society, so the apron began to reflect ownership, and its decorative and fashionable qualities become more interesting to the contemporary collector. Different levels of domestic service demanded a variety of decorative attributes. The serving parlour maid was on show to visiting society and a freshly laundered apron signified the financial ability of the house owner to be able to dress their servants well. A petite and delicately embroidered half-apron worn by the mistress of the house was an indication of a domesticity that was only for show; these ornate aprons were simply an example of fine needlework protecting exquisite fashions beneath.

As the silhouettes and hemlines of 20th-century fashions streamlined and shortened, the apron naturally adapted.

Encouraged by participation in the First World War, more women joined the workforce and the introduction of domestic appliances removed some of the drudgery from housework, but the apron still retained its popularity and displayed a new character with fashionable qualities.

The working apron of the late twenties, thirties and forties took on a new shape: a complete overall that wrapped over and was usually sleeveless. Made from serviceable fabrics, they were nevertheless covered with diminutive florals and often decorated with jaunty pockets, braided trimming and sometimes lace or ribbons. Worn daily, aprons became fashionable items and, as can be observed from the many dressmaking patterns that can still be bought, they were often designed to complement a fashionable dress. Whether handmade or purchased from catalogues or department stores, the apron was darted, seamed and shaped to rival the seventies sensation of Diane von Furstenberg's wrap dress.

These serviceable housecoats and aprons embodied fashionable femininity

and the frills, flounces and heart-shaped bib fronts that can be found today in embroidered ginghams, faded florals, fruit and vegetable prints or kitsch novelty images, have been softened with years of frequent washing and use. Many are so shapely and decorative that they are chosen for contemporary wear as summer dresses. The austere years of the Second World War ignited imaginative and creative approaches to home dressmaking and retaining a fashionable wardrobe. Three large floral handkerchiefs could be transformed into a bib-fronted patchwork apron, while faded dresses had their sleeves removed. Countrywomen in the United States utilized durable printed feed sacks once emptied of their contents. Acknowledging this trend, astute manufacturers sourced attractive prints to ensure continuing sales of the animal feed, flour and sugar contained within the sacks.

During the late forties and early fifties, McCall's, Simplicity and Butterick issued paper dressmaking patterns dictating elaborate appliqués, embroidery transfers, pleating

1 This American magazine illustrates dress patterns for aprons, showing how aprons were designed to blend with the outfit they protected.

2 Beautiful late twenties housecoats or smocks indicate the pride women took in their everyday appearance. This hand-printed floral design is a worthy summer dress for today's vintage enthusiast. HANDMADE. COTTON. c. LATE 1920s.

2

Page 34

THE DELINEATOR, August, 1922

Apron 3860-A
Embroidery design 10982

Apron 3858
Embroidery design 10982

Combination 3851

Apron 3857

Apron 3878

Apron 3860-B

1

3, 6 The blouse-style smock dates to the thirties and was popular for gardening and hobbies such as painting or flower arranging before being replaced by the sleeveless pinafore style in the forties. The print styles of these aprons are more sophisticated while their construction is simpler than that of apron **2**, indicating their later age.

4, 5, 7 Many aprons of the forties and early fifties were enveloping wraparound styles, barely distinguishable from a modern summer dress. The diminutive prints of **4** and **7** indicate that they were made in the forties, while the full-blown rose print and shorter length of **5** are typical of fifties design.

4 HANDMADE. COTTON. c. 1940s.

5 HANDMADE. COTTON. c. 1950s.

7 HANDMADE. COTTON. c. 1940s.

techniques, lace insertions and new ways with crossover straps. The domestic apron of the fifties became a commercial and fashionable commodity, in tune with 'domestic goddess' aspirations and a significant trend for home entertaining. Always quick to commercialize a trend, American manufacturers in particular released designs for Thanksgiving, Christmas and Easter, matching tablecloths and aprons, coordinating mother and daughter aprons, as well as designs that were simply chic for the glamorous hostess.

Sixties youth rejected the domesticity of an older generation and the apron returned to its serviceable status. Terence Conran arrived on the British high street with Habitat in 1964 and transformed the design attributes of domesticity. Clean lines, simple stripes and natural fabrics were the buzz words for interior design that amplified the concerns of sixties fashion, and in the midst of it all was the navy and white striped butcher's apron proudly worn by Conran himself in archive promotional footage of the opening of the first London store.

The 2012 *Schiaparelli and Prada: Impossible Conversations* exhibition curated by Andrew Bolton and Harold Koda at New York's Metropolitan Museum of Art illustrated a new and sophisticated interpretation of the working apron. A section of the exhibition 'Waist Up/Waist Down' juxtaposed Schiaparelli's attention to decorative detail on the upper body (part of restaurant dressing for thirties café society) with the below-waist focus of Miuccia Prada. Prada explained that her inspiration derived from the apron, a domestic garment that generates a low focal point. Garments selected to illustrate Prada's inspired 'below-the-waist' emphasis displayed elaborate embellishment, Art Deco and biomorphic prints, and play with proportions. The designs are a far cry from the obvious kitchen-sink characterization or the derivative kitsch and cute connotations usually associated with a domestic apron.

The heyday of the vintage apron really spanned the twenties to the fifties when so much effort was given to their personalization and decoration. Their careful construction and coordinated fabric choice turned them into fashionable garments for everyday wear. The variety of prints offer an archival reference for the textile designer, but ultimately it is their simple charm that attracts the collector.

1 Two women pose in thirties housecoats, with only their cleaning utensils indicating they are wearing protective aprons rather than summer dresses.

2 The wrapover apron was frequently manufactured in sophisticated prints. GLAZED COTTON. c. 1950s.

3–6 The variety of inspirational printed textile designs that can be found on aprons is evident from the forties designs. Like the garments they decorate, the small busy prints are hard-working and refreshingly different from the fashion styles of the day. Women in the United States in the forties would utilize the attractive prints found on animal feed sacks while dress fabric was in short supply during the war years. Durable cloth made for practical aprons and other garments was enlivened by the attractive printed patterns. Aprons bearing the British government's utility label were just as attractive (**6**). With many fashion houses today utilizing archive print designs, it is useful to see the patterns at work.

3–5 HANDMADE. COTTON. c. 1940s.

6 COTTON. c. 1940s.

1

2

3

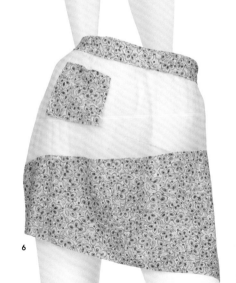

6

7

8

4

5

11

9

10

1–11 By the fifties, the job of 'domestic goddess' was taken seriously. Home entertaining became the new popular social activity, and women selected their pert half-aprons to coordinate with their ensembles accordingly. Aprons were designed for daytime or even cocktail wear and dressmaking patterns offered ingenious new ways with pockets, trimmings and fastenings. A popular style was the 'handkerchief apron' (**2**), made from a series of matching handkerchiefs. Manufacturers in the United States in particular took apron design seriously. The garment was a valuable commodity and could be marketed to coordinate with national holidays centering around the kitchen such as Thanksgiving, Christmas and Easter. Even matching mother-and-daughter styles were marketed. HANDMADE. COTTON. c. 1950s.

1

2

3

4

5

6

7

8

1, 2, 5, 6 These aprons display some of the variety of styles on offer in the fifties. Embroidered, pleated and printed designs mean the vintage apron offers a wealth of often-overlooked inspiration. Discarded in the sixties as a garment that helped tie women to their kitchens, the vintage apron – with all its nostalgic appeal – has again returned to favour. HANDMADE. COTTON. c. 1950s.

3, 4 More women of the sixties had careers, and washing machines and other labour-saving devices had become standard in the modern home. The use of the domestic apron was dwindling but this early sixties editorial celebrates integrated aprons designed for the hostess.

7, 8 Vintage apron patterns offer an invaluable resource for studying garment construction and imaginative finishes, trimmings and pocket details.

KNITWEAR
WARM NOSTALGIA

'KNITTED CLOTHES HAVE BECOME INTERNATIONAL STATUS SYMBOLS, LIKE VUITTON BAGS AND GUCCI SHOES.' *NEW YORK TIMES*

1 Three-piece cardigan suits (shown here with the cardigan removed) provided popular daywear during the twenties. Easy to wear, they were perfect for the relaxed style of dressing introduced by Chanel and Patou. The influence of Art Deco is evident in this knit's angular block patterning, and its rich, vibrant colours are indicative of the United States as opposed to the subtler colouring seen in Europe. HANDMADE. RAYON. c. 1920s.

The unique design and craftsmanship of a piece of vintage knitwear make it highly sought after and wearable today. However, vintage knitwear is hard to find in wearable condition, as so many pieces are destroyed by moths or have become shrunken or misshapen with age. Even dealers of vintage fashion have resorted to selling copies of knitwear patterns while holding on to the originals. The reproduction of appealing designs, with emphasis on the thirties and forties, is in serious demand, particularly if the pattern has been updated to modern sizing. The cardigans and jumpers, and even the dresses and skirts, which have survived in good condition, can command high prices due to their relative scarcity.

Each decade offers creative knitwear with identifiable characteristics and details that are intertwined with the mode of the day, and yet knitting is an area of fashion set apart by its own tradition and craft. Such were the skills of yesterday's knitter, the vintage sweater, cardigan, twinset, slipover tank or even bed jacket does not need a label of distinction to mark it as a collector's piece worthy of contemporary wear.

Surprisingly, the origins of commercial knitwear are buried within the centuries before the industrial revolution. Decades of fine and luxurious mechanically manufactured undergarments, stockings and socks rival the traditions of hard-working knitting needles. The quality of ancient silk and cashmere underwear worn by nobles and royals make exquisite outerwear today, if one is lucky enough to find it unshrunken and without moth holes. Pastel-coloured vests rival the modern T-shirt, while knitted silk stockings of the twenties and thirties are found in astonishingly vibrant colours.

Paintings as early as the 14th century depict hand-knitting as a pastime of nobility as well as being a craft of necessity. Hand-knitting was an essential skill utilized by both men and women: the rudiments were taught to schoolchildren as the production of warm, utilitarian, even waterproof clothing was a part of survival.

Out of the hard-working communities and cottage industries scattered around harsh British and Scandinavian landscapes came the indigenous patterns and stitches that have inspired contemporary knitwear designs. Intricate Fair Isle patterns, Guernsey sweaters with identifying parish stitches worn by fishermen and sailors, distinctive Irish cabled patterns inherited from families of the Aran Islands and fine web-like woollen lacework from the Shetland Isles: these designs steeped in history and culture are reinterpreted

3

2 A forties knitwear pattern for a dress and matching hat in a colour-blocked design. The bold use of colour is indicative of forties American styling, and it is easy to see the inspiration behind much of eighties design.

3 This spectacular sweater suit shows the lengths the fashion industry went to in order to provide clothing during the war years. Ribbon was manufactured in soft tubular or single rayon with a soft sheen, specifically for knitting purposes. The finish was surprisingly elastic, achieving a tailored and glamorous style that could be achieved by home knitters as well as manufacturers. This suit was one of a series sold in the American department store Bergdorf Goodman and is an example of the way patriotic insignia was used on clothing made in the war years. BERGDORF GOODMAN. RAYON RIBBON. c. 1940s.

2

by contemporary designers and their connotations of heritage embraced by brands such as Ralph Lauren.

Equally effective was the jersey fabric produced on the fine-gauge, circular knitting looms of the industrial 19th century but this was still the preserve of those who could afford fine undergarments, vests and stockings. Modernists Coco Chanel, Jean Patou and Elsa Schiaparelli utilized this fluid knit for fashionable sportswear and the long suits of the twenties, replacing corseted styling with easy chic. Chanel, often portrayed as more of a stylist, even negotiated exclusive rights to the fine jersey produced for men's underwear by textile industrialist, Eugene Rodier, to outdo her competition.

Each couturier added their individual style to this new genre of fashion. The *trompe-l'œil* patterns of Schiaparelli's jumpers introduced a typically playful aesthetic. Her designs featured ties and skeletons but she wore her first and most famous jumper, featuring the optical illusion of a bow, to a society luncheon and the impact was such that she subsequently received her first orders. Patou is known for the jersey sportswear and swimwear he championed, while Chanel, in her constant search for chic, easy styling, was inspired by the simple jerseys worn by French fishermen.

● The plain black lines on the plan are the garter-stitch ridges formed in the knitting. Choose your own colour scheme for the embroidery, using your odds and ends of wools. Coloured embroidery on a white background would make an attractive summer jumper.

Knitwear of the twenties helped to change the silhouette of fashion, adapting it to the active lifestyle of the modern woman. It is designs from the United States that can still be found with relative ease and their long and lean forms, along with their mono-coloured, striped, colour-blocked motifs in simple chevrons, Cubist or Art Deco patterns, display the influence of Parisian fashion.

The traditional Fair Isle that has rarely wavered in its original stitchwork escalated from being a humble local product of Shetland crofters to a fashionable garment in the twenties. The style was chosen by the Prince of Wales, later the Duke of Windsor, as his choice of golf jumper to play in a match in 1922 at St Andrews, Scotland. The jumper received considerable attention and has remained an item of sartorial choice ever since, with continuing popularity throughout the forties and a resurgence during the seventies, a decade that embraced historical fashion and a nostalgia for crafts. Both the traditional Fair Isle of the Shetlands and the cable stitch of the Aran Islands remain in constant demand as a vintage trend.

Hand-knitting was a skill of many and provided a way of achieving a high-fashion look for women of ordinary means who would not otherwise have been able to afford Parisian style. The forties saw the introduction of metallic yarns, and the many boleros and knitted jackets featured large novelty celluloid buttons moulded in intricate patterns or shaped to imitate florals and animals. The company Pringle of Scotland, established in 1815, developed the twinset – matching jumper and cardigan sets. A simple concept in soft yarn and colouring that became a fashion staple of the following decades, it was at its heyday in the fifties when Pringle opened a twinset bar in the prestigious department store, Harvey Nichols. They were also responsible for the introduction of the famous Argyle pattern in the twenties.

Among the abundance of kaleidoscopic pattern, jewelled embellishment and traditional knots and

1 Embroidery and knitted stitchwork involving the use of multicoloured threads are typical of designs found in the austere years of the Second World War when every scrap of yarn was utilized, resulting in the delightful array of colourful knitwear found today.

2 A late thirties pattern for a hand-knit designed by Schiaparelli exclusively for *The Needlewoman*. Advertised as being ideal for 'Sportswear or Spectator Sports', the cardigan has all the hallmarks of a structured jacket, including patch pockets, revers and a tailored shape.

3

4

5

6

7

3-5 Fair Isle has become a generic term that is, today, applied to all patterned knits that resemble the traditional patterning created by home knitters on the Scottish Shetland island, Fair Isle. Along with the Guernsey sweater and Aran patterning, it is one of the knitwear traditions of the British Isles that dates back several centuries. Fair Isle was popular during the austere years of the Second World War as the pattern utilized all the leftover odds and ends of coloured wools when new supplies were hard to obtain because of wartime rationing. HANDMADE. WOOL. c. 1940s.

6 The knitted tabard, a mid-seventies style that has rarely resurfaced in fashion, arrived alongside ponchos and fringing with patterns referencing Native American and Aztec designs. JUMP. SYNTHETIC. c. 1970s.

7 Printing on knitwear was a technique that was not fully explored until the eighties. Although select garments can be found, there are few as sophisticated as this Italian design from the early seventies. Damon Creations was established in 1942 and ceased trading in the eighties. FRANCESCA FOR DAMON CREATIONS. WOOL. c. EARLY 1970s.

cables, the humble bed jacket should not be ignored. Worn for warmth, in the days before central heating, these have survived far better than their daytime counterparts and, particularly those from the twenties and thirties, often display an intricacy of stitchwork, refined colouring and beguiling construction. When mixed with a modern wardrobe, it is only the connoisseur who would ascertain their original use.

'Remember Pearl Harbor … Purl Harder' was one of the American slogans of wartime. Hand-knitting became a wartime obsession in the effort to keep warm at a time of fuel shortage, and every worn sock or lost glove was utilized. Clothing was unravelled and reknitted and consequently jumpers from the forties can be found in multicoloured stripes and variations of the Fair Isle, or interesting designs, sometimes sleeveless, that incorporated openwork and crochet in an effort to use less yarn. Trimmings were not restricted by rationing, so jumpers of the forties may well be found featuring embroidery, flowered corsages, appliqué, and even sequins or beadwork.

The famous 'sweater girl' look arrived at the end of this decade, epitomized by American actress Lana Turner and inspired by the pin-up sweethearts of wartime. Stars of the silver screen exploited the voluptuous style in fitted cashmere, fluffy angoras and lambswool. The flattering dolman sleeve was a new feature seen at the end of the forties, a feature that experienced huge popularity on its revival during the eighties. The eighties was also notorious for its reintroduction and enlargement of another feature of forties fashions: the shoulder pad. While many dismiss the oversized exaggerated knitwear of the eighties, the era experienced several divergent trends. Knitted stretch jersey fabrics helped to achieve the body-conscious look of the decade, a style that has been enjoying a recent resurgence. Many notable designers embraced the sophistication of the original trend and arguably the designs most sought after and wearable today are those of Azzedine Alaïa and the early work of Joseph Tricot. Also highly collectable is the deconstructed knitwear of Rei Kawakubo, founder of the Comme des Garçons label, which challenged the conformity of eighties excess.

Many vintage enthusiasts enjoy the decorative, embellished styling produced in the fifties and the beaded cardigans have seen so many reinterpretations that it is often hard to distinguish from originals. Obvious indications are that both beaded cardigans and jumpers from this decade were often lined in silk to prevent stretching caused by the weight of elaborated beadwork. Labels, if they remain, will read 'Made in Hong Kong', not 'China' like later designs.

1 Helen Bond Carruthers knitwear from the early fifties is much sought after today and commands high prices. Her elaborate garments used what was, even at the time, vintage material. She bought good quality cashmere cardigans (thought to be from Bergdorf Goodman), shortened them by removing the waist welts, turned up the sleeves, changed buttons for pearl or glass, before covering the cardigans and sweaters with ornate embroideries she had taken from antique Chinese shawls and Belgian lacework. She became so successful that she employed a whole workforce of women from her house. Her label is found sewn into the waistband of her garments. HELEN BOND CARRUTHERS. CASHMERE. c. MID-1950s.

2 A 1948 pattern from the British range Stitchcraft, illustrating the emerging trend for non-traditional integral intarsia patterning. The simple lace-like look created with two contrasting colours was a modern effect for the time.

3 An exciting assortment of knitwear designs from a 1952 Spanish clothing catalogue shows the development of industrially knitted fashion. The styling is inspired by the hand-knits of the forties, but the tailoring effects achieved on the machine were superior.

4 Fully fashioned cardigans and jumpers (knitwear that was knitted to shape, rather than being cut and sewn from panels) were intricately decorated for cocktail wear during the fifties and usually made from the finest of wools – angora, cashmere or lambswool. The embellishments of pearl and sequin beading and silk thread were often manufactured and imported from Hong Kong. A silk lining would prevent the knitwear from stretching and sagging under the heavy weight of the beadwork. Later examples can be distinguished by their 'Made in China' label. LAMBSWOOL. c. 1950s.

5 It is hard to find fifties printed knitwear in a wearable condition. By the sixties, the use of synthetic yarns made printing on knitwear a viable option and many polyester jumpers can be found covered in printed florals. Earlier printed knitwear is far superior both in the quality of the yarns (mohair and lambswool were most commonly used) and in the complexity of the printed image. PRINTED MOHAIR. c. 1950s.

6 This style of embroidered flower was common in the fifties, seen in raffia on handbags and ribbon-work on skirts and dresses, as well as on knitwear. WOOL. c. 1950s.

7 Italian businesswoman Luisa Spagnoli initially sold chocolate before turning to knitwear. She is famous for breeding her own Angora rabbits, using their wool in her designs. Early labels for the company, still in business today, bear a rabbit image in addition to the company logo. LUISA SPAGNOLI. ANGORA. c. EARLY 1950s.

8 Intricate embroideries are the sign of high-end fifties knitwear. Couture houses began their early flirtation with ready-to-wear by marketing exquisite knitwear. Knitwear was constructed on a machine and could not be fitted in the same way as a bespoke dress or coat, making it the ideal ready-to-wear garment for the couture houses. PRINTED MOHAIR. c. 1950s.

1 This mohair cardigan is by the celebrated French designer Claude Montana. Known for his strong use of colour and shape, Montana was at his peak in the eighties. Mohair could be easily dyed, making it the ideal yarn for the strong vibrant colours used throughout the eighties and early nineties. CLAUDE MONTANA. MOHAIR. 1991.

2 Two brothers founded the hugely successful French company Naf Naf in 1973. Although not a specialist knitwear company, it stayed at the forefront of young international fashion and partook in the trend for knitted leggings that appeared towards the end of the eighties. Worn with flat ankle boots or desert boots, the trend was not enduring, probably because it required a sylph-like figure to wear them. NAF NAF. WOOL MIX. c.1980s.

3 This cardigan is a British imitation of American 'preppy'-style chunky cardigans featuring novelty images. This design promotes the Birmingham Small Arms Company, a business that started as a gun manufacturer but went on to become the world's largest producer of motorcycles. The cardigan would have been worn to a competitive event or on a promotional tour. BIRMINGHAM SMALL ARMS COMPANY. WOOL. c.1950s.

The sweater dress introduced in the fifties continued to be worn during the following decade, but was updated by being made in intricate knitted jacquards, a modern machine reinterpretation of traditional patterning. Barbara Hulanicki of Biba used the jacquard knit to interpret her signature moody Art Nouveau patterns, a contrast to the androgynous jersey dresses of Courrèges and Cardin. The American purveyor of androgynous styling was Rudi Gernreich, who, as the son of a hosiery manufacturer, was well positioned to develop the highly collectable simple and unstructured knitwear he designed in this period. The British high street, meanwhile, championed the crochet lacy dresses that can easily be found today, often in white cotton or Lurex yarns. The 'skinny-rib' synonymous with sixties youthful confidence was an interesting style that arrived, along with other trends, from borrowing characteristics of children's clothes. In her 1966 autobiography, *Quant by Quant*, Mary Quant claims her wearing of an eight-year-old's sweater sparked a trend, resulting in 'within six months, all the birds wearing the skinny-ribs'. A slightly later arrival on the design scene, Ossie Clark also had a penchant for wearing his childhood jumpers, knitted for him by his mother.

Knitwear in the seventies diversified to give two trends worn today: the highly detailed hand-knit styling and the slinky sophistication seen in the decade's Grecian trend. The decade continued to enjoy the vast array of patterning and intarsia inspired by back-to-nature trends. Led by the connoisseurs of knitwear, the Italian Missoni family, it was a style indulged in by many, including, notably, British designer Bill Gibb. Gibb proved his dexterity by also experimenting with the possibilities of Qiana, the slinky heavy jersey that enabled the lustrous Grecian styling seen as part of the decade's disco fever and immortalized in the designs of Halston.

Reinterpretations of the patterns in each decade make it difficult to ascertain the original date of a garment.

Material is one indication, as the use of synthetic yarns increased as the decades progressed, seeing an influx of poor imitations in the sixties and seventies. Length is another obvious clue: jumpers of the thirties and forties are shorter than the long *garçonne* silhouette of the twenties, designed to sit cropped at the high waist of woollen skirts and trousers of the following forties. It is also worth looking at the neckline of the garments, as each decade has its own unique style, be it the the deep V of the twenties, the elaborate jabots and double collars of the thirties, the forties round high-necked button-throughs and the multiplicity of turtlenecks, square necks, V-necks and Peter Pan collars of the fifties. Many necklines introduced during the fifties continued through the early sixties, but additionally the single and double machine-knit jersey fabrics developed in this decade saw an increase in jacquard patterning, often using metallic threads influenced by Space Age modernist fashion. Necklines, too, were streamlined and simplistically modern, with a continuing trend for the turtleneck and polo neck.

The lexicon of knitwear presented by the 20th century should be enjoyed for its highly individual styles, which, when taken out of the context of fashion, become unique and timeless garments.

4 Knitwear designer Mary Farrin owned a boutique in London's South Molton Street in the early seventies. Her designs were manufactured on the island of Malta and typify the slinkier side of seventies knitwear that was often worn as eveningwear. MARY FARRIN. RAYON. c. 1970s.

5 Space-dyed yarns were fashionable for creating the psychedelic patterning of the sixties. The multicoloured yarns created interesting effects with no need for complicated jacquard or stitch technique. WOOL. c. 1970s.

6 The dolman sleeve remained fashionable well into the fifties but, by the end of the decade, fashion-conscious teenagers were creating their own casual 'beatnik' style, as far removed as possible from the elegant styles of the older generation. Large jumpers were borrowed from brothers and cardigans were worn back to front, setting a fashion where manufacturers actually produced back-fastening cardigans. WOOL. c. 1950s.

1 Home-knitting was a skill passed down through generations and was used by many women as a way of remaining fashionable, taking advantage of the numerous free patterns then issued in women's magazines. The thick braided welt and oversized floral Bakelite button (a distinctly thirties feature) help to pinpoint the age of this piece. HANDMADE. WOOL. c. 1930s.

2, 3 Early bed jackets, lovingly hand-knitted for warmth in the days before central heating, should not be ignored by today's vintage fashionista. Surprisingly they are more plentiful than daytime knitwear, and usually are in better condition. They can be found in a huge variety of creative and beautiful stitches, such as the variation of the wave pattern illustrated on the left (**2**), and a fascinating variety of forms, including soft wrapovers, batwing sleeves and even caplets, all designed for comfort, warmth and freedom of movement. Combined with their colouring, a gentleness synonymous with bedtime, these jackets are eminently wearable as knitwear today, regardless of their original use.

2 HANDMADE. WOOL. c. 1930s.

3 HANDMADE. WOOL. c. LATE 1920s/ EARLY 1930s.

4, 5 Knitwear became increasingly decorative during the thirties, losing its sportswear image and being more frequently worn as part of fashionable ensembles. Hand-knitting was prolific and patterns such as these feather and fan patterns were constructed in vibrant colourways before wartime rationing restricted the use of coloured dyes. HANDMADE. WOOL. c. 1930s.

6 Imaginative crochet and embroidery stitches used up leftover yarns following British government advice to 'Make do and mend' in the austere war years. HANDMADE. WOOL. c. LATE 1930s.

1 Cocktail cardigans became a staple of fifties eveningwear, decorated to enhance décolletages and necklines without the need for much additional jewelry. They were frequently worn draped over the shoulders of a low-cut dress. LAMBSWOOL. c. 1950s.

2 A cutaway midriff is an indication of sixties design, as are the metal circles seen across all forms of fashion in this youth-led decade. ACRYLIC. c. 1960s.

3 After establishing himself within the circle of haute couture, Christian Lacroix, the former head of Jean Patou, founded a ready-to-wear line in 1988. His knitwear was as flamboyant as the clothes in his main collections. Lacroix's multicoloured knit uses an irregular hand-knit looping technique that references the deconstructed looks achieved by several of his contemporaries, such as Japanese designers Kenzo and Junko Koshino and the British duo Body Map. CHRISTIAN LACROIX. SILK. c. LATE 1980s.

4 The dolman sleeve of the forties was revisited during the eighties under the guise of the 'batwing' sleeve. Here the fabric has been used sideways to add interest to the pineapple stitch. ACRYLIC. c. 1980s.

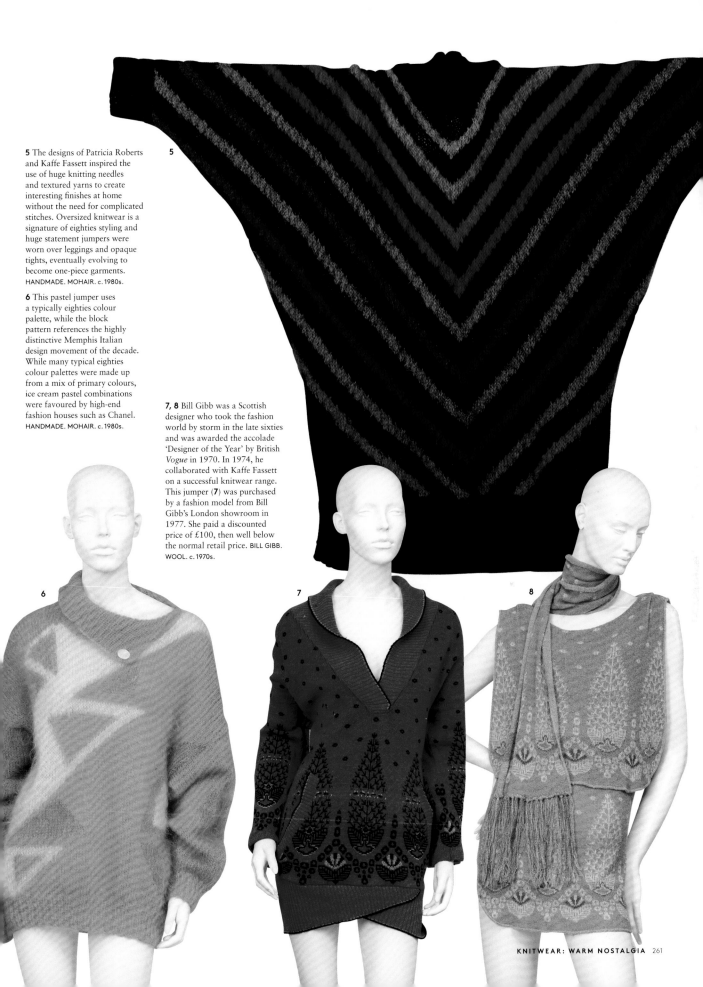

5 The designs of Patricia Roberts and Kaffe Fassett inspired the use of huge knitting needles and textured yarns to create interesting finishes at home without the need for complicated stitches. Oversized knitwear is a signature of eighties styling and huge statement jumpers were worn over leggings and opaque tights, eventually evolving to become one-piece garments. HANDMADE. MOHAIR. c. 1980s.

6 This pastel jumper uses a typically eighties colour palette, while the block pattern references the highly distinctive Memphis Italian design movement of the decade. While many typical eighties colour palettes were made up from a mix of primary colours, ice cream pastel combinations were favoured by high-end fashion houses such as Chanel. HANDMADE. MOHAIR. c. 1980s.

7, 8 Bill Gibb was a Scottish designer who took the fashion world by storm in the late sixties and was awarded the accolade 'Designer of the Year' by British *Vogue* in 1970. In 1974, he collaborated with Kaffe Fassett on a successful knitwear range. This jumper (**7**) was purchased by a fashion model from Bill Gibb's London showroom in 1977. She paid a discounted price of £100, then well below the normal retail price. BILL GIBB. WOOL. c. 1970s.

1 This knitted dress has no label but bears a strong resemblance to the style of knitwear designed by Issey Miyake in the eighties, especially his sculptural rib-work and kimono-style sleeves. Miyake was one of several legendary Japanese fashion designers who challenged the status quo of eighties aesthetics. SYNTHETIC. c. 1980s.

2 Since their humble beginnings with three knitting machines in a small Italian studio in 1953, the Missoni family have been synonymous with knitwear. Their distinctive multicoloured pattern-work is created using a warp-knitting technique and continues to be manufactured in the countryside near their home in Sumirago. MISSONI. WOOL. c. 1970s.

3 The dolman sleeve of forties knitwear typifies the 'sweater girl' look, a favourite of screen stars such as Marilyn Monroe, Lana Turner and Jane Russell. WOOL. c. 1940s.

4 The alpaca flocks of Peru produce a soft wool, similar to a fluffy cashmere, that was used by local textile mills from as early as the 1800s. Not unlike the traditional patterns of the British Isles, the indigenous knitting designs of the Incas were exported and adopted as fashionable knitwear during the early seventies. HANDMADE. ALPACA. c. 1970s.

5, 6 The sweater dress that arrived during the fifties really took off in the sixties as synthetic yarns became more sophisticated, enabling machine-knit techniques to mass-produce finishes such as the 'skinny rib' to give a sleek and flattering fit. The popularity for Lurex and metallic fibres was a high-street derivative of the Space Age-inspired fashions introduced by French couturiers André Courrèges, Paco Rabanne and Pierre Cardin. A belt defined the sleek sweater dress, which was often worn with long, over-the-knee socks or coloured and patterned tights. SYNTHETIC. c. 1960s.

1

2

264 PART TWO: ELEMENTS

1

2

EVENINGWEAR
RED CARPET GLAMOUR

1 A model displays a couture pale satin halterneck dress designed in the mid-thirties.

2 Heavy duchesse satin, a popular choice for both wedding and evening dresses in the fifties, is often a hallmark of couture as the high thread count makes it an expensive fabric. HANDMADE. DUCHESSE SATIN. c.1950s.

3 Lurex was developed in the United States in 1942 as a way of preventing the tarnishing of metallic threads by coating them with brightly coloured aluminium. Looking for Lurex is a way of dating garments for the vintage collector.

'FINDING A BEAUTIFUL VINTAGE GOWN CAN EVOKE THE VISION OF A TECHNICOLOR MOMENT. REAL GLAMOUR ONLY EXISTS IN THE PAST.'

JENNY PACKHAM

The most coveted of all vintage fashion items is the glamorous gown designed to celebrate the feminine form, a timeless creation that gives the merest nod to trends. Decade becomes irrelevant in the quest for the perfect ballgown, dinner dress or even a dress for the red carpet, and with careful selection the vintage evening dress can become a worthy investment. Whether it is the allure of the rarest of couture, the fame and history of a previous owner, a considered ethical statement or simply the appeal of being distinctively unique, the charm of vintage eveningwear lies in the discovery of a forgotten style that may be half a century old yet never looks out of date and rarely appears out of place amidst contemporary fashion. Today spectacular occasions provide an arena for a multiplicity of sophisticated design, yet the silhouette of glamour has remained consistent since the start of the 20th century. Notable designers of historic eveningwear, such as Vionnet, Dior, Valentino, Balmain and many more, collectively provide some of the most utilized references for today's designers. Since the early decades of the 20th century, the style, cut, fabric, decoration and detail of evening dresses have all focused on the creation of a beauty not influenced by trends, but instead designed for specific occasions, be that the debutante ball of the fifties or the New York nightclub of the seventies. The defined selection of silhouettes is frequently repeated, so that a frothy ballgown of the fifties may be barely distinguishable from those on the current catwalks and we can be assured the sensual, liquid contour of the thirties will slip into the collections of the future.

It is the arena for this wear that has changed throughout the decades and, in turn, this has influenced the style of evening gowns that have been worn. Whether the carefree decadence of the Jazz Age, the *bon ton* of the debutante Season or the wild bohemian parties of the seventies, each era contains designs that make exciting formalwear today. Despite much academic discussion of French 17th-century court dress, it is twenties French and American fashion that really revolutionized eveningwear. For the first time women wore their evening dresses as short as their calf-length day dresses until briefly, mid-decade, when knees were revealed for dancing. And despite the observation of one of the world's most notable designers of the couture evening dress, Valentino, that, 'an evening dress that reveals a woman's ankles is the most disgusting thing I have ever seen', it is the style of the twenties flapper dress that is repeatedly revisited by mainstream fashion. Necklines plunged both back and front, arms were bare and the boyish *garçonne* silhouette of the flapper appeared, championed by Coco Chanel. Dresses from this era are fragile and hard to find in wearable condition and their elaborate and detailed embellishments including ruffles, fringing and beading, appliqué and embroidery are sourced for modern inspiration. But

3

The thread of the story is LUREX

THE LEGEND OF THE GOLDEN ROSE inspires a gown of modern enchantment...in fabric woven with a new Lurex®—supple as molten gold; fashioned with inimitable magic by Philip Hulitar. At Bergdorf Goodman, New York; Scruggs-Vandervoort-Barney, St. Louis; Julius Garfinckel & Co., Washington, D. C. Lurex, non-tarnishing metallic yarn, made only by the Yarn Division of The Dobeckmun Company, Cleveland 1, Ohio . . . New York: 250 West 57th Street

1

an original flapper dress has an intensity
not easily found in modern garments,
which are constrained by the expense
of manufacture. The hand-decorated
evening dress of the twenties shone
with sequins, diamanté, crystal and the
metallic thread used to create intricate
floral motifs or cubist patterns in stripes
and zigzags. Allegedly, these evening
dresses were so illuminated by their
own embellishment that the nightclubs
frequented by their wearers had little
need for lighting.

It is the sultry silhouette of the thirties
evening dress that is perhaps the most
sought after for contemporary wear.
The glamorous sophistication of the
simple bias cut that flatters so many
body shapes – a signature of the designer
Madeleine (Madame) Vionnet – arose at
a time when there was a greater need
for financial restraint and this is reflected
in the absence of decoration and a
necessary emphasis on cut. Vionnet
was inspired by geometry and ancient
Greek dress, and she experimented with

2

1, 2 Early dresses of the twenties were ankle-length; by mid-decade the impact of the Charleston and other vigorous dances caused hemlines to rise to the knee. The ankle and the back became the focal points, as the new *garçonne* style replaced the curves of the previously idealized Gibson Girl. Both this handmade example and the illustration show how metallic threads, embellishments and laces were used to sparkle in evening soirées of the twenties. Unless the dresses have been carefully stored, the metallic threads can become brittle and tarnished, although they can sometimes be buffed to their former glory using a soft cloth. HANDMADE. SILK/METALLIC JACQUARD. c.1920s.

3 Susan Small was a British manufacturer of cocktail wear. Belted evening dresses were common from the forties through to the sixties and are a style that has seen a recent resurgence. SUSAN SMALL. SILK SATIN. c.1960s.

4 Screen star Jane Russell's famous curves are enhanced by the figure-hugging 'mermaid'-style evening dress. This style, popular in the fifties, cinched the waist into shape, then clung to the hips before flaring out like a mermaid's tail.

creating twist and tension in her designs by making toiles cut for two-foot-tall wooden dolls. Her revolutionary one-seam bias-cut dress was inspired by the conviction that as the female body has no side-seams, neither should a dress. Believing that 'when a woman smiles her dress should smile too', she made fluid dresses of satin and crepe de Chine that moved with their wearer. It was a style that dominated the thirties, loved by the stars of stage and screen. Hollywood style icons of the era, Marlene Dietrich, Greta Garbo, Joan Crawford and Barbara Stanwyck all wore the bias cut, both on screen and on the all-important red carpet that has been synonymous with glamorous gowns since the days of the first Academy Awards in 1929.

Many spies infiltrated Vionnet's atelier, and her clothes were widely imitated, so she instigated countless copyright lawsuits. But many of her contemporaries, as well as designers

1 This dress shows the reduced simplicity of early forties evening dresses in Britain necessitated by the government's CC41 scheme. CHIFFON. c. 1941.

2 The full-skirted simplicity of a fifties evening dress is enhanced with heavily embroidered ribbon on a deep waistband. This is an Australian dress, although Melbray was also a popular British manufacturer. MELBRAY. SILK. c. 1950s.

3 Layers of appliquéd floral print fabric create an inset décolletage typical of the intricate and sculptural house style of the British company London Town. Their younger offshoot label, Miss London, focused on streamlined versions of the successful, more elaborate 'grown-up' styles. LONDON TOWN. SATIN. c. LATE 1940s.

today, acknowledge her influence and architectural prowess. Cristóbal Balenciaga was a great friend and considered her a mentor, while Azzedine Alaïa, a legend in his own right, applauds her artistry and has gathered one of the largest private collections of her work.

The sinuous appeal of thirties glamour retained a refined sexuality indirectly inspired by the introduction of the Hays Code. Brought about collectively by leading film studios in 1930, the Motion Picture Code outlined the rules of behaviour for on-screen conduct, including suitable dress for female stars. The amount of cleavage on display was restricted to two inches between the breasts, and belly buttons could not be revealed at all, even if a midriff was bared. Hollywood's designers were left to use clinging fabrics to flaunt the sexuality of their screen sirens, who often wore no underwear under their bias-cut gowns. Backlighting shone through the shimmering fabrics, revealing a hint of the erogenous zones beneath.

With the onset of the Second World War, the evening dress was transformed, reworked and remade. Fabric, particularly luxury silks and crepes, was severely restricted. Home dressmakers looked to printed rayons to add interest to their limited means. Sequins, beading and similar decorative trims were surprisingly not restricted by rationing restrictions in Europe and many dresses cut with limited fabric can be found with embellished décolletages and bodices. Although wartime patriotism restricted an exuberance of dress, looking one's best was a loyal obligation and an evening occasion a time to indulge in a little joyful dressing up. Nevertheless, the evening dress of the forties holds a place in contemporary wear, its refined subtlety in satin-backed crepes of midnight blue, tobacco brown and black offering sophistication. Colour is one of the easiest ways of distinguishing between European and American fashions of this period. As the United States was less affected by wartime rationing, their clothes are brighter,

with a wider selection of dyes readily available.

The sumptuous silhouette of the fifties evening gown endures as a favourite of today's fashionista. The floaty silk tulles and crisp georgettes were first introduced by Dior, who, unlike other post-war designers, had little trouble finding the expensive fabrics needed, thanks to his backer, the textile magnate Marcel Boussac. The blossoming dresses of this time were an expression of joy after the austerity of war and it is hard to find a design that does not make a grand statement even in today's showground of red carpet style. Dior was not alone in his creation of stylish post-war fashion. 'If a woman came into a room in a Balenciaga dress, no other woman in the room existed,' observed fashion editor and devotee Diana Vreeland.

By the sixties and seventies the etiquette of dressing up had been lost to a nightlife of clubs and discothèques, producing a diversity in evening dress not seen before – a fusion of short and long, kaftans and slinky jersey Halston halternecks, both patterned and plain. Emilio Pucci had introduced his first printed evening dress as early as 1951 and by the seventies pattern prevailed, prior to the slick black creations of the statuesque eighties.

Investment dressing comes into its own from a century of classic design: Jacques Fath, Dior, Givenchy, Hartnell, Balenciaga and Bellville Sassoon are all labels that will only increase in value, unlike a design of today that devalues the very second it leaves the shop floor. But among the dresses worn for the dance floor, the theatre and the red carpet are many beautiful interpretations of couture fashions. Some will be identical licensed copies made by easily obtainable labels such as Susan Small, others will be handmade with very personal touches. All are unique designs that inspire the designer of today and hold a much-loved place in the contemporary wardrobe.

4 Pierre Cardin, along with Yves Saint Laurent, was one of the first couturiers to establish ready-to-wear labels, sensing the arrival of youth-led fashion that was to govern the sixties. By the late sixties, Cardin had licensed his label to over 800 companies. JERSEY COUTURE BY PIERRE CARDIN. SILK JERSEY. c. LATE 1960s.

2 This crepe evening dress by John Bates is decorated with diamanté embellishment in the futuristic style associated with the designer's Jean Varon label. JEAN VARON. SILK. c. 1960s.

3 The 1982 Valentino evening dress worn by Julia Roberts to the 73rd Academy Awards in 2001 made fashion headlines. It heralded the start of vintage as something that could be worn on the red carpet alongside the very latest from the world's leading designers. Renée Zellweger wore a canary yellow silk chiffon dress from the fifties, designed by Jean Dessès, to the same event.

1 British fashion house Marcel Fenez adopted a French name, as did many companies who wanted to be associated with the style of Parisian couture. The oversized bow is a feature that was frequently employed on sixties evening dresses. MARCEL FENEZ. SATIN. c. 1960s.

4 Military uniform has long been an inspiration for fashion design. The appliquéd chain work, achieved with embroidered ribbons and metallic tassels, is an unusual find for the sixties but enhances the hourglass silhouette of the dress. CREPE. c. 1960s.

5 Delicate Lurex threads have been used to embellish the front of a heavy wool cocktail dress in a design style reminiscent of the twenties. The slight overhang of the bodice helps to date this as a dress from the end of the fifties. WOOL. c. LATE 1950s.

6 This dress displays the Eastern-style embellishment that was so prevalent in late sixties fashion. The hippy ethos freely adopted and adapted traditional clothing from the Far East, and kaftans and indigenous embroidery were echoed in both high-street and couture fashions. BLANES. SILK JACQUARD. c. 1960s.

2 Many names have designed under the Halston label since the death of its founder, the renowned Roy Halston Frowick, in 1990. This sought-after label has been reinstated as Halston Heritage under the discerning eye of Marios Schwab. HALSTON. SILK CHIFFON. c. 1970s.

3 The 'prom' dress, a classic of fifties American youth, is a design that never seems to date and has been revisited by mainstream fashion so often it is often only the fabric and finish that distinguishes the original. CHIFFON. c. 1950s.

4 The puffball was not a phenomenon of the eighties as is often supposed. Seen here in printed chiffon, the interior has inserted hoops like an early crinoline, taking the place of voluminous petticoats. CHIFFON. c. 1960s.

5 The classic shape of this dress makes it relevant in any decade. Many of Jean Allen's designs were intended for an older audience, meaning the label is often overlooked. However, the occasional design, such as this one, would not look out of place on the red carpet. JEAN ALLEN. SILK CHIFFON. c. 1960s.

1 British company Susan Small was known for its glamorous but affordable eveningwear and party attire. Its manufacturing standards were of sufficient quality that the company was given licence by Christian Dior to reproduce selected designs. SUSAN SMALL. CREPE. c. 1960s.

1

1 David Sassoon is known for his many dresses made for the British royal family (including Princess Diana) and for high society and celebrities. Nancy Dell'Olio wore this corseted design on the cover of the book, *The Glamour of Bellville Sassoon*. BELLVILLE SASSOON. SILK TULLE. 1990.

2 Many evening dresses from the fifties incorporate a structured bust, either formed by pleating or boned, like this design. SILK. c. 1950s.

3 Eighties fashion borrowed many features from the forties, in particular shoulder pads and peplums. The flocked print is also an identifying feature of its age. JINTY'S. SILK. c. 1980s.

4 The interesting design on this integrated jacket and dress appears effortless, belying its complicated construction. Such design is the mark of a superior dressmaker or a couture garment whose label has been lost over time. Garments such as this are unique and, by comparing signature design styles, their origin can often be traced back to a fashion house. SILK CHIFFON. c. EARLY 1940s.

1

1 This intricately embellished cocktail dress is made of silk satin, with the velvet roses depicted in three-dimensional appliquéd work. HANDMADE. SILK SATIN. c. 1950s.

2, 4, 5 These three cocktail dresses show the subtle development of style through the sixties. **4** dates from the early part of the decade, with the sophisticated embroidery and a deep waistband created from ruched chiffon. It would have been worn with a corset or a girdle to help accentuate this structured silhouette. **2** illustrates the relaxing of the silhouette in the early to mid-sixties with the telltale oversized bow, a favourite design feature of the period, and the informal trimming in the form of rows of silk fringing. By the mid- to late sixties (**5**), jacquard had become a big hit, metallic fabrics reflecting Space Age styles. The silhouette has become looser and less formal.

2 SILK SATIN. c. MID-1960s.

4 HANDMADE. SILK SATIN. c. EARLY 1960s.

5 GLOBAL. SYNTHETIC. c. LATE 1960s.

3 The psychedelic trend of the sixties was evident in every aspect of fashion from daywear to nightwear. Fringing was a common decoration, an influence of the Native American decorative elements adopted by hippy fashions. ALFRED KERR. SILK. c. 1960s.

1, 3 Two evening dresses illustrate the influence of the romantic medieval style on late sixties fashion. Often colloquially referred to as the 'Princess' style, the bodices are fitted and the sleeves are free-flowing, either anchored into a cuff or, by the bohemian seventies, left wide and loose.

1 QUAD. CHIFFON. c. LATE 1960s.

3 KATY. SILK CHIFFON. c. LATE 1960s.

2 A dress with Indian-inspired embellishment. Original Indian fabrics, trimmings and garments were worn extensively as a part of the hippy trend, and then glamorized by design houses who created an upmarket, more commercial version of the style. The beaded fringing combined with a loose overhung bodice was a significant trend for eveningwear in this decade. SATIN. c. 1960s.

4 The bolero helps to date this dress to the forties or early fifties, while the wide width of the skirt also suggests that it was made after rationing regulations were relaxed. The bolero was also seen in the early part of this decade as a popular item of daywear, and is an item that adapts well to contemporary wear. HANDMADE. RAYON CREPE. c. 1940s.

4

5 Soft fluid single-knit jersey dresses were widespread at the start of the seventies. While couture and high-end designs were made in luxurious silk jersey, the high street was easily able to emulate the look in cheaper versions of the fabric. Consequently its overuse meant its popularity was short-lived. HERSHELLE. c. 1970s.

5

1

2

3

1 Bill Gibb's work is renowned for his unique mix of fantastical designs, incorporating historical and global influences. The knife-edge pleated skirt, inspired by Egyptian designs, is used as the basis for a series of outfits where it was worn with different extravagant jackets. The jacket sleeve seen here is formed from a series of petal shapes that move gracefully with their wearer. BILL GIBB. SILK. c. 1977.

2 This jacket is made using silk devoré. Devoré is the technique of applying a paste to the fabric through a designed screen. Layers of fabric are burnt away leaving behind the silk in the desired pattern. Many evening dresses of the decade can be found in the fabric, often in a more free-form image than the spotted design seen here. It is worn over an evening dress with an embellished neckline. HANDMADE. SILK DEVORÉ. c. LATE 1920s/EARLY 1930s.

3 Frederick Starke was a British designer of high-end ready-to-wear, established in the early twenties. He designed costumes for the lead actress Honor Blackman in the 1964 season of *The Avengers* television programme (the often-cited John Bates designed for the subsequent series, featuring Diana Rigg). Starke also had a more affordable, younger line whose labels read 'Fredrica Starke'. FREDERICK STARKE. WOOL AND LUREX. c. 1960s.

THE WEDDING DRESS
A VINTAGE AFFAIR

The vintage bridal gown is a garment unrivalled in its sentimental appeal. The romance and history evoked by the combination of fragile tulle and lace, silk and satin, waxed orange blossom and delicate veils sees future brides searching for their 'something old' among rails of antique clothes in the hunting grounds of internet sites, auction rooms and vintage fashion fairs. Select modern wedding ateliers even curate collections combining contemporary models with beautiful bridal dresses from every decade in a barely distinguishable mix.

The well-documented bridal styles of glamorous weddings from past decades serve as inspiration for a modern romance that is intrinsically linked with the past. Wedding dresses give merely a nod to current trend, so the timeless designs embedded in the styles of their own eras offer a variety of silhouette choices to the vintage-wearing bride of today. The sartorial benefits of wearing a vintage bridal dress are manifold: for the most part, the dresses are unique; they will have been worn only once and stored with care; and, with the exception of those made during the world wars, they are exquisitely constructed in the finest of fabrics and with painstakingly applied detail and decoration. The potential disadvantage is that many vintage wedding dresses were made by hand specifically to fit their bride, much as a modern bridal dress is today, and are therefore full of idiosyncrasies that relate to their original owners, such as a tiny waist or a shorter length. Many are small, designed for the slighter female figure of past decades. However, much as a modern dress may be bespoke or adapted to fit the bridal figure, so a bridal gown from the past may be altered and even remade to create a

'THE HISTORY OF BRIDALWEAR IS FASCINATING AND A VINTAGE BRIDAL DRESS CAN BE AN INSPIRATION ON SO MANY LEVELS.' JENNY PACKHAM

1

2

3

1 Princess Dmitri of Russia wearing a Chanel wedding dress for American *Vogue*, May 1932, photographed by George Hoyningen-Huene.

2 Dresses completely made of lace were a favourite bridal style of the fifties. Synthetic lace fabrics do not have the same softness of touch as silk or cotton but are not as fragile and therefore last longer. HANDMADE. COTTON LACE. c. 1950s.

3 The new youthful trends of the sixties were reflected in many wedding dresses of the decade. HANDMADE. METALLIC SYNTHETIC LACE. c. 1960.

unique and finely crafted piece of history for a contemporary bride.

The seemingly age-old tradition of wearing white has not always been natural wedding etiquette. Until the mid-19th century, white was a colour rarely seen at the altar. It was in fact the colour of mourning for French royalty, while black was a favourite of Scandinavian brides. The average Western bride wore a patterned dress that was specially made for the occasion but worn again for social celebrations, such as church events or dances. Working-class women simply wore their best dress and bonnet, often in colours that did not show the dirt, as regular laundry was a luxury reserved for the women they worked for. The colour white, long associated with purity and spirituality, became an 18th-century status symbol that was used for all types of clothing by those who could afford servants. Gradually introduced for society weddings, an important international precedent was set when it was chosen as the colour for Queen Victoria's dress on her marriage to Prince Albert in November 1840. Ironically it was as a sign of frugality that Queen

Victoria opted for the pure colour, not wishing to appear ostentatious in front of her British subjects. Royal weddings have long inspired bridal fashion, and her choice of orange blossom wreath and tulle veil rather than the more common bonnet instigated a fashionable following in civil weddings of later decades.

The ambience of the twenties is one often recreated in modern weddings: the simple sheath, dropped waist and loose bodice is a silhouette that flatters many figures. In this decade, dresses of fine silk and delicate handmade lace were worn with long tulle veils, closely fitted low over the forehead to echo the fashionable cloche hat. They were held in place by a tiara or simple wreath, and the look was often completed with a bouquet made from the stems of lilies and streaming satin ribbons. The 1923 society wedding of Lady Elizabeth Bowes-Lyon and the Duke of York in London's Westminster Abbey epitomized the style. She wore a longer-length dress in the style of the decade made from moiré chiffon and Brussels lace, which was shaped with a belt of silver leaf wound with green tulle.

Following the high death rate endured in the First World War, many weddings of the thirties were second marriages and there was a shift in traditional wedding attire. The famed 1936 marriage between the Duke of Windsor and twice-divorced Wallis Simpson took place in France. Wallis wore a simple silk dress designed by Mainbocher, who was responsible for much of her everyday wardrobe, in a specially dyed, pale blue that became known as 'Wallis blue'. It was one of the most copied dresses of the era. The traditional bridal silhouette of the thirties also shows a fashion for heavy duchesse satin cut on the bias, imitating the distinctive style of Vionnet.

The wedding of the forties is often described as rushed, as military leave allowed little time for planning and fabric was scarce. For a lucky few, parachute silk or the heavier silk used to contain supplies dropped from airplane to battlefield was reused to create dresses. In Britain, manufactured

1

2

1 The Mainbocher dress worn by Wallis Simpson for her marriage to Edward, Duke of Windsor, in 1936 is often cited as being the most copied dress in couture history. Made in pale blue, a shade that subsequently became known as 'Wallis blue', the dress has a simple design that seems 'right' for any decade.

2 A simple wedding dress, handmade using added trims and decorative covered buttons that also act as weights to anchor the bodice of fine silk. HANDMADE. SILK. c. 1920s.

3, 4 This handmade dress with intricate embroidery may have been worn for a special occasion in the past. It would make a unique contemporary wedding dress. HANDMADE. SILK. c. 1920s.

5 A wartime wedding dress with the 'dinner plate' rationing label. Less is known about this label that was introduced after the first CC41 design, but it is thought the later label may have been introduced to indicate slightly more luxurious clothes, although still under government restriction, to counteract the negative connotations of utility clothing. HANDMADE. SILK. c. 1940s.

1

2

3

4

1 Seventies bridal style encompassed the trend for the romantic historical, a style led by companies such as Laura Ashley. COTTON. c. 1970.

2 The innocent 'baby doll' of the sixties looked particularly effective as a little white dress. Celebrity brides such as Raquel Welch, Sharon Tate and Yoko Ono made headlines in white wedding minis, a look that was easily imitated by the home dressmaker. HANDMADE. COTTON BRODERIE ANGLAISE. c. 1960s.

3 Audrey Hepburn wore a remarkably simple Pierre Balmain dress for her 1954 wedding. This helped to popularize the shorter 'ballerina'-length bridal dress. HANDMADE. SYNTHETIC. c. 1950s.

4 Bianca and Mick Jagger married in 1971. The untraditional ensemble of jacket and skirt designed by Yves Saint Laurent typifies the personal and often irreverent approach to wedding styling in the seventies.

designs in synthetic rayon and satin were produced under the government CC41 label, utilizing valuable clothing coupons. Even Queen Elizabeth II reportedly saved ration coupons to buy the heavy duchesse satin for her 1946 wedding dress, which was embellished with 10,000 imported pearls. Many wartime brides wore suits that matched the military styling of their husband's uniforms. In Europe and the States, hats, which were not rationed, were sumptuously decorated to soften the effect.

The sweetheart neckline, seen in many traditional forties wedding dresses, continued to be fashionable throughout the fifties. Heavy satin and lace were the favourite of the full-skirted dresses that imitated Dior's 1947 'New Look'. Celebrity weddings were scrutinized and the Balmain dress worn by Audrey Hepburn in 1954 for her first wedding set a fashion for the shorter 'ballerina'-style wedding dress. It was a length she

echoed as an on-screen bride in the 1957 film *Funny Face*, in a stunningly simple design that was an early collaboration with Givenchy. But perhaps the most admired dress of the decade, even the 20th century, was that worn by Grace Kelly for her marriage to Prince Rainier in 1956. Designed by cinematic costume designer Helen Rose, it is thought to have returned the traditional wedding dress to the height of popularity, making international headlines with its elegant design that used 24 metres (80 feet) of silk taffeta and 270 metres (890 feet) of antique Valenciennes lace, no longer in production today.

In true late sixties and early seventies fashion, weddings of the era broke with tradition. Divorce was acceptable and wedding ensembles for second and even third marriages were designed in an array of whites, silvers and ivories in minis and maxis and even trouser suits. The vogue for a return to the free-flowing, romantic and historical gave many an opportunity to invest in contemporary and favourite designers and to marry in an Ossie Clark or Bellville Sassoon evening dress. Memorable celebrity brides of the era included Yves Saint Laurent muse Loulou de la Falaise, who wore a bohemian creation by the designer complemented with a white turban for her 1977 wedding, and Bianca Pérez-Mora Macias who wore a white 'Le Smoking' jacket and wide-brimmed hat, also by Yves Saint Laurent, for her unconventional wedding to Mick Jagger. (Reportedly her original wedding ensemble was a dress designed by Ossie Clark, of whom she was a great devotee, but it did not fit on the day because she had omitted to tell him she was four months pregnant.)

Often contemporary choice relates to a dress of indeterminate era. As silhouettes have been repeated so often throughout fashion, date becomes irrelevant and it is merely choosing a shape that flatters that is important in the search for a dress of unfathomable beauty, worn for one day and passed on as an heirloom to become the vintage of future generations.

1 This wedding dress by the designer John Bates for his Jean Varon label utilized the seventies 'bishop sleeve' trend. JEAN VARON. SILK CHIFFON. c. 1970s.

2 The layered pleating and contrasting silk yoke on this cocktail dress make for an unusual wedding dress today. PARIGI. SILK. c. 1980.

3 A simple vintage dress in white, not originally designed for bridalwear, offers a unique style for the modern bride. PARIGI. SILK. c. 1970s.

4 This late seventies cocktail dress makes an understated but beautiful contemporary wedding dress. Rose Bradford was the designer responsible for translating many of Ossie Clark's designs for Radley into commercially viable garments for the high street. ROSE BRADFORD FOR RADLEY. SYNTHETIC. c. 1970s.

5 A handmade dress for a sixties wedding is appliquéd with intricate daisies, the flower of the decade. HANDMADE. SILK. c. 1960s.

6 Bill Gibb was one of the many designers who enjoyed working with Qiana. The substantial weight of this jersey was particularly effective for the drapery and gathering techniques explored in this white dress with an asymmetrical shoulder strap. BILL GIBB. QIANA. c. 1970s.

1

2

1 The traditional post-war wedding dress used a profusion of lace and tulle. The nipped-in waist and covered arm were popularized by the spectacular dresses designed by costume designer Helen Rose for Grace Kelly's wedding to Prince Rainier and for Elizabeth Taylor's costume in the 1950 film *Father of the Bride*. HANDMADE. NYLON LACE. c. 1950s.

2 It is common to find British fifties ballgowns in white, dating to the time when the debutante 'coming out' ball was the height of the social season. This elite practice did not end until 1958 and girls traditionally wore virginal white evening dresses with a glamour appropriate for a contemporary wedding. EMBROIDERED SILK SATIN. c. 1950s.

3 A more traditional wedding dress by John Bates, a designer known for his youthful, cutting-edge styles. The empire line and central bow are key features of wedding dresses from the sixties. JEAN VARON. SILK. c. LATE 1960s.

3

Part Three

HALLMARKS

1 Horrockses Fashions was launched in 1946 and found success through the fifties and sixties, renowned for their cotton printed frocks. This dress from the seventies uses pattern very differently from the designs traditionally associated with the brand. HORROCKSES FASHIONS. COTTON. c. 1970s.

2 Although the early synthetic rayons are stiff to wear today, the colours retain their vibrancy. Rayons were easy to print on and reflected the true colour of dye pigments. RAYON. c. 1930s.

3 Many artists found work as textile designers during the post-war depression and their influence is felt in the painterly 'watercolour' treatment often given to fifties printed florals. COTTON. c. 1950s.

'A FEMININE BRAND LIKE OURS RELIES ON FLORALS, WHICH DELIGHT OUR CUSTOMERS EVERY SEASON. FROM DELICATE 19TH-CENTURY BOTANICALS TO PAINTERLY THIRTIES FLORALS, CHINTZED FIFTIES ROSES OR STYLIZED SIXTIES DAISIES, EVERY ERA HAS SOMETHING TO INSPIRE.'
CLIVE REEVE, DESIGN DIRECTOR, OASIS STORES

3

BEAUTIFUL BOTANICALS
THE POWER OF THE PETAL

The floral motif is one of the most extensively employed decorations in fashion history, whether printed, knitted, embroidered, embellished or woven. The floral is a perennial favourite in spring/summer catwalk presentations, reappearing in forms borrowed from past decades, and an original printed floral frock is always a coveted vintage classic. Floral patterns have blossomed differently in each fashion era and, as pattern and palette characterize the style of an era, it is the style of a floral – be it flamboyantly thirties, futuristically sixties or boldly eighties – which makes for easy identification of the moment in fashion.

Floral fabric was rarely used for the construction of an entire garment until the 20th century. Clothes were generally made from plain dyed cloth with little embellishment, and even the elaborate 'tea gowns' of the 18th and 19th centuries were usually made from more than one fabric, employing the expensive intricate jacquards and woven floral fabrics as decorative details. In addition, the printed floral was not considered to be a decoration worthy of a grand dress and delicate sprigs and simple blossoms were instead used for working clothes such as aprons, housecoats and overalls made from hardy cotton or linen. As printing methods were perfected, printed florals began to be used on lining fabrics and as decorative panels for dresses inserted between lace and plain silks and satins.

Always a pattern associated with the spring and summer seasons, floral prints began to be used on full ensembles in the twenties, as summer holidays became a regular activity requiring a new style of clothing. Pretty chiffons and silks covered with colourful blossoms suited the stylish beachside fashions of loose 'pyjama' palazzo trousers, bandeau tops, soft unstructured jackets and kimono-style robes.

2 Twenties florals were predominantly romantic and whimsical, often printed on a black or white ground. They were mainly used for insertions and decorations or as linings for eveningwear and it wasn't until the late twenties that floral fabric was used for a complete dress. HANDMADE. SILK CHIFFON. c. LATE 1920s.

3 The floral of the thirties is generally recognizable by its small scale. The June 1939 issue of British *Vogue* commented, 'The Paris Collections this season were inspired by the Edwardian period, we're told', a comment reinforced by this dress, which evokes early 20th-century styles. HANDMADE. CHIFFON. c. 1930s.

4 This jacket dates from around the start of the twenties. The embroidered floral work has a feel of the Arts and Crafts movement, a style championed by John Ruskin and William Morris in the late 19th century. The simple construction – an identifiable quality of this movement, which rejected industrialization and fussiness in favour of hand craftsmanship – makes it easily wearable today. HANDMADE. WOOL AND SILK. c. EARLY 1920s.

1 Floral prints of the thirties were busy all-over patterns, worn for day as well as evening. Couturiers such as Paquin started using floral fabrics in their collections at the start of the decade and their designs were shown as beautiful fashion illustrations in magazines. As collections were rarely photographed at this time, it was illustrations that conveyed the latest trends. HANDMADE. SILK CHIFFON. c. 1930s.

3

4

For many women, home dressmaking was the means of keeping up with fashions, making obtaining sewing patterns crucial. As the collections of Parisian couture were not photographed, illustrative newspaper adverts and dressmaking patterns were the only way to visualize changing fashions. Decorative fabric was expensive, an investment that was treasured, stored away carefully to be used and reused, even long before wartime austerity and rationing. So it is not unusual to find a forties blouse made from a delicate thirties chiffon or even a fifties evening coat made from an early brocade.

Resourceful women in the countryside of the United States collected feed sacks to be cut up. These were cotton bags of approximately 36 by 44 inches (90 x 110 cm) containing animal food and usually bought by farmers. The bags were usually printed with simple floral motifs and, during the Great Depression and the Second World War, discerning wives would persuade their husbands to look for sacks made from the same design, allowing them to make a complete dress from two or three bags. Smaller printed bags that contained flour, sugar or grains were perfect for making blouses or children's clothes. Feed sack clothing became such a success that the sack manufacturers began to compete over their choice of designs. Clothing made from feed sacks remained popular all the way through until the fifties, when the bag companies found it was more cost-effective to use paper instead of fabric.

Floral fabrics of the twenties were often surprisingly large in scale, though delicate in appearance due to the popularity of the fine silks, chiffons and light gauzy cottons on which they were printed. Both diminutive and buoyant motifs were evident in fashion 'to be seen in' – those outfits worn for socializing and eveningwear. The simple flora of country gardens typifies the print style of this decade and retains a gentleness that can also be found in beadwork and embroidery from the era. Coco Chanel's emergence as a designer saw the introduction of her favourite white camellia in many of her designs. The flower was beautifully recreated as stylized embroideries and later as a printed textile design. The camellia, as would be worn in a gentleman's buttonhole at the time, appeared on several of her designs during the twenties and, by the thirties, it formed the basis for black and white floral prints. Today it is still the flower associated with the fashion house and has inspired the design of watches and fine jewelry.

During the course of the thirties the printed floral became widely worn, both in styles that were acceptable for day and wildly flamboyant by night. This celebrated style saw soft organic blooms covering dresses made with matching printed shoulder capes or large attached motifs, cut round the shape of the flower and reapplied in layers that draped softly over shoulders and around necklines, creating a profusion of print on print and flower on flower. The feminine style of thirties fashionable florals ran riot over ruffles and flounces and the pretty prints, previously the confine of working clothes, began to appear in collections of the Paris fashion houses, notably Paquin and Vionnet.

Manmade rayon became widely used during the thirties as an artificial replacement for silk and, although many surviving dresses display vivid colouring (as the fabric was so receptive to printed dyes), it has a stiffness making it inferior wear when compared to the delicate crepe de Chines, silks and chiffons of the decade. By contrast forties fabrics were necessarily hardy. Wartime practicality dictated the style of the day and the all-important suit became the mainstay of working women. As textile manufacturing faltered, home dressmakers in Britain and France reverted to hardier linens and cottons, often using a wider-width furnishing fabric that

1 A model wears a white linen floral evening dress by Paquin from the spring/summer collection of 1950. The Iris print is typical of the light-hearted mood of post-war fashion.

2 The floral of the forties was denser than the looser style of the previous decades. The halterneck, introduced mid-thirties, continued to be fashionable and is indicative of forties styling for evening dresses. HANDMADE. RAYON. c.1940s.

3 Virginia Bates, vintage blogger for *Vogue*, is rarely photographed wearing anything that does not date to the twenties or thirties. She is seen here with her daughter, actress Daisy Bates, and both are wearing printed floral chiffon dresses from the thirties.

4, 5 These two early thirties dresses both display the smaller-scale prints that defined eveningwear of the era. It is unusual to find linen printed in an all-over design and used for eveningwear but it illustrates the changing attitude to cotton, hitherto perceived as the 'country cousin' of silk.

4 HANDMADE. COTTON. c. LATE 1920S/EARLY 1930s.

5 HANDMADE. SILK. c. LATE 1920S/ EARLY 1930s.

6 Despite the growth of department stores offering ready-to-wear, in the thirties home dressmaking, or employing the services of a seamstress, was vital for most to remain fashionable. Beautiful fabrics were frugally used and it is quite common to find a handmade dress echoing the fashionable silhouette for its time but made from fabrics of the previous decade, as in this forties evening dress made from a thirties printed silk chiffon. HANDMADE. SILK CHIFFON. c. EARLY 1940s.

1 This day dress from the United States dates to the early forties. The pleated neck that forms a cowl, the puffed sleeve and the translucent green side-zip (unseen), matched to the floral print, all help to date it. The zip or 'slide fastener', as it was first called, was introduced for fashionable wear during the thirties. Zips were not hidden away but shown off as a design feature. HANDMADE. CREPE DE CHINE. c. LATE 1930s/EARLY 1940s.

2 Flowers of the English garden were popular for use on silk, rayon and cotton. Irises, carnations, anemones and poppies inspired textile designers during the thirties. As wartime rationing took hold, 'make do and mend' became the slogan of the time, as shown in this forties dress made from thirties silk. HANDMADE. SILK. c. 1940s.

3 An illustration from the forties depicts a lady gardening in overalls so decorated with floral motifs that she blends in with the garden.

4 This handmade fifties summer dress has been personalized with red accents for the lining of the pockets and shoulder reveres. HANDMADE. COTTON. c. 1950s.

5 Cotton sprigged florals were the mainstay of fifties summer dresses, many of which were handmade. COTTON. c. 1950s.

6 The post-war floral reflected a joyful mood. Although rationing continued for several years after the war, coloured printing dyes could be utilized again and were particularly suited to the full skirts prompted by Dior's triumphant 1947 collection. VICTOR JOSSELYN. COTTON. c. LATE 1950s/EARLY 1960s.

1 Synthetic rayon became commercially available during the thirties. Widely used for its durability and cost-effectiveness, it was better at reflecting the colour of printed dyes than natural fabrics. The result was astonishingly vibrant prints. HANDMADE. RAYON. c. 1940s.

2, 3 Increased travel for leisure after the Second World War resulted in the use of exotic flora, such as the hibiscus or the Chinese poppy, as prints. RAYON. c. EARLY 1940s.

4 The evening dress of the fifties was sophisticated, but shorter than in previous decades and with an added element of fun. Dior's 1947 'New Look' collection inspired full skirts in vibrant colours worn over rustling net petticoats. BLANES. SILK. c. 1950s.

5

5 This maxi dress is from the late sixties, as indicated by its square pinafore cut. Maxi dresses continued to be popular well into the seventies but were typically fitted and shaped. Pierre Cardin was the first couture designer to initiate a ready-to-wear label, and was a master at licensing. Care should be taken when investing in the label as not all garments would have been made in the fashion house. PIERRE CARDIN COUTURE. COTTON. c. LATE 1960s.

could be bought with the same amount of ration coupons as the fabrics being produced for fashion. In the United States, a trend for exotic tropical flora emerged, a fashion propelled by artist and designer Tina Leser, whose work is described in 'Global Inspirations' (see p. 379). Sidestepping wartime restrictions, Leser worked with imported fabrics from Hawaii and Tahiti to recreate sarong-style evening dresses and tropical silhouettes. In Europe, meanwhile, a naturalistic style prevailed for eveningwear, using designs printed on Celanese rayon or cotton on occasion.

Post-war fashion changed quite dramatically, led by the reopened houses of Parisian haute couture. The celebrated 1947 'Corolle' collection of Christian Dior, which was dubbed the 'New Look' by fashion journalists of the day, challenged the spare sophistication of wartime styles and conveyed Dior's love of gardening through his designs for 'women flowers'. As the world of fashion embraced his timely departure from the neat, austere silhouette of wartime, fashion on every continent also rejoiced in the jubilant full-bloomed florals. The flora of vibrant cottage gardens and diminutive posies covered the wide-skirted fashions from Christian Dior and Balmain as well as the popular dresses manufactured by the Northern English cotton mill Horrockses, a company who introduced beautifully made cotton dresses to their business in 1948, dresses that were desired by all, even the royal princesses Margaret and Elizabeth.

Dior, who always filled his showroom with mixed white bouquets, continued a floral theme with his 1953 collection, which featured an array of floral prints and was coined his 'Tulip' line. His favourite flower, the lily of the valley, became the central theme for his spring collection of 1954, and he would have little sprigs of it sewn into the linings of his creations on the first day of a show for good luck. However, it was to be the rose that became the 'it' flower of the fifties. The rose print designed by Cecil Beaton for textile company Ascher in 1946 was used by Balmain in his collection, and the rose continued to retain its popularity throughout the decade.

As the rose was the flower of the fifties, so the daisy became the flower of the early sixties. Its naïve simplicity suited the streamlined youth fashion of the era, epitomized in the abstracted logo designed by graphic designer David McMeekin for Mary Quant for her highly successful cosmetic range. The bright abstracted florals of the early sixties morphed into the 'Flower Power' hippy culture, an ethical movement with wild overtones, as expressed in flowing, free-spirited textile designs in complete contrast to the simplicity of the early 'mod' culture. Floral styles began to diversify and, as the era moved into the seventies, the whimsicality of Celia Birtwell florals sat next to Art Nouveau-inspired poppies and the intricate heritage of Liberty prints.

While the boldness of eighties design saw the end of the flowing forms of the seventies, the floral of the eighties returned to the romance of the fifties, adding a modernity to the full-blown blooms. The formality of the furnishing floral was a significant influence on the era and the combination of brightly coloured feminine prints with body-conscious styling, as typified in the collections of Kenzo, Ralph Lauren and Christian Lacroix, was a powerful union.

The ultimate stamp of femininity, the floral motif remains a constant throughout each fashion era. Its continuing reinterpretation defines the mood of the time, as well as providing a nostalgic whiff, evocative of summer holidays and afternoon tea. Whether worn for their originality or sought after as inspiration for designs of the future, the floral frock is one of the most loved items of vintage clothing.

1 A mid-sixties range of button-through summer coatdresses by Originals. The styling plays on the childlike spirit inspiring fashion in the era. Psychedelic swirls and florals softened the square, geometric cut but need careful accessorizing when worn today to not look like items from a dressing-up box.

2, 3, 4 The style of a floral
print is often one of the easiest
ways to date a garment. The
abstracted daisy typified sixties
textile design. Popularized by
Mary Quant's logo – a flat five-
petal daisy – abstracted florals
suited the simple styling of the
era. The abstract floral was, of
course, not the only floral style
of this period. Vivid psychedelic
swirling florals are seen in no
other era unless adapted by
designers of today.

2 PETER BARRON. COTTON. c. 1960s.

3 ST MICHAEL, MARKS & SPENCER.
NYLON. c. MID-1960s.

4 COTTON. c. MID-1960s.

1 This thirties blouse is covered in the popular appliqué technique of the decade. Floral prints would be cut up around the shape of the flower and placed in a random pattern on plain blouses, dresses and even coats. HANDMADE. RAYON. c. 1930s.

2 Small, busy, all-over floral patterns were popular in both the thirties and forties. A blouse like this is easily worn as part of a contemporary ensemble. HANDMADE. CREPE. c. LATE 1930s/EARLY 1940s.

3 The rayon fabric of this thirties evening dress enhances its rich colouring. Although rayon was often called the poor man's silk, it was not really considered to be an inferior fabric and was undeniably popular during this decade because of its brilliant sheen. HANDMADE. RAYON. c. 1930s.

4 The silhouettes of the thirties and forties were hugely influential for many designers, including Ossie Clark and Barbara Hulanicki. The styling and cut of the late thirties housecoat (**5**) is echoed in this early seventies design by Clark. OSSIE CLARK FOR RADLEY. MOSS CREPE. c. 1970s.

5 Housecoats and dressing gowns of the thirties were made for relaxed daytime dressing around the house. The zip or zipper, initially named the 'slide fastener', was used as a design feature. HANDMADE. SILK. c. LATE 1930s.

6 Seventies border prints were often used on long maxi dresses and wide-leg palazzo trousers. The brilliance of these trailing hollyhocks is indicative of the influence of hallucinogenic patterns on textile design from the late sixties. HANDMADE. COTTON. c. LATE 1960s/EARLY 1970s.

1 Raffia embroidery was a popular decoration from the late fifties, used on baskets, straw hats and other summertime accessories. The style was often imitated on clothing such as knitwear and jackets with thick woollen embroidery thread, but rarely is it found with such intensity as seen on this dress. HANDMADE. COTTON AND RAFFIA. c. 1960s.

1

2 The rose is the characteristic flower of the fifties, fashionable in Britain, France and North America. Dior's 'Tulip' collection of 1953 contained many floral prints and inspired an international trend. The layered styling of the skirt on this summer cocktail dress was named 'tulip' due to its shape and is typical of the period's vogue for shorter evening dresses. FRANK USHER. COTTON. c. 1950s.

3 Nylon was a common fabric for post-war fashion and the synthetic, originally used to make wartime parachutes, became so refined that it was proudly worn for both day and evening, its silky stiffness maintaining the fashionable full circle silhouette, particularly when placed over a fine net, as with the example shown. HANDMADE. NYLON. c. EARLY 1950s.

4 As the rose was the flower of the fifties, so the daisy was the floral print of the sixties. Florals from the United States often had a bold sophistication in comparison to English garden-style florals. BLO. SILK. c. 1960s.

1 It is unusual to find an Ossie Clark dress that is not a Celia Birtwell print. Although his designs with a Radley label bear the Ossie hallmark of design, they were the diffusion line made for a mass market and therefore were sometimes made from cheaper fabrics. OSSIE CLARK FOR RADLEY. CHIFFON CREPE. c. 1970s.

2 Many printed textiles of the seventies referenced a soft, romantic and historical style and imitated the work of artists such as Aubrey Beardsley. The print on this synthetic dress shows an illustrative floral garden in linear repeat, reminiscent of the paintings of Monet. SYNTHETIC. c. 1970s.

3 Using one floral print but in multiple colourways was in keeping with the patchwork styling adopted by hippy fashions. This skirt is shown with a thirties embroidered peasant blouse. POLLY PECK. SILK. c. 1970s.

4 This is an unusually diminutive floral for John Bates, whose label Jean Varon was at the forefront of sophisticated youth-led fashion in the sixties alongside designers such as Mary Quant. JEAN VARON. COTTON. c. EARLY 1970s.

5 Thea Porter was a painter-turned-designer who opened a shop in London's Soho selling exotic fabrics, kaftans, trimmings and beadwork. Her tastes suited the bohemian trend of the time and clients included the Beatles, Princess Margaret, Jackie Onassis, Bianca Jagger and Elizabeth Taylor. This dress is one of Porter's more commercial designs, referencing the Romany gypsy style that inspired a mid-seventies trend. THEA PORTER. COTTON. c. 1970s.

3

4

5

COUNTRY CLASSICS
SHABBILY CHIC

1 Today's vintage style drawn from images of forties frugality is achieved using a combination of textures taken from a mix of eras, often borrowing garments from a masculine wardrobe. MALE SUEDE JACKET, ARMY ISSUE KHAKI SHORTS AND WOODEN BELT. ALL c. 1940s; LISLE (COTTON) STOCKINGS. c. 1920s; JUMP ACRYLIC JUMPER. c. 1970s.

2, 3 The costumes worn by Sienna Miller and Keira Knightley in the 2008 film *The Edge of Love* portray a style easily recognized by vintage enthusiasts today. Small woollen jumpers are used over faded floral dresses and the borrowed touches of male fedoras and cuffed wellingtons coincide with a modern trend that would pass unnoticed at a music festival today.

'DESIGNERS REVISITED ALL THE COUNTRY CLASSICS: CORDUROY JACKETS AND JODHPURS, TWEEDY PLUS-FOURS, FAIR ISLE KNITS AND STURDY LEATHER BOOTS, BUFFED TO A CONKER SHINE.' *VOGUE,* COMMENT ON WINTER 2012 COLLECTIONS

It is a style given many different names – including 'Land Girl', 'Home Front', 'Shabby Chic', 'Country Style' and 'Heritage' – but it is the combination of old-fashioned florals, battered check tweeds and darned wool worn with distressed velvets, corduroy and leather that creates what might be considered the quintessential 'vintage' look. The style is reliant on the perfect mismatch of garments drawn from a diversity of eras and is instantly recognizable from fashion photographs showing the apparently carefree clothing combination of granny's hand-knitted jumper, a boyfriend's tweed jacket and a whimsical mid-20th-century printed floral against romantic backdrops of meadows and windswept landscapes. Meanwhile, evocative commercials for the traditional essentials of family life (such as bread, cheese, milk and washing powder) rely on the muted tones of ginghams and Fair Isle, ancient tweeds and worn corduroys to capture the nostalgia of 'the good old days'.

Beautiful examples of this vintage style can be seen in films such as *The Edge of Love* (2008), based on the life of Dylan Thomas. Keira Knightley and Sienna Miller tread the Welsh beaches dressed in cuffed wellingtons, sprigged dresses and elaborately textured cardigans. Although the film is set in the forties, several scenes consciously reference modern vintage styling, such as when Miller dons a man's grey fedora or Knightley slips her husband's military jacket over her floral dress.

The rustic style, a frequent inspiration for contemporary fashion collections from designers such as Ralph Lauren, comes from a blend of ancient craftsmanship and the ingenuity of wartime. It is a fashion that arrived because of wartime austerity, the forties 'make do and mend' objective that some still aspire to today. In 1941, *Vogue* featured inspirational images of society beauties including Lady Diana Cooper, pictured running her own three-acre farm, exuding elegant country style in trousers and a tailored shirt, with a 'peasant kerchief' tied to protect her hair.

4, 5 Faded summer florals juxtaposed with heavy textured knitwear achieve a 'country' style, epitomized in the film *The Edge of Love.* COTTON CULOTTES AND HANDMADE COTTON DRESS. c. 1940s. WORN WITH JAEGER BLUE AND GREEN WOOL CARDIGANS. c. 1950s.

Forties wartime fashion editorials gave instruction on ways to revitalize old clothing through the use of decorative patching, ribbon replacement collars and the addition of spotted or striped cotton sleeves to replace threadbare woollen ones. Wool unravelled from worn-out socks and gloves was reknitted into multicoloured Fair Isle-patterned jumpers and sleeveless tanks. Ankle socks, meanwhile, were neatly donned to replace the nylon or rayon stockings that were scarce. 'Mrs Sew and Sew' was a well-known illustrated character created by the British Board of Trade, and government-led fashion editorials created an internationally appealing style. Ration coupons were introduced in Britain at the end of 1941, with each person issued with sixty-six clothing coupons. By 1945, this had reduced to a mere thirty-six. Faced with such severe restrictions one commonly employed tactic was to make dresses from furnishing fabrics: these fabrics were wider than a standard dress fabric and therefore enabled more to be made from the length of one yard available with three ration coupons.

Government restrictions were also imposed on fabrics and goods made from the raw materials needed for uniforms and military equipment. Clothing factories had to adhere to the imposed austerity measures that restricted frivolous trimmings, belt and hem widths and the number of pleats or buttons used, pocket sizes and collars. A label

1 This illustration from a 1927 edition of US magazine *Ladies' Home Journal* shows suitable weekend outfits. According to the accompanying commentary, 'dust-coloured gabardine' was considered ideal for the 'comfort and correctness' of a social outing to the countryside.

2 The traditional equestrian jodhpur was used as an eighties fashion statement, inspired by two big-screen costume dramas, *White Mischief* and *Out of Africa*, both set in colonial Africa. COTTON JODHPURS. 1918. WORN WITH SUEDE WAISTCOAT AND TWEED JACKET. c. 1960s.

3 The cut of the jodhpur has rarely changed, though exaggerated to the extreme as a fashion of the eighties and pared down for contemporary equestrian wear. Worn by women after riding sidesaddle ceased to be etiquette in the early twenties, jodhpurs were first borrowed for fashionable wear by Coco Chanel and more recently by Ralph Lauren, an American fashion house that has cultivated English traditions. WOOL JODHPURS. c.1940s. WORN WITH PRINGLE LAMBSWOOL TWINSET. c.1950s.

4 The rustic paisley wrapover blouse complements the heavy weave of forties jodhpurs, especially when accessorized with a wooden belt. PRINTED RAYON. c.1940s.

5 The British Women's Land Army uniform was only issued in a limited range of sizes. Uniforms were belted and cuffed, nipped and tucked to create the glamorous poster girl image that still inspires trends decades later.

For a healthy, happy job

Join the
WOMEN'S
LAND
ARMY

printed with the letters 'CC41' was issued to mark clothes made to government-stipulated restrictions, and spotting this label is an easy way to date clothing from the early forties. However, it is thought that many people removed their label in an attempt to hide the fact that their garment was not couture, or even blessed with designer finesse. A later label, known as the 'double elevens', is thought by some to represent more expensive and slightly more elaborate utility garments (see the section on the forties for examples of both these labels: p. 57).

A host of resourceful improvements created a stylish mix of looks. Shortages of material encouraged innovation in shoe-making too, as can be seen in the designs of Salvatore Ferragamo, working in Italy during the Second World War. He experimented with materials such as raffia, hemp and even Cellophane confectionery wrappers. In the absence of rubber and leather, wedge heels made from cork proved to be hardwearing, comfortable and, fortuitously, stylish, and they maintained a fashionable presence throughout the following decades.

This appealing mix of aesthetics was underpinned by the government-issued clothing for women who took over manual labour in countries bereft of a male workforce.

1 This tweed hacking jacket is complemented by leather elbow patches and the soft fan stitch on a scarf. A hacking jacket from any decade has a flattering cut: the waist and shoulders are fitted, but the inverted central back vent means the jacket does not bunch. Likewise, the slanted pockets and longer line are designed to accentuate height and move with the wearer. HARRIS TWEED. c. 1950s. WORN WITH WOOL SCARF. c. 1940s.

2 The Fair Isle tank, traditionally a male jumper, is an important component of this look. Early patterns can be distinguished by the use of only three or four colours, unlike their modern counterparts that use more colours and sophisticated stitchwork. HANDMADE. WOOL AND CHENILLE. c. 1940s. WORN WITH LEATHER BELT. c. 1980s.

The uniforms worn by women in the Allied countries had a universal practicality that was transformed with feminine guile to become the internationally renowned style of the early forties. Inner-city factory workers wore overalls and nearly everyone wore the siren suit (the forerunner of fashion's jumpsuit) over their ordinary clothes or nightwear when sirens called civilians to the air raid shelter. Churchill even wore one made specially from glamorous red velvet. The British issue for the Women's Land Army, designed by Lady Denman, was distinctive and only manufactured in a limited selection of sizes. It inspired similar uniforms in the Allied countries. Consisting of green woollen jumpers, brown breeches, two Aertex shirts and dark green dungarees, the 'uniform' was worn with felt hats or headscarves and a thin mac for winter. This helped shape a poignant image for the female workforce that continued throughout the war and well after it ended. The land girls of Britain known as 'Cinderellas of the soil', the 'lumberjills' of Scotland and the 'Rosie Riveters' of the United States formed the domestic armies and, even while the battles of the 'home front' were severe, women were encouraged to maintain as glamorous an image as possible.

Forties advertising used alluring female silhouettes to promote everything from cigarettes to Coca-Cola and femininity was seen as a tool to boost the morale of the troops. Government campaigns promoted the importance of an appealing appearance, encouraging women to 'be his pin-up girl'. Even the most practical of uniforms could be customized for a more attractive look. Dungarees and overalls were altered and belted to fit, while make-up, then in short supply, was encouraged both as a protection against dirt and a way of adding glamour. Hair, meanwhile, was styled beneath scarves tied turban- and bandeau-style.

In the sixties, traditionally rustic tweed fabric was reworked into chic silhouettes for city style. Used in high-street collections as well as by designers from Quant to Balenciaga, tweed knickerbockers and kilts were accessorized with knitted tanks, 'Granny' glasses and flecked schoolboy caps. By the seventies increased environmental awareness and a desire for frugality encouraged by the recession once again inspired 'country clothes for the city' in 'layered' and 'nostalgic' styles, as reported by British *Vogue* in 1973. The styling of fashion editorials, featuring chunky knits offset by romantic chiffons, helped shape this classic vintage look.

While this look does not have the splendour of couture or the luxury of expensive decoration, its mismatch of styles and reappropriation of traditional fabrics does have a nostalgic appeal. In its successful blend of heritage and tradition, the contrast of ancient tweeds with faded florals, crucial details of antique leather and lace, mixed with quintessential quirkiness, it offers an endlessly adaptable look, robust enough to respond to the demands of the 21st-century wardrobe.

3 Military-issue flying jackets, worn by pilots in both world wars, have been popular as fashionable outerwear for both sexes since their invention. Their American creator, Leslie Irvin, stopped manufacturing at the end of the Second World War, but the second-hand market for these jackets remains buoyant even today. The distinctive style was designed for warmth and easy movement in a small cockpit. The copyright of the original 'Irving' design (the 'g' was reportedly added accidentally by a secretary) was sold during the war, as wartime demand was so high. LEATHER. c. 1950s.

4 This dress was worn by women in the WVS (Women's Voluntary Service) and dates to around 1942 when Brilkie, a fashion manufacturer, took over the production of uniforms originally designed by Digby Morton. BRILKIE. WOOL. c. 1942.

5 Archive photographs show contrasting leather belts worn with coats of the thirties and forties, a combination that works well with tweed. The interesting collar on this coat was a style seen in the late forties and early fifties. WOOL. c. EARLY 1950s. WORN WITH LEATHER BELT. c. 1960s.

1 The sixties explored the potential of tweed beyond being the reserve of elderly elegance. DURETTA LONDON. WOOL. c. 1960s.

2 The fashion house Valditevere was founded in Florence in 1951 and remains at the forefront of Italian fashion today. The fine dog's-tooth check is knitted silk and Lurex used at varying scales. VALDITEVERE. SILK AND LUREX. c. 1960s.

3 Tweed, a fabric with country connotations, is given a glamorous image shown as a three-quarter-length sightseeing jacket with the defining shoulder pads of the forties.

5

6

7

4 The Lammermuir Hills are situated in southern Scotland, near the River Tweed. This area is traditionally the home for the production of a wide variety of woven textured fabrics and has supplied international fashion houses since the forties. The Lammermuir label on this dress proudly declares its heritage. WOOL. c. 1960s.

5 Abercrombie & Fitch dates back to 1892 New York. Traditionally a company that designed 'sportswear', its classic leisurewear, as seen above, remained popular until the original company closed in 1976. Its subsequent relaunch in the nineties saw a high-fashion makeover.

6 Jaeger was founded in 1883 as a company that promoted the use of natural fibres for clothing. By the sixties the company epitomized fashionable London and garments with the label 'Young Jaeger' are highly prized today. The collarless tweed suit was the height of sixties chic. JAEGER. WOOL. c. 1960s.

7 The tweed checks that became an iconic sixties look were popularized by the designs of fashion house Christian Dior in 1959 under the helm of Yves Saint Laurent. Dior wrote of checks, 'There are so many styles of checks to choose that there will be one to suit every age and figure … the older woman will have a broken check in a soft silk or woollen material … for the country there are beautiful, classic check tweeds.' COTTON. c. EARLY 1960s.

1 An expertly crafted hand-knitted dress by the first British designer to produce hand-knitted garments commercially. Marjorie Tillotson also wrote knitting patterns and the famous Woolcraft books, which were at the heart of British home knitting. MARJORIE TILLOTSON. WOOL. c. 1940s.

2 The textured knit and embroidered collar of a forties jumper sit effortlessly with the pink woven tweed of sixties trousers. HANDMADE WOOL JUMPER. c. 1930s/1940s. WORN WITH WOOL TROUSERS. c. 1960s.

3 Even when sixties designers gave 'country' fabrics a high-fashion makeover, the distinctive tweeds and checks maintained a rural and natural feel. WOOL. c. 1960s.

4 A handmade woven check jacket uses a soft caped sleeve and fringed hem (the finish commonly used on scarves) to create a soft silhouette, offset by polished leather buttons. WOOL. c. 1950s.

5 The combination of twenties brogues, long Argyle-patterned knee socks, heavy wool overcoats and cardigans creates a rustic style many aspire to today.

6 The woven fabrics associated with British country pursuits, such as hunting, fishing and golf, were used for traditional wear, until hound's-tooth tweed and its smaller variation, the dog's-tooth, were revived by fashion designers such as Mary Quant during the sixties. WOOL. c. 1960s.

7 Working overalls, common wear during wartime, became a fashion statement of the seventies. The adopted workwear of the forties was redesigned in luxurious fabrics such as velvet and satin as well as in durable denim and corduroy. COTTON CORDUROY. c. 1970s.

8 A tweed coat with leather piping and buttons blends with a jacquard knitted dress that has been constructed to resemble a woven fabric. WOOL AND LEATHER COAT. c. 1960s. WORN WITH GIBSON WOOL DRESS. c. 1960s.

ANIMAL INSTINCT
WILD FASHION

'THE TIGER IN THE JUNGLE AND THE BROKER IN THE CITY BOTH ASSUME THE COLOUR OF THEIR SURROUNDINGS; WHILE THE BRIGHTNESS AND THE BEAUTY OF FASHION FIND THEIR ECHO IN THE MATING SEASON OF BIRDS.' JAMES LAVER, *TASTE AND FASHION*, 1937

Animal skins have adorned humans and their homes for centuries. Esteemed for their decorative pattern and sophisticated coloration, originally real animal skins were worn as a mark of distinction, rather than as a decorative fashion, and were used to award ceremonial status, a display of rank and power in scale with the ferocity and scarcity of the animal. Snakeskin, lizard, zebra or monkey were all highly prized, but the distinctive leopard has always reigned fashionably supreme, even more sought after than ermine – the white winter coat of the stoat – that has long been the traditional wear of royalty and those of political and academic standing, or even mink, valued for its rarity and luxurious softness.

Real fur skins were used as warm, practical linings for cloaks worn in earlier centuries, only becoming fashionable when they began to be selected for their aesthetic qualities and made into hats, gloves and muffs or used as a trimming for winter garments. The fur coat, as known today, became a fashionable garment during the 19th century, although more common were the caplets worn with evening dress and made from the delicate hues of rabbit skins. Early French fashion houses Paquin and Poiret added to the opulence of their garments by using fur stoles and trims, giving them a fashionable glamour associated with the rich clientele who wore the clothes to theatres, balls and fashionable soirées.

Luxury skins were favoured for their distinctive markings, in particular the leopard, and twenties fashion revelled in exotic decoration. Actress Marian Nixon enhanced her

1 Early sixties fashion continued to enjoy the leopard prints that were so popular in the fifties. But, as the decade progressed, realistic animal prints seemed dated compared to the startling modernist styles introduced by designers such as André Courrèges and Paco Rabanne. This Dalmatian print cloak with contrasting red lining is a modern interpretation of the traditional animal patterning. WETHERALL. WOOL. c. 1960s.

2 The fifties were the heyday of the simulated leopard-print three-quarter-length jacket or coat and these are easily found today. SIMULATED SNOW LEOPARD PRINT. c. 1950s.

3 This fashion editorial from 1942 shows a model wearing a coat with imitation leopard-skin lining and a matching hat.

celebrity by matching her fur coat to the pet leopard she walked on a lead along the boulevards of Hollywood, a pursuit also allegedly enjoyed by Josephine Baker, Gene Tierney and Carole Lombard, albeit without the dubious addition of matching coats. However, leopard really became a familiar sighting among Hollywood's starlets following the successful series of *Tarzan* films that began in 1932. Highly patterned cheetah and leopard skins were translated into jacket collars and pocket inlays, worn with matching hats and gloves. The house of Paquin, meanwhile, caused a sensation with a complete coat of leopard skin in 1941.

1

The debate that surrounds the use of 'real' fur in the 21st century was not a consideration in this era and when Christian Dior introduced his acclaimed leopard-print dresses in 1947, 'Jungle' for day and 'Afrique' for evening, they were designed in celebration of his model and muse Mitzah Bricard, rather than being a fashionable alternative to wearing real skins. Madame Bricard, employed at the house of Dior essentially to be in charge of hats, was renowned for her elegance, love of pearls, turbans and leopard pattern. Dior believed in surrounding himself with beauty and said of his muse, 'Madame Bricard is one of those people, increasingly rare, who makes elegance their sole *raison d'être*. I knew that her presence in my house would inspire me towards creation.'

Dior often used leopard for cuffs on velvet coats, on hats and outerwear but his 1947 collection was considered to be the first in Europe to truly spark the trend for leopard print. In the early fifties Roger Vivier experimented with leopard-like patterns on vibrant blue satin for shoes and bags, and it is still possible to find leopard-print scarves from this era with bottle green and blue grounds. In the United States, Norman Norell took the leopard print for his signature look. Considered to be ahead of European trends throughout his career, Norell worked with both real fur and printed leopard throughout the forties. Even earlier, dating back to 1936, is a printed leopard crepe dress held in London's Victoria and Albert Museum. Cut on the bias with an asymmetrical neckline that only covers one shoulder, the dress is highly reminiscent of the untailored skins used for costumes in the *Tarzan* films that first popularized the trend, and would not look out of place on a contemporary catwalk.

As manufacturing and printing techniques improved, animal print became a part of mainstream fashion, no longer reserved solely for the rich and famous. The fifties is the era in which it was most prevalent: both leopard and cheetah prints work incredibly well in photographs (particularly for black and white footage) and this photogenic quality was exploited by stars of the silver screen. Gene Tierney, Marilyn Monroe, Brigitte Bardot and Catherine Deneuve were all regularly photographed wearing the striking pattern. By the late fifties and early sixties animal prints had become so overused that they began to lose their glamorous appeal. Happily for vintage collectors today this means animal print coats and jackets are readily available.

1 Dior was one of the first couturiers to popularize printed animal patterns rather than actual skins. Inspiration came from his muse and house model, Mitzah Bricard, who had a penchant for leopard prints. This evening dress, pictured in the *Evening Post* in August 1953, was from his autumn/winter collection of that year.

2 A fifties knitting pattern for matching animal-print gloves and hat.

3 Double-breasted leopard-skin jackets from the fifties bear a striking resemblance to those manufactured in the early eighties. Quality of the simulated fur is no obvious clue, as this varied extensively in both decades. The writing style of the label, if there is one, and lining fabric are good indications. Linings from the fifties will be stiffer with a taffeta feel, while those from the eighties are still usually synthetic but are softer and silkier. DACRON. SIMULATED LEOPARD PRINT. c. LATE 1950s.

4 A structured jacket with an exaggerated peplum defines the waist in typical eighties style. Leopard print in this era often reflected the trend for all things kitsch. JEAN PAUL GAULTIER. COTTON. c. 1980s.

5 The collar and cuffs of this forties jacket are highlighted with synthetic leopard-print fabric. Worn with narrow 'cigarette'-style trousers from a later decade it makes a real statement for contemporary wear. HANDMADE WOOL JACKET. c. 1940s. WORN WITH SYNTHETIC TROUSERS. c. 1950s.

HELANCA *Helanca leopards by Cole of California.*

1 Cole of California was a United States swimwear manufacturer known for its attention to glamour and style. Using Helanca (the name given to nylon fibres treated so they become elastic) for swimwear was revolutionary in the fifties and sixties. It has a sprung stretch that retains its shape and it could be dyed or printed with brilliant colours.

2 Leopard prints were a signature of eighties style, softened here by using them in floral combination from an eminent design studio. JAEGER. SILK. c. 1980s.

3, 4 The sophistication of leopard prints from the late fifties to early sixties trends have been reinterpreted for the contemporary catwalk by designers such as Dolce & Gabbana and Roberto Cavalli.

3 SILK. c. 1960s.

4 HANDMADE. COTTON. c. 1960s.

8 Realistic animal-skin interpretations did not suit the flowing feminine fashions of the seventies. Softer interpretations included animal-like patterns or whimsical animals and insects. SILK JERSEY. c. 1970s.

5 This cleverly constructed wrapover blouse, made from Lurex featuring a hazy leopard print, engineers a double cowl neck. SELFRIDGES. SYNTHETIC LUREX. c. 1960s.

6 Both removable real and simulated fur collars were manufactured during the fifties. Occasionally worn with raglan-sleeved jumpers or on winter dresses, they added a luxurious softness to checked tweed suits WOOL AND FUR. c. 1950s.

7 An illustrated advertisement for the US department store Lord & Taylor displays a range of leopard-print lingerie and loungewear from the early sixties. In particular, slips and half-petticoats were popular.

The Jungle Girl

1 Ribbed imitation-fur pile was a fashion of the sixties, rarely seen in any other decade. SIMULATED FUR AND LEATHER. c. 1960s.

2 The sophistication of a fifties swagger coat is here achieved using simulated animal skins. SIMULATED FUR. c. 1950s.

3 Imitation animal prints were more common in the thirties and forties than often realized. Rarely found today, early animal prints may not have been realistic interpretations of animal skins but the quality of the simulated fur is surprising. HANDMADE. PRINTED VELVET AND SIMULATED FUR. c. 1940s.

4 When animal prints were used in the seventies, they conveyed a decadence in keeping with bohemian styling. SILK JERSEY. c. 1970s.

5 The classic eighties label Cockney Rebel manufactured dresses for both day and night. The wrapover tulip-shaped dress was a principal style that, like many fashions of the mid-eighties, imitated a shape of the fifties. COCKNEY REBEL. SYNTHETIC. c. 1985.

6 Virtually every animal-skin pattern featured in eighties fashion. New synthetic metallics were able to absorb intricate prints, such as the featured imitation snakeskin print on this disco dress. DAVID BUTLER. SYNTHETIC. c. 1980s.

The animal world has always been a reference for fashion, but noticeably absent from printed fashion textiles before the fifties are birds of any sort. Although particular birds such as peacocks have always been synonymous with Liberty prints, fashion, between the war years, took its lead from the French couture houses. The French believed birds to be unlucky and it took the formidable combination of Christian Dior and textile converter Zika Ascher to break with tradition. In 1953 Dior produced a matching dress and coat for his spring/summer collection from Ascher's 'blue bird' print and sales were so successful that former *Vogue* editor Alison Settle commented, 'by their sales, they realize that those painted ones fly with fortune in their beaks'.

Butterflies are a mainstay of fashionable wildlife imagery, but it is hard to find much evidence of their use before the forties. The late sixties and seventies used all manner of printed fauna and flora on the hippy fashions that embraced an ethical and social awareness. The humble bumblebee was selected to be the signature motif of celebrated Scottish designer Bill Gibb. In line with the mood of fashion in the period, Gibb's bumblebee evolved to be a sophisticated design resembling a beautiful butterfly wing towards the end of his career. While many of his early designs do not carry the motif, it is always exciting to find one of his exotic creations with the bee insignia. Another seventies sensation, Diane von Furstenberg, was also a perpetrator of wildlife imagery in fashion. 'All my inspiration comes from nature, whether it's an animal or the layout of bark or a leaf,' said Furstenberg, whose classic wrap dress was first introduced in 1974. It was released in leopard print the following year.

The seventies treatment of animal markings took a softer approach than that of the subsequent decade. The sharply defined silhouette of the eighties used distinct patterning to enhance its ostentatious fashions. Leopard print, in particular, was adopted by mainstream fashion for use on dresses and blouses, but it also enjoyed a revival popularized by the anti-fashion followers of the Punk street fashion, and the distinctive style of musician Debbie Harry created a vintage vibe for the animal pattern. It was also during the eighties that animal print once again became a signature of many notable fashion houses, whose use of the pattern continues today. Christian Lacroix, Roberto Cavalli, Leonard, Dolce & Gabbana and Alaïa are all associated with the timeless, enduring animal print that has spanned a whole century, and shows little sign of being tamed.

4 This detail is from a handmade silk kimono jacket dating to the early twenties. The metallic-thread embroidery depicting dragons and exotic birds shows the influence of the Orient on fashion, as well as an Art Deco influence in the floral border. EMBROIDERY ON SILK. c. EARLY 1920s.

5, 6 Soft plumed bird feather prints can be found on many silk and nylon scarves from the fifties but rarely on garments, as superstition considered birds to be an unlucky motif. This changed in 1953 when Dior incorporated a bluebird print from the Ascher collection.

5 NYLON. c. 1950s.

6 KREIER. SILK. c. 1950s.

1 The density of a border print depicting fluttering birds is softened by the translucency of sheer chiffon. The off-the-shoulder style would have been worn over a fitted slip. SID GREENE. SILK CHIFFON. c. 1970s.

2 Bird feather prints were hugely popular during the seventies, either as literal repeats or as abstracted designs emulating a feathery pattern. POLYESTER. BRITISH. c. 1970s.

3 The peacock and feather motif first popular in the twenties was revisited with vigour during the seventies. The exotic plumage suited the fluid styles of the era and was popular for both interior and fashion use. PHOOL. COTTON. c. 1970s.

1 A snake curls around the shoulders of eighties shoulder pads. Electric blue was a defining colour of the decade. POLYESTER. c. 1980s.

2 A handmade dress from the fifties is made in a woven jacquard depicting the faces of Siamese cats and is identical to the printed image on a silk scarf by Pierre Baccara. WOVEN SILK JACQUARD. c. 1950s.

3 Bill Gibb adopted the humble bumblebee as his emblem, often but not always incorporating it into his designs. The motif is reminiscent of the oversized insect brooches designed by Schiaparelli in the 1930s. BILL GIBB. METAL. c. 1970s.

4 Tropical fish swimming over coral reefs pattern this unusual Hawaiian textile design. Alfred Shaheen is a much-loved name among collectors of the Hawaiian clothing that was enormously popular during the fifties. Among the first to promote the Hawaiian shirt for fashion post-Second World War, Shaheen built both a successful textile printing and garment manufacturing industry, adapting Hawaiian textiles for a commercial US market. While this dress has no remaining label, it can be identified by the sophisticated design; it also bears the name of his company Surf 'n Sand Handprints on the selvedge. ALFRED SHAHEEN. COTTON. c. EARLY 1950s.

5 This model wears a European interpretation of Hawaiian textile design. Dachshund dogs decorate a full-circle skirted dress from 1955. Although an unusual motif for fabric, the dachshund was a popular breed in the period and the subject of many household ornaments.

6 The poodle was the most popular breed of dog portrayed in fifties fashion, a particular favourite on North American teenage clothing. Although sometimes used as a print, as seen here on cotton, it was most commonly seen as an embroidery motif on dirndl skirts and cardigans.

1 Butterfly prints personified the mood of free love and a fondness for all things natural in the late sixties and early seventies. COTTON. c. 1970s.

2 Butterfly prints were not a common pattern on fifties fabrics even though fashions of the decade enjoyed every type of floral motif imaginable. COTTON. c. 1950s.

3 Butterflies, birds, feathers or quaint animals such as owls and hedgehogs formed the core of animal-inspired patterns in early seventies fashions. LANVIN. SILK. c. 1970s.

4 Simone Mirman was a French-born milliner who trained under Elsa Schiaparelli, moving to London to run the Schiaparelli millinery department in Mayfair before the Second World War. After some years establishing her own business, she was given a royal warrant for her designs for the British royal family. Here a pair of shorts has been customized to match an appliquéd butterfly hat from her 1971 spring/summer collection.

5 This dress exhibits unusual commerciality for Thea Porter, known for her exotic and bohemian designs. The elaborate print, inspired by butterfly wings, translates well for contemporary designs. THEA PORTER. COTTON. c. 1970s.

NICE
NAUTICALS
SEASIDE SPIRIT

1 A thirties portrait of Gabrielle Chanel and her dog Gigot in the garden of La Pausa, her villa in Roquebrune in the south of France. She is wearing the sailor-style trousers and striped T-shirt she championed as fashionable wear.

2 The twenties was a time of travel and cruise ships, and the seaside promenade was the catwalk for the latest in holiday style. COTTON DRESS AND RAYON SCARF. c. 1920s.

3 Nautical stripes and sailor collars have inspired fashionable dress since the sailor suit was first adapted for a four-year-old Prince of Wales in 1846. POLYESTER MIX. c. 1970s.

Crisp nautical style is a perennial of spring/summer fashion collections on both the catwalk and the high street. Despite the long history of this look, the distinctive nautical palette is unvaried and red, naval blue and, always, white are used with anchor motifs, sailors' knot insignia, sailor-style collars and cuffs, brass buttons and military braids. Stylistically more whimsical, but equally charismatic, maritime ephemera have decorated hats and handbags and were a staple of the novelty print at its heyday during the fifties.

Although the French Navy has a longer history of using colours and accessories to distinguish officers from general crew, historical legend suggests that it was the British monarch, King George II, who formulated and selected the colours of the distinct and much-imitated British naval uniform in the 18th century. The King's final colour choice was apparently inspired by his wife's navy blue and white riding habit. The US Navy took its lead from Britain, and fashion soon followed suit. The appealing characteristics of naval dress began to also appear on children's clothing and in the leisurewear of the upper classes.

By the late 19th century, naval-inspired fashion had become a popular style worn for boat trips and visits to the seaside, and nautical stripes were used for the heavy bathing costumes worn to take a dip in the sea. Early 20th-century dress adopted nautical details such as sailors' collars and cuffs, triple-stripe braiding and brass-buttoned jackets. Ribbon-trimmed flat straw boaters began to be worn as everyday fashion. The 'middy' blouse, the style borrowed from the loose-fitting shirt with wide flat collar worn by the lowest-ranking naval seaman, the midshipman, was the first garment to reach truly fashionable status. The blouse became a staple of early 20th-century casual wear, worn for sporting activities, country visits and gardening due to its comfortable, loose-fitting construction. Made in cotton, silk or even jersey, it was featured in many illustrated advertisements of the day, trimmed with contrasting buttons and cuffs, sometimes a lanyard and always a sailor collar, fastened with knotted neck bows or toggles. The sailor collar remained an elegant feature of nautical fashion well into the thirties and remains an essential of the theme.

However, the garment most closely associated with nautical fashion has to be the simple yet distinctive, boldly striped Breton. Established as the uniform for all seamen in the French Navy during the late 19th century, the navy blue and white knitted shirt was initially named a *matelot* or

2   3

'OVER THE LAST 150 YEARS, THE ENDURING INFLUENCE OF NAUTICAL AND NAVAL-INSPIRED STYLES HAS SPREAD FROM THE UK AND THROUGHOUT EUROPE TO AMERICA AND INTO WARDROBES OF MILLIONS, PERMEATING HIGH STREET AND HAUTE COUTURE FASHIONS ALIKE.' AMY MILLER, CURATOR, NATIONAL MARITIME MUSEUM

marinière and always used twenty-one navy blue stripes to represent Napoleon's victories. Manufactured in Brittany, it became established as the working wardrobe for many seafaring workers and fishermen of the region, eventually becoming known as the Breton (the dialect of Brittany). Its distinctive stripes made it easy to spot any unfortunate man who fell overboard.

It is said that Coco Chanel was inspired by the Bretons worn by local fishermen she saw while on a boat trip in the French Riviera. Adopting the chic striped jumper and bell-bottomed trousers for her own wardrobe, Chanel created a nautically inspired fashion collection in 1917. Adapting masculine garments for feminine attire was progressive for the time and the *garçonne* style has often been attributed to Chanel. The so-called 'boat-necked' Breton became a fashion fixture in many eras, popularized by a variety of celebrities. Screen sirens Brigitte Bardot and Marilyn Monroe were often seen sporting the nautical stripe during the glamorous fifties, while the notable costume designer of the big screen, Edith Head, introduced a new silhouette by putting Audrey Hepburn in a Breton with slim-line ski-pants in the 1957 film *Funny Face*. The famous shirt has also become the trademark of notable designers such as Jean Paul Gaultier (whose press team has worn versions of it during his shows) and of artist Andy Warhol (who dressed model Edie Sedgwick in a Breton and opaque black tights for his film, *Kitchen*). Warhol's sixties celebration of the Breton was a reflection of the reactionary beatnik trend that adopted army surplus and utility wear. The sailor's three-quarter-length naval reefer jacket or pea-coat, double-breasted and brass-buttoned, was a huge trend of the sixties and inspired the designs of a young Yves Saint Laurent, who completed his 1962 collection with Breton striped T-shirt and white bell-bottomed trousers.

Fashion in the late thirties and forties was patriotic in its interpretation of naval influences, and Hollywood films dressed starlets in stripes and anchors and shirts laced with jaunty white cords running through metal eyelets. American *Life* magazine ran a feature on nautical fashion in October 1940, and slogans such as 'Give a fashionable salute to the navy in this engaging new sailor dress' were used in newspaper adverts. Even stockings of the forties bore rope and anchor patterns in vertical lines from the heel. By the fifties, nautical style took on a subtlety, using a varied colour palette in crisp cottons for sailor-collared

1 This risqué illustration from *La Parisienne* shows the popular beach 'pyjamas', part of the *après*-swim wardrobes worn on sociable beach promenades of the late twenties and early thirties. Often glamorously flared in cool fabrics of crepe de Chine, silk or loosely woven cotton, these trousers for women were considered too racy for every day. They are rarely found today and are much sought after for contemporary wear.

2 Wide-leg bell-bottoms have been stylish since Coco Chanel first adopted the trousers of French sailors. COTTON. c. 1970s.

3 The luggage labels associated with early travel have frequently inspired 20th-century fashion prints. POLYESTER SHIRT. c. 1970S. WORN WITH DENIM JEANS. COTTON. c. 1950s.

4–6 Three skirts from the sixties display the use of nautical emblems as the novelty print for holiday wardrobes. While swimwear itself was often designed using sophisticated patterns, the rapidly developing genre of leisurewear used designs with a light-hearted joviality and displayed obvious clues that their wearer was able to enjoy holidays and day trips. COTTON. c. 1960s.

dresses and blouses. Sailor style remained fashionable, fuelled by Hollywood films such as 1958's *South Pacific*, while the popular novelty print was used for the canvas of the full-circle skirt, reflecting seaside holidays with images of bobbing boats, starfish and painterly seascapes. Three-dimensional shells, crabs and anchors decorated belt buckles, straw baskets and jewelry, a style that reemerged during the eighties.

By the eighties, the nautical look was used both for mainstream fashion in the form of stripes, sailor collars and seaside regalia and for the revolutionary style of Vivienne Westwood and Malcolm McLaren's 1981 'Pirate' collection that immortalized the New Romantic fashion, part of street style and seen in the pop charts on musicians such as Adam Ant, Duran Duran and Spandau Ballet.

1 Even Biba, better known for its bohemian and decadent reinterpretation of thirties and forties fashion, referenced nautical style. A sophisticated and pared-down styling under the design helm of Barbara Hulanicki saw the reinvention of the twenty-one-striped Breton as cool coats, jumpsuits and dresses with just a hint at the nautical. BIBA. SYNTHETIC CHIFFON. c. LATE 1960s.

2 Mid-sixties colour blocking references chic nautical style, with a highlighted yoke and striped belt, offset by the brass buckle. BANCROFT. WOOL. c. 1960s.

3 An unusual tailored suit displaying ingenious pattern-cutting from the disbanded English Eccentrics label. The nautical stripe and style of suit are both reminiscent of the striped Edwardian boating blazer. ENGLISH ECCENTRICS. WOOL. c. LATE 1980s.

4. This Royal Marines bandsman jacket has been customized with braiding to resemble the jacket famously worn by Jimi Hendrix. Hendrix bought his jacket from the boutique 'I Was Lord Kitchener's Valet' on London's Portobello Road in the sixties. WOOL. c. 1980s.

1 A nautically inspired fashion shoot from 1940 uses the naval colours of red, white and blue. Wartime fashion was continually patriotic, and the cheering colours and chic insignia of the navy lent themselves more easily to fashionable interpretation than the austere colours of the military.

2 Vintage seaside novelty prints are some of the most sought after today. Naval insignia translate easily onto fabric, evoking seaside holidays. COTTON. c. 1970s.

3 The nautical look was a recurring feature of forties wartime designs, and international fashion editorials encouraged 'Sailor Style'. HANDMADE. RAYON. c. 1940s.

4–7 Chic nautical colour combinations and military styling in the form of epaulettes, contrasting buttons, belts and sailor bows are intrinsic features of sixties fashion, reinterpreted with graphic simplicity.

4 FRANK RUSSELL. WOOL. c. 1960s.

5 MANSFIELD. WOOL. c. 1960s.

6 WOOL. c. 1960s.

7 SYNTHETIC. c. 1970s.

1 Red and blue linear stitchwork on a divided skirt evokes the cruise-ship holidays popular in the thirties. HANDMADE. COTTON. c. 1930s.

2 The 'middy' blouse (seen on the right of the illustration) was a popular twenties interpretation of sailor style. The blouse had been favoured since the early 20th century and saw many variations, worn in practical jersey or cotton for sports and active wear or luxury silk for more formal wear. Initially a youth fashion, by the twenties the versatile blouse was so popular it was worn by both young and old.

3, 4 Seaside imagery never loses its appeal, whether it is a literal translation of sailor uniform or a picturesque print, and the sailing boat has been one of the most popular motifs since the thirties. While many modern versions can be found, it is the quirkiness and naïvety of the original that has special charm.

3 COTTON. c. 1960s.

4 COTTON. c. 1970s.

5, 6 Summer prints of the thirties and forties depicted a medley of seashore images, using everything from jellyfish to seaweed. The styles from these eras are often looser interpretations than the literal illustrations so popular during the fifties. Cotton, hitherto the fabric of working clothes, became increasingly important for cruisewear and holiday ensembles.

5 HANDMADE. RAYON. c. EARLY 1940s.

6 HANDMADE. COTTON. c. 1930s.

2 A late thirties fashion illustration highlights the growing area of leisurewear. Beach games, suntanning and other outdoor activities needed the new style of 'play' clothing that had manufacturers experimenting with new fabrics such as towelling and seersucker.

3, 4 The dirndl skirt of the fifties provided the perfect canvas for depicting seaside scenes and frequently utilized border prints illustrating holiday destinations. COTTON. c. 1950s.

5 The style of illustrative print on this seventies dress could easily be mistaken for a design from the fifties. However, the soft synthetic fabric and nylon zip are obvious clues as to its real date. HANDMADE. SYNTHETIC. c. 1970s.

6 Ropes and sailors' knots form a sinuous print on this cotton shirt by Fredrica Starke, the affordable label from couturier Frederick Starke. FREDRICA STARKE. COTTON. c. 1950s.

1 This gentle print, evocative of seaweed, is a typical thirties design, where these were in keeping with the softer feminine fashions of the era. Even the styles adopting details of sailor uniform used combinations of pastel pinks and soft browns as well as the original crisp contrast of navy and white. HANDMADE. SILK. c. 1930s.

SEA SHORE WEAR

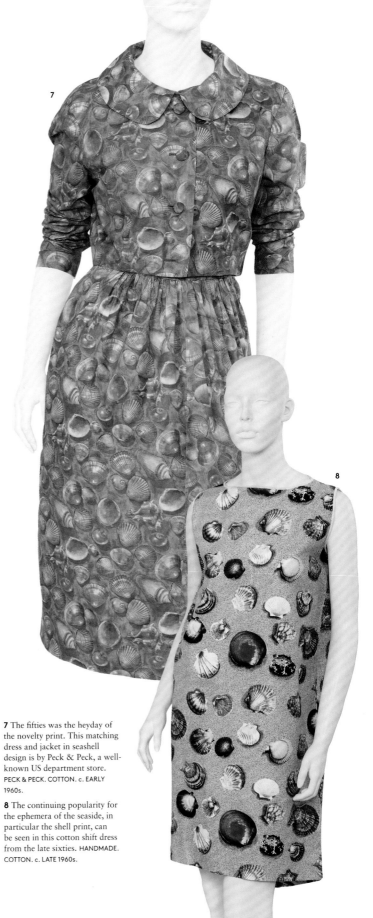

7 The fifties was the heyday of the novelty print. This matching dress and jacket in seashell design is by Peck & Peck, a well-known US department store. PECK & PECK. COTTON. c. EARLY 1960s.

8 The continuing popularity for the ephemera of the seaside, in particular the shell print, can be seen in this cotton shift dress from the late sixties. HANDMADE. COTTON. c. LATE 1960s.

1, 2 Lace is one of the most appealing of vintage fabrics. Whether in weighty cotton or silky gossamer, even modern interpretations retain a nostalgic quality. As it has been manipulated into the silhouettes of each decade, designers have consistently explored its diaphanous quality, exploiting the allure of décolletages, shoulders, backs and arms when glimpsed through its delicate pattern. **1** is a heavy silk, sleeveless dress from the twenties, while the Chantilly lace cocktail dress in **2** demurely covers arms and shoulders.

1 HANDMADE. SILK. c. 1950s.

2 SILK. c. 1950s.

3 Actress of screen and stage Patricia Morrison poses provocatively wearing a sleeveless lace dress mounted on a coloured underslip. She was never a major star, and her looks meant that she was often cast as the 'other woman', an image that would have been reinforced by wearing black lace, still considered to be a little risqué in 1950, the time of this portrait.

LACE FRAGILE FEMININITY

Lace, synonymous with a fashionable femininity throughout the 20th century and into the 21st, has a much disputed history. The origins of lace-making are thought to come from the elaborate twisting and plaiting of threads at the ends of unhemmed drapery and the practice of drawn threadwork creating open patterns in fabrics, held in place with embroidery. This traditional craft is steeped in tradition, with unique patterns found in villages, towns and convents across Europe. The use of lace emerged as a fashionable trend in the 16th century, the ornamental fabric a requisite of wealth and status, and male and female royalty and nobility equally wore lace collars, cuffs, ruffs and handkerchiefs.

The very nature of its intricate handmade manufacture ensured that all examples of lace were expensive and rarely produced in sizeable lengths before the industrialization of the textile industry in the 19th century. Both bobbin and needle laces (the terms encompassing an almost infinite variety of traditional techniques) were used to form decorative trimmings and trappings so valued that they were used as portable accessories of fashion for many centuries, moving from garment to garment. Such was their worth that they were bequeathed in wills and wedding trousseaus, their decorative beauty an indication of social standing as well as being obligatory wear in the French court of Napoleon.

With a historic craftsmanship and a unique, ethereal beauty, it is no surprise that lace has a strong connotation with vintage fashion. It is found in every decade of the 20th century in all its forms: Chantilly, Flanders, Brussels, Venetian and Duchesse. Even the humble cotton, nylon and printed versions are sought after for contemporary wear and have been reappropriated by contemporary fashion houses. Inspirational swatches from the 18th and 19th centuries fetch as much as a couture gown at auction but wearable dresses and blouses from the 20th century can still be bought in good condition at affordable prices. Fashion has always supported and propelled lace manufacture: Italian duo Dolce & Gabbana are known for their celebration of the traditional lace mantilla of the Sicilian woman. Several of their runway shows have included projected images of

'I CONSIDER LACE TO BE ONE OF THE PRETTIEST IMITATIONS EVER MADE OF THE FANTASY OF NATURE; LACE ALWAYS EVOKES FOR ME THOSE INCOMPARABLE DESIGNS WHICH THE BRANCHES AND LEAVES OF TREES EMBROIDER ACROSS THE SKY.'
COCO CHANEL, 1939

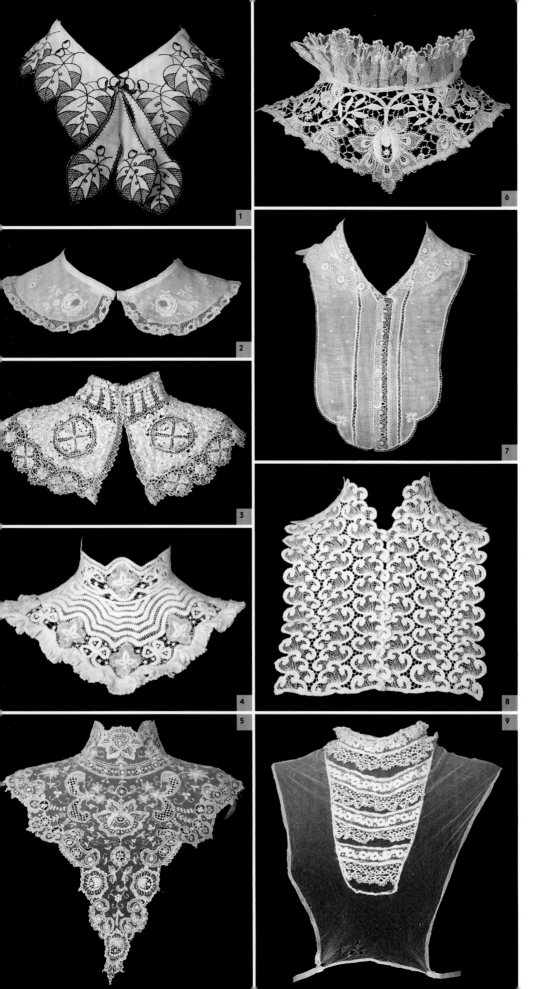

These lace collars, taken from different decades, also make a contemporary fashion statement. Worn as they were first intended, as removable collars on plain blouses and sweaters, they become the focal point of an outfit, as decorative as an expensive piece of jewelry. In previous centuries, lace collars and cuffs were purchased as luxury accessories and moved between different outfits – a practice that will still lift a plain jumper or enhance a dress.

1 COTTON BLACK-EDGED COLLAR. c. 1920s.

2 COTTON EMBROIDERED COLLAR WITH LACE EDGING. c. 1930s.

3 SILK MALTESE LACE SHOULDER CAPE AND COLLAR. c. 19TH CENTURY.

4 COTTON RIBBON OR LACE TAPE COLLAR. c. EARLY 20TH CENTURY.

5 HANDMADE. CHEMICAL LACE COLLAR IN COTTON. c. EARLY 19TH CENTURY.

6 CHEMICAL LACE AND TULLE COLLAR IN COTTON. c. EARLY 19TH CENTURY.

7 COTTON INFILL WITH NEEDLEPOINT CENTRAL FRONT AND COLLAR. c. 1920s.

8 MACHINE MADE LACE COLLAR IN COTTON WITH THE APPEARANCE OF HEAVY BATTENBURG STITCH. c. EARLY 20TH CENTURY.

9 Rows of cotton lace edging and trimming are applied to an infill of fine tulle netting to create a delicate underblouse. COTTON. c. EARLY 20TH CENTURY.

10 This delicate embroidered needlepoint day dress would have been worn over a fine white cotton lawn underdress for special occasions such as afternoon tea or a picnic. HANDMADE. COTTON. c. EARLY 1920s.

11 This blouse from the United States has elaborate embroidered lace insertions and pleats known as French seams. HANDMADE. COTTON. c. EARLY 20TH CENTURY.

traditional lace-makers at work, highlighting the historic craftsmanship that supplies the eminent names of fashion and couture.

With the British city of Nottingham at the forefront of 19th-century industrialized mass production, virtually every handmade lace had a machine copy that could be cut without unravelling. Lace became widely available, although still expensive, and it became entirely a prerogative of 20th-century feminine fashion. It is rare to find a dress of complete lace from the twenties – panelled inserts are more common, placed particularly between the chiffon handkerchief points of delicate day dresses – as this was the reserve of the wedding dress. Here lace was usually employed in tiers or rows of frills rather than as a whole panel. Lace from this time was fine and delicate, sometimes handmade for this occasion of a lifetime. Still an interchangeable fashion accessory, machine-made lace collars and cuffs could be purchased in department stores, while wide embroidered lace ribbons were used to adorned hats and lace infills preserved modesty on a V-shaped neckline on a dress. Many delicate laces can be found shaped into what appear to be sleeveless blouses with plain cotton or linen backs. These were worn underneath deep-fronted dresses or jackets and can be worn in the same way today. Occasionally dresses can be found that have deep lace 'medieval' sleeve inserts, or fitted lace undersleeves that emerged from a shorter sleeve and finished in a fingerless mitten. Metallic laces in gold and silver can often be found trimming eveningwear but these are often the most fragile.

While lace tints of the twenties were mostly natural or pastel, the sophistication of the thirties saw full-length lace dresses dyed in deep rich colours for evening and worn over sheeny satin underslips, sometimes of a contrasting colour and thereby displaying the lace patterning. Lace was still used as delicate insertions and trims during the thirties, decorating bias-cut silk and satin evening dresses. Nightdresses of the era can be just as beautiful, with combinations of lace also placed over satin underslips and, as the colours of underwear became more adventurous, the natural tones of lace ribbon inserts complemented the pastel lilacs, duck egg blues and jade green satins and silks.

While the expense of lace meant it was not viable during wartime, by the fifties it became a fabric explored to the full. Tailored into suits with matching jackets, embroidered and appliquéd for evening, it was considered by American

Vogue in 1953 to be 'less dependent on the whims of fashion than almost any other fabric ... in brilliant colours it becomes sophisticated, in pastels it becomes naïve'.

The sensuality of lace's transparency began to be explored in evening dresses that exposed shoulders through both real and printed laces down to a sweetheart neckline. In 1954 Nina Ricci, a designer known for her frilly

1

femininity and, as described by British *Vogue*, 'coquettish' use of lace, designed a collection of cocktail dresses with lace backs. Unlined and clear to the waist, they created, as the *New York Times* reported, a 'sensuous element of surprise'. The printed lace pattern became an inexpensive alternative to real lace dresses, often effectively flocked onto nylon, and the fine Chantilly lace evening dresses of Dior, Balmain, Givenchy, Norman Hartnell and others inspired a host of lace-covered evening dresses. Still the requisite party dress of every vintage lover's wardrobe, the style is epitomized by the dress Audrey Hepburn wore to receive her Oscar for *Roman Holiday*. (The dress was, in fact, a remake of a costume designed by Edith Head for the film: Hepburn simply had the shawl collar and sleeves removed.) Hepburn's lace creations, many of which were designed by her favourite designer Givenchy, have sold for huge sums, not least the striking black Chantilly lace ensemble from *How to Steal a Million* that fetched £60,000 at a UK auction. The costumes in the film epitomize the change from feminine fifties to chic sixties styling, with the unusual addition of lace eyemask and lace tights. Also highlighted is the profound effect Hepburn had on fashion, not just as a clotheshorse but as someone who so effectively manipulated her screen style that it had an international impact. 'She had an eye for design,' commented film director Stanley Donen on the Audrey effect.

Lace tights, lace printed boots, trousers, coats and little dresses perfectly suited the sixties trend for Lolita-like fashion. Lace construction took on a heavier feel, in line with the decade's embrace of traditional craft techniques such as crochet and macramé. Heavy cotton 16th-century-style lace collars sat on velvet and cord, and ruffles and jabots decorated the shirt fronts of both men and women, a historically referenced styling that continued into the early seventies. While the eighties manipulation of fine stretch lace underpinned the era's body-conscious styling, with electric-coloured bodies that have inspired high-street fashion in recent years, the decade does not offer the revered delicate gossamers of mid-century. Witnessing the scramble for a fifties ballerina length evening dress of charcoal Chantilly, or a thirties oyster silk nightdress with organic lace ribbon inserts, reinforces the phenomenon of vintage fashion and the delicate beauty of antique lace, seldom recreated with such finesse by any but the elite fashion houses.

1 Heavy machine made Brussels lace has been placed over a blush lining in this early sixties cocktail dress. HANDMADE. COTTON. c. EARLY 1960s.

2 Audrey Hepburn famously adapted her lace dress for the film *Roman Holiday* to wear to collect the Oscar she won for the film. The film's costume designer Edith Head found Hepburn's sylph-like frame difficult to dress, being more accustomed to the voluptuous figures of her other screen clients, and tried to cover her up with collars, sleeves and frills.

3 This boned cocktail dress is made from unbleached lace forming a delicate butterfly pattern offset by pink silk braiding. COTTON. c. 1960s.

4 While lace can have a nostalgic feel, the metallic laces of the sixties and early seventies also reflect the era's obsession with futuristic Space Age design. By marrying the two influences, sixties designers created a new style for both evening and day wear. HANDMADE. SYNTHETIC. c. LATE 1960s.

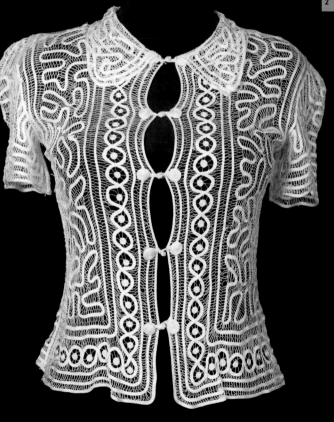

1 The delicate crewelwork on this sheer blouse creates a lace-like pattern and would have been worn over a camisole of the same colour. HANDMADE. SILK. c. EARLY 20TH CENTURY.

2 This silk ribbon blouse has been influenced by Asian style, with Chinese knotted 'plate' buttons. The play of pattern on pattern looks particularly effective with this style of lace work. HANDMADE. COTTON. c. 1920s.

3 The heavy machine laces used for mini dresses of the sixties took inspiration from 19th- and early 20th-century design. Braver followers of fashion often wore them without petticoats, deliberately exposing their underwear. LADYBIRD. COTTON. c. 1960s.

4–9 Feminine blouses from all decades, especially the forties and fifties, made entirely of lace or with lace insertions can be found with relative ease today. While there have been many modern reproductions, the originals can be bought fairly inexpensively.

4 COTTON. c. 1950s.

5 COTTON. c. 1940s.

6 COTTON. c. 1960s.

7 COTTON. c. 1930s.

8 COTTON. c. 1940s.

9 RAYON. c. 1940s.

1

2

3

1 Early 20th-century summer garments were favoured by alternative fashionistas in the seventies. Combined with hard-edged fabrics, such as the flannel of a striped boating jacket, denim or the leather of a pair of brogues, they created a style that was alternative but, unlike the hippy movement, not anti-fashion. HANDMADE. COTTON LAWN. c. 1900s.

2 Jacqmar was a British company primarily known today for their scarves. However, they also produced both garment and fabric ranges, some of which were sold wholesale to other garment manufacturers. This advertisement is for a lace fabric made from wool lace, a dense lace that is rarely heard of today, although still available.

3 The use of crochet and knitted lace work in fashion has seen several revivals. While this knitted Arrowhead lace stitch dress in rayon thread dates to the late twenties, the decade that really exploited this kind of open stitch was the sixties. Crochet, macramé and other transparent hand-knits were the start of a craft revival sympathetic to the naturalistic ethos of hippy fashion and continuing well into the seventies. HANDMADE. RAYON. c. LATE 1920s.

4 Machine lace work creates a decorative décolletage neckline for this cocktail dress. SILK. c. 1960s.

5 The full-circle collar of lace tatting on this Edwardian wool coat creates a romantic style. HANDMADE. WOOL. c. 1900s.

6 A summer linen dress with floral cutwork and mother of pearl buttons is an easy piece for contemporary wear. LINEN. c. 1940s.

1 The natural edge of the heavy Guipure lace of this sixties cocktail dress has been used to form a decorative hem and matching bolero jacket. COTTON. c. LATE 1960s.

2, 3 By the sixties, designers began to treat lace fabric with less formality and reverence. Cotton lace dresses from the era can be found dyed in vibrant colours such as turquoise, orange and even canary yellow. The Italian shirtdress (**2**) with covered buttons is from the later part of the decade, while the prom-style dress (**3**) is an earlier design that allows the silk lining to show through the pattern of the lace to create an eveningwear look.

2 COTTON. c. LATE 1960s.

3 HANDMADE. COTTON. c. EARLY 1960s.

4 A 1967 trouser suit by Jules-François Crahay for Lanvin illustrates a sixties modernist design approach to a fabric that had previously usually been given a traditional treatment. Suddenly lace fabrics reflected the forward look of the decade.

5 This asymmetrical evening dress has lace daisy pattern with a sequin at the centre of every flower set over a pale pink silk lining. The dress has the finish of a high-end designer but has lost its original label. COTTON AND SILK. c. 1960s.

1 The three-dimensional quality of this lace dress with appliquéd lace flowers demonstrates the same technique and lace of an extravagant cocktail dress by London couturier Michael Sherard, exhibited in the Victoria and Albert Museum's exhibition *The Golden Age of Couture* in 2007. Sherard, originally a painter, was famed for the formal lace wear displayed in his Connaught Street atelier. SWISS LACE. c. 1957.

2 The shocking pink lining of this heavy cotton lace dress helps to define the floral pattern and creates a sophisticated style. HANDMADE. COTTON. c. 1960s.

3 Chantilly lace has been used extensively for fashionable wear since its conception in 17th-century France. Mittens, shawls, fichus and even parasols have all been made from this fine, traditionally black lace. HANDMADE. SILK. c. 1940s.

4 The popularity for new synthetics such as nylon after the Second World War meant every purse could afford the distinctive patterning of lace. Nylon, originally introduced as a replacement for silk during the war, had become a refined fabric and could be dyed and printed with a variety of effects. This exciting new fabric held its shape and could be washed frequently and left to dry. HANDMADE. FLOCKED NYLON. c. 1950s.

SEEING SPOTS
POLKAMANIA

'I DON'T THINK THERE IS EVER A WRONG TIME FOR THE POLKA DOT.' MARC JACOBS

Whether it is a fine and delicate twenties spot, a sixties 'Itsy Bitsy Teeny Weeny' dot, or a large and bold eighties statement spot, the simple polka dot is the pattern that arguably is most strongly associated with vintage style.

Spots originated as decorative features in delicate woven muslins and lace, but it wasn't until around 1850 that printing machines could cope with the regularity of a simple printed spot. At the same time, a popular new dance believed to have derived from Czechoslovakian folk culture was sweeping through the ballrooms of Europe, heading from Prague and Venice to Paris and London, and finally on to the United States. This craze for the 'polka' was fully capitalized on by businessmen. 'Polkamania' not only gave its name to the new printed spot pattern but also to the polka jacket, the polka hat (neither were spotted), polka puddings and polka sauce.

By the twenties, a simple and usually small-scale polka dot decorated the silks and fine cottons of pastel-coloured day dresses, blouses and bows. A gently playful print that suited the youthful fashions of the Jazz Age, the polka dot was perfect for the many bows and accessories that were becoming an integral part of a fashionable wardrobe. Walt Disney films introduced Minnie Mouse as a love interest for its starring character, Mickey, in 1928. Minnie was based on the flapper girl of the twenties and wore a polka dot skirt with oversized shoes and a hat that was later redesigned to be a playful polka dot hair bow. Meanwhile, the appearance of Miss America 1926, Norma Smallwood, in a spotted knitted swimsuit marked the start of a trend for polka dot swimwear set to continue for many decades.

While the polka dot print is usually associated with this irreverent, youthful quality, in the thirties spotted prints were created in stark colour combinations such as brown, green or navy and white, or in soft pastel combinations on

Eisenberg Originals

OLKA DOT

1 A small printed white spot (pin dot) on black was a favourite for evening dresses in the forties. SILK SATIN. c. 1940s.

2 This American advertisement for Eisenberg Originals shows not only the sophistication that could be obtained with this playful motif but also the varying effects that could be achieved by simply enlarging the size or compacting the print.

3 A pin dot print, offset by inverted coral pleats, has been used for this forties bolero jacket and dress combination from the United States. The heart-shaped décolletage is a clue to its age. HANDMADE. CREPE. c. 1940s.

4 By the fifties and sixties the polka dot was used at a larger scale, in keeping with the playful mood of the fifties and the irreverence of the sixties. SATINIZED COTTON. c. EARLY 1960s.

flowing chiffon to match the sophisticated glamour of the decade. For eveningwear, it was not unusual to see black satin with dainty printed or embroidered white spots and, by the late forties, polka dot prints were used in couture, in particular by the houses of Jacques Fath and Christian Dior. Dior presented several polka dots in his renowned 'New Look' collection of 1947, the fabric used being an Ascher Studio design. Ascher Studio, a textile company that inspired and supplied many of the leading names of fashion, was renowned for its seemingly infinite variety of spot prints designed by Lida Ascher, the wife of the manufacturer. Her often irregular and freehand designs were produced in numerous colourways and proved to be timeless classics.

By the fifties, as with many other post-war patterns, the polka dot became fun and frivolous again, larger in size and bolder in colour. This era was the heyday of the polka dot, always regular in placement but diverse in scale. The pattern was a favourite of many eminent names in fashion. Christian Dior, the couturier followed by every fifties fashion editor, described the benefits of using the polka dot in his designs: 'According to their colour ... they can be versatile... Black and white for elegance; soft pinks and blues for prettiness; emerald, scarlet and yellow for gaiety; beige and grey for dignity.'

The eye-catching polka dot worked well on camera and many celebrities of the era were pictured sporting polka dot fashion. American comedienne Lucille Ball's on-screen wardrobe was rarely without a spotted print, maximizing the playful associations of the pattern. The dot worked for glamorous occasions, too. Marilyn Monroe and Jane Russell both wore halterneck spotted dresses to the 1953 première of *Gentlemen Prefer Blondes*. Almost sixty years later, Natalie Portman wore a 1954 Christian Dior red silk organza evening dress, printed with black polka dots, to the 2012 Oscars.

A radical approach to art and fashion typified the sixties. Both the Op Art and Pop Art movements had an enormous influence on boutique culture fashion, particularly the comic strip paintings of Roy Lichtenstein, who reproduced the 'Ben Day' dots (from the printing process named after illustrator and printer Benjamin Day) of comic books in his work. The monochromatic spots used in the paintings of Bridget Riley also translated easily into avant-garde sixties fashion. Design looked to the future, and the head-to-toe

elegance of earlier fashion was rejected in favour of a streamlined youthful style. The Space Age styles of André Courrèges and Pierre Cardin used unconventional materials such as plastics, metallics and paper, and required a different style of spot to the feminine forties and fifties polka dot. In this decade, polka dots appeared in a multitude of bright colours and were reproduced in a huge variety of sizes. They were used in psychedelic patterns to suggest the hallucinogenic effects of drug taking, or as diminutive dots for the doll-like pinafores and shift dresses filling the rails in the boutiques of London's Carnaby Street and King's Road. A seemingly effortless modernism dominated early sixties fashion and the simplistic spot suited the mood. Contrasting bold round buttons continued the theme, a complement to the patterns created from a mix of spots and squares or spots and stripes. Used in abundance by notable designers Mary Quant and Rudi Gernreich, the spot became a signature of cutting-edge fashion. Accessories continued the circular theme: earrings were round, as were sunglasses and handbags, and even tights were covered in spots!

1 Marilyn Monroe poses in a risqué two-piece polka dot swimsuit in 1951. The fashion for polka dot swimwear inspired the song *Itsy Bitsy Teeny Weeny Yellow Polka Dot Bikini*. It was released in 1960, by which time the two-piece swimsuit was commonly known by the name 'bikini'.

2 This late forties dress uses an unusually bold polka dot for the time. The central-fastening covered buttons continue the multi-toned lilac print. MOYGASHEL. LINEN. c. LATE 1940s.

3 The pattern of this dress, a fine etching over a variated lilac spot, is in tune with the painterly quality of many early fifties textile designs. This quality was inspired by the work of several notable artists who were invited to design for textiles after the Second World War. COTTON. c. EARLY 1950s.

4 A classic polka dot by the quintessential British company Horrockses, who had cotton mills for many years before they made a name for themselves for impeccably made cotton dresses. HORROCKSES FASHIONS. COTTON. c. 1950s.

1 Styles of the seventies used the polka dot far less than in the previous decades when it had suited the Op Art, graphic trends. Here the subdued metallic spot defines the plunging neckline of a disco all-in-one from the cusp of the sixties/seventies. LUREX. c. EARLY 1970s.

2 This sixties day dress, with inverted kick-pleats and matching bow in a shaded spot print, demonstrates the influence on fashion of Pop Art and work by painters such as Roy Lichtenstein who often imitated the printing process, echoing 'Ben Day' dots (the graphic dots seen when comic strip illustrations are blown up) in his work. POLYESTER. c. 1960s.

While, courtesy of Norman Hartnell, the female officers of the 1969 London Metropolitan police force wore white blouses printed with a black polka dot, the motif fell from grace during the back-to-nature fashions of the early seventies. An occasional earthy brown or purple spot may be found among the maxi dresses of the hippy culture, but the polka dot was too simplistic and bold to sit comfortably within the intricate textile designs of the era when high fashion instead referenced the romantic and the historical.

The eighties meant the return of bold statement trends and a revival of fifties style saw the polka dot once again at the forefront of fashion. Mid-eighties style demanded attention and polka dot prints covered everything from suits and dresses to shoes and hats in bold contrasting colours. Between the distinct tartans, checks and stripes of the era, the polka dot covered the designs of both couture and the high street, revered in the 1985 'Mini-Crini' collection of Vivienne Westwood and the designs of French fashion house Emanuel Ungaro.

As the mood of fashion moved towards the understated chic of nineties styling, the flexibility of the spotted print was demonstrated in the dress and accompanying hat worn by Julia Roberts in the 1990 film *Pretty Woman*, the outfit selected by her character to demonstrate her change from prostitute to sophisticated love interest. The longevity of the simple spot design relies upon nothing more than dexterously changing colour and scale to ensure its success. While the date of a spot can be recognized in an instant, it is a style that does not date.

3 The spot has been a feature of woven fabric and embroidery for centuries, but it was not used as a screenprint until around the 1850s when printing processes improved and enabled the success of such a regular pattern, which would have previously highlighted any flaws in the repeat. SILK. c. 1920s.

4 Natalie Portman made fashion headlines when she wore a polka dot silk chiffon evening dress from Christian Dior's spring 1954 collection to the 2012 Oscars. The dress had an inbuilt waist-corset, as was common in Dior's designs from the early fifties.

5 Although the eighties revived the fifties silhouette, prints of the decade were seldom re-employed, with the exception of the polka dot. Here the embroidered spot pattern is in the neon colours fashionable in the eighties. RADLEY. POLYESTER NET. c. 1980s.

1 The increasingly experimental style of forties fashions can be seen in the simple spot combined with a different type of print on this dress. MERWYN. COTTON. c. 1940s.

2 These illustrations for thirties dressmaking patterns suggest using different colourways with a polka dot print for spring fashions.

3 This loosely spotted underblouse would have been worn beneath a plain overblouse or jacket to create a small area of decoration. HANDMADE. SILK. c. 1920s.

4 Combined with sharp linear and geometric patterns, the polka dot of the sixties looked new and contemporary. SUSAN SMALL. POLYESTER. c. 1960s.

5, 6 Two spotted prints highlight how colour and design can convey different moods. The variated small pink spots on the navy blue ground of the cocktail dress (**5**) suggest a grown-up glamour; enlarging the spot against a white ground gives the print a freshness for daywear.

5 SILK. c. 1960s.

6 SYNTHETIC. c. 1960s.

7 Although forward-thinking in many ways, British boutique fashion of the sixties was littered with historical references. Lace collars and cuffs, harking back to 16th-century fashions, became a trend of the decade. POLLY PECK. SILK. c. 1960s.

4

5

6

7

1 Alice Edwards is a little-known label of British origin, but the dresses, mainly cocktail or sophisticated daywear, are always expertly constructed from exquisite fabrics. This dress, as with many designs from the fifties, displays the influence of continental chic, also illustrated in the two labels used by the company, 'Alice Edwards "Italians"' and 'Alice Edwards goes places…' ALICE EDWARDS ITALIANS. SILK. c. LATE 1950s/EARLY 1960s.

2 The sixties explored the effects of spotted prints like no other decade, adapting the style of the pattern to suit the modernist trend. FIONA. MOSS CREPE. c. 1960s.

3 Bright contrasting spots were one of the key prints of the mid-eighties. Seen everywhere from the catwalk to the high street, the large-scale polka dot did not seem out of place on an oversized fashion silhouette. CHELSEA COBBLER. POLYESTER. c. 1980s.

4 The polka dot of the forties was diminutive and rarely ostentatious, even when printed in contrasting colours, as on this dress. The attributes of forties styling that inspired designers of the seventies, such as Ossie Clark, are evident in this dress's moss crepe, fitted waist and shoulder pads. It could easily be mistaken for a dress from the seventies, but the heavy texture of the crepe and the oversized chunky side-zip are evidence of its true age. MOSS CREPE. c. 1940s.

5 This dress is from the United States and uses a bolder spot print than would be used in Europe at that time. Though retaining a delicate femininity, American vintage items can be recognized by their stronger colouring and sharply defined details. CHIFFON CREPE. c. 1940s.

6 The vibrant colour combination of red with embroidered white spots suggests the handmade skirt is probably an American design. COTTON. c. 1940s. WORN WITH RAYON BLOUSE. c. 1940s.

1 Brightly coloured polka dots and humorous conversationals were representative of the jubilant post-war mood. COTTON. c. EARLY 1950s.

2 While the polka dot is an unusual motif for Ossie Clark, the peephole shoulder detail is a common decoration of late sixties and early seventies design. OSSIE CLARK. MOSS CREPE. c. LATE 1960s.

3 This wrapover blouse by Hardy Amies uses the 'Blarney' fabric by Gillian Farr, designed in 1960 for Liberty and based on the discontinued threepence coin. HARDY AMIES. SILK. c. 1964.

4 Hollywood actress Eleanor Parker poses in a polka dot halterneck for a 1954 studio portrait.

5 The diminutive spot can portray a childlike innocence and was a frequent print of the sixties trend for Lolita-style fashion with its shift dresses, shorts and pinafores. COTTON. c. 1960s.

6 The spot appeared in every scale and style in the sixties and was used equally for both daywear and eveningwear. ROBERT DORLAND. SILK CHIFFON. c. 1960s.

7 The polka dot print is a lighthearted motif in any era. Seen here in wavy stripes on a forties dress, the playful design is complemented by a diminutive sailor collar and puff sleeves, distinguishing characteristics of the period. COTTON. c. LATE 1930s/ EARLY 1940s.

4

5

6

7

GLOBAL INSPIRATIONS
INTERNATIONAL HERITAGE

'EVERY TIME SCHIAPARELLI BUYS A RAILWAY TICKET THERE ARE FRUITFUL CONSEQUENCES FOR THIS WORLD OF OURS.' *VOGUE*, 1936

1   2

1 This late thirties evening dress is embellished with embroidery and beadwork in a paisley formation, a traditional motif of both Iran and India. HANDMADE. CREPE. c. 1930s.

2 In this photograph from the thirties, Hungarian women are shown posing in traditional dress. The brightly coloured mix of embroidery and print has inspired designers in every decade, particularly the seventies.

3 The hibiscus was the flower most used in the tropical prints of the seventies. Kaftans and other loose robes were imported from India and Morocco and other African cultures, worn as part of the hippy style that, in turn, influenced mainstream fashion. POLYESTER. c. 1970s.

3

Traditional clothing drawn from around the world has inspired Western fashion for centuries. Dense embroideries, lavish metallic threads, opulent colour combinations and cultural motifs have been reworked in every fashion era, adapted for Western tastes but used to evoke ancient cultures. Throughout fashion history, cultural appropriation has mixed Russian capes with Persian jackets, Indian saris, Hungarian peasant blouses and other 'folk' garments to provide the templates for catwalk themes.

The start of the 20th century saw a considerable demand for all things inspired by the East. The move away from the tailored silhouette in pastel colouring towards the relaxed silhouette of the Jazz Age saw a bohemian mode adopting the rich colour palettes and elaborate embroideries of South Asian textiles, Kashmiri shawls and Japanese kimonos. The department store Liberty & Co., formally named East India House, focused on imports, selling a wealth of textiles from Japan, China, Indonesia and Persia. Under the helm of Arthur Lasenby Liberty, the store was noted for offering delicate Japanese printed fabrics subsequently purchased by dressmakers alongside less expensive copies of the intricate Asian embroideries that Liberty also stocked, produced by northern Britain's textile mills. Although partly responsible for popularizing the paisley motif, Liberty did not focus on commercial fashion in the early decades; a precursor of the Aesthetic movement, the store provided artistic 'costume' (the name they gave to ladies' clothing) for women who did not slavishly follow fashion. It wasn't until the twenties that they hired the renowned 'King of Fashion' and initiator of oriental-inspired designs, couturier Paul Poiret, to give a new dimension to their 'costume department'.

As with all trends, it is timing, collaboration and inspiration that are key to bringing about an international phenomenon. The Ballets Russes, the Russian ballet company directed by Sergei Diaghilev, created a sensational impact thanks to the opulent oriental sets and costumes designed by Russian artist Léon Bakst, with further contributions from other notable international names of art and fashion, Picasso, Matisse, Derain, Braque, Miró and Coco Chanel. An emphasis was given to the aesthetic of the costumes that varied from simple Russian folk dress to the exotic Arabian Nights fantasy of the hugely influential ballet, *Scheherazade*. A new obsession for all things Eastern had arrived. Poiret's interpretations of Arabian harem trousers, kaftans and Japanese kimonos echoed Bakst's costumes (although Poiret vehemently denied taking any inspiration from the Ballets Russes). The daytime lounge dressing of the decadent rich embraced the wearing of oriental silk pyjamas and loose kimonos, richly embroidered or even hand-painted with designs evoking the mystic Orient.

The widely publicized discovery of Tutankhamen's tomb in 1922 expanded the craze to include Egyptian influences and, such was the demand, representatives from Western textile companies were sent to gather inspiration from the tomb's excavation sites. The resulting textile designs inspired by Egyptian hieroglyphics were printed in scarab colours of jade green, gold and lapis lazuli, and were particularly favoured by women in the United States. Among the most collected and worn today are the Assuit shawls made from woven Egyptian cotton and adorned with hundreds of hand-appliquéd metal pieces to form intricate, geometric patterns. These large shawls can be found transformed into simple shift dresses and loose unstructured evening jackets of the time, fetching high prices today if they are in good condition. Newspapers and periodicals christened the craze 'Egyptomania' or 'Tutmania' and ran adverts for 'Luxora' frocks, Egyptian embroidered squirrel fur coats and jewelry inspired by the treasures of the tomb. Egyptomania swept through the United States and became so over-commercialized that, sadly, it was eventually considered to be vulgar and common. It was thought that the States were more receptive to the craze, as Europeans were too embroiled in the First World War.

The trend for all things opulent continued as Hollywood's silver screen reflected the fashions in the films of Cecil B. DeMille, *The Ten Commandments* (1923) and later *Cleopatra* (1934). Throughout the twenties and thirties the vogue for lavish 'dressing-up' parties fuelled demand for extravagant costumes suitable for 'masked parties, Savage parties, Victorian parties, Greek parties, Wild West parties, Russian parties, Circus parties, parties where one had to dress as somebody else,' as observed by Evelyn Waugh in his thirties novel, *Vile Bodies*.

The fascination with the seemingly exotic styles of distant continents came to a halt with the onset of the Second World War. However, easy continental travel and a desire for post-war exploration was reflected in forties fashion, as consumers observed the traditional costumes of easily reachable travel destinations first hand. The villages of the Tyrol revealed embroidered blouses, and the

1 Thirties fashion illustrations display oriental floral prints as well as the influence of the kimono on garment construction.

2 This twenties illustration, *Les Chinoiseries à la Mode*, depicts the eye-catching fashion for all things oriental. Chinese- and Japanese-style dragons were one of the most common motifs.

3 A twenties advertisement for French gloves displays the Egyptian influence particularly evident in embroideries and embellishments after the discovery of Tutankhamen's tomb.

4, 5, 6 In the fifties and sixties, Europe and North America delighted in the sophisticated beauty of oriental patterns, fabrics, furniture and *objets d'art*. Elaborate brocades were ideal for the newly important cocktail dress. A shorter version of the evening dresses of the forties, the cocktail dress was worn for early evening functions and home entertainment.

4 HANDMADE. BEADED SILK. c. 1960s.

5 SILK. c. 1960s.

6 SILK JACQUARD. c. 1950s.

1, 2, 3 The cheongsam dress originated in twenties Shanghai, a development of a traditional style that was no longer practical for contemporary Chinese women. The style became hugely popular in the thirties and forties in North America for evening and cocktail wear. The cheongsam seen here from the forties features a bold hand-embroidered golden dragon and would have been worn to an evening function, while the cotton sixties version by Miss Mod (**2**) would not have been out of place in the office.

1 HANDMADE. SILK EMBROIDERED. c. 1940s.

2 MISS MOD. COTTON. c. 1960s.

4 There was a seemingly short-lived trend for using Chinese calligraphy as a print in the late fifties. The design is used boldly here on red silk satin, giving the piece a modernity ahead of its tulip-shaped skirt. RICHARD GROSSMAN. SILK. c. LATE 1950s.

5 This black polyester jersey dress reflects the sixties/seventies love of paisley print. Paisley patterns, originating in Persia and India, were fully explored during this period – embroidered, magnified, used singularly and in repeat. The paisley as shown here reflects not only the influence of global travel, but also the impact of hallucinogenic drugs on design at the time. POLYESTER. c. 1960s.

traditional family stitchwork became so popular that the designs started to be published as patterns in the weekly magazines. Knitwear, as seen on Austrian ski slopes, was taken home for winter wear and embroidered dirndl wool skirts were adopted for everyday fashion.

The woman of the forties and fifties maintained her traditional role within the home and family, but now she was also managing it alongside work. Fashion needed to be practical. Cocktail dresses and hostess attire were essential for the new vogue of entertaining at home. Prêt-à-porter cocktail dresses were ideally suited to the mass-produced, oriental-influenced brocades that glistened with an understated glamour. The cheongsam began to be worn in the forties but became a widespread fashion in the fifties and sixties when the figure-skimming style became an acceptable mode of sophistication. What began as the *qipao* in twenties Shanghai remains unchanged in the Western world today, still featuring a high mandarin collar, lavishly printed or embroidered imagery and frogged fastenings.

Also at this time, there was a trend for 'tiki', due to the impact of increased travel to Hawaii. Tina Leser, a trained artist who settled in Honolulu, was particularly influential in the promotion of Hawaiian wear. She opened her first shop in 1935 selling sportswear and eveningwear made from Hawaiian and imported Filipino cloth, many featuring prints she had designed herself to order. Saks of New York put in an order for 500 garments in 1940. An avid traveller, Leser created designs not only inspired by traditional Hawaiian wear but also by Guatemalan weavings, Indian Punjab trousers and silk Chinese pyjamas. Alfred Shaheen, son of a Hawaiian clothing manufacturer, is also associated with promoting the island's traditional textiles for fashionable wear. Labels bear either his name or the 'Surf 'n Sand Handprints' name of his company. At his most prolific during the fifties, both he and Leser were responsible for the popularity of the Aloha prints of tropical fauna and florals and the particularly popular hummingbird that were taken home on cotton sarongs, halternecks and the cheongsam for fashionable summer wear.

Tropical prints saw a resurgence during the seventies and eighties, when dense prints inspired by patterns from South America and Indonesia were offset with khaki and beige safari styles. Kenzo Takada, a designer also greatly influenced by his extensive travels, opened his first boutique, Jungle Jap, in 1970. Laura Ashley was also known for its

tropical prints during this era. But it is the eastern influence on late sixties fashion that is probably the most documented of all globally influenced trends. It was an era that celebrated inspiration drawn from outside the Western world; a time when designers reinterpreted traditional embroideries and printed motifs to capture the bohemian mood of fashion. The paisley, the kaftans, beadwork and fringing,

2

1

1 A lamé trouser suit evokes Eastern influences with its exotic colour mix of purple and gold. The hippy movement that began as a socio-political reaction to a bourgeoisie establishment was anti-fashion. However, their adopted dress had such widespread appeal that it became commercialized and was worn in all fashion capitals and by all ages and was no longer a political statement of the 'flower people'. HANDMADE. SILK LAMÉ. c. LATE 1960s.

2 This 1970 fashion editorial shows a model reclining in a mini dress by Hanae Mori, the first Japanese designer to be invited to join the revered circle of haute couture. The dress is accessorized with a rope belt by Yves Saint Laurent.

the patterns of Native Americans and Aztecs, all contributed to a cultural revolution. Kaftans first appeared in Persia in around 600 BC as robes worn by ambassadors and notables, embellished with embroidery and jewels. Seen by the influential American *Vogue* editor Diana Vreeland on a trip to Morocco, the kaftan was promoted as a fashionable garment to be worn by both sexes during the sixties. It was popularized by stars such as the Beatles and interpreted by Yves Saint Laurent, Pucci, Marc Bohan at Christian Dior, Halston, Zandra Rhodes and many others.

At the height of bohemian hippy fashion, the Italian-born, United States-based designer Giorgio di Sant' Angelo worked in suede and leather, incorporating the tie-dye techniques, fringing and feathers associated with Native Americans. The model Veruschka was his muse, and inspiration also came from Greek goddesses, Amazonian queens, and tribal and Aztec patterns. His early work was a reaction to the structured, futuristic shapes of the sixties and is much sought after and worn today: the rust suede two-piece worn by Nicole Kidman to the 1999 première of *Eyes Wide Shut* is an understated example.

Contemporary references to 'ethnically inspired' pattern and design risk losing the individual cultures that have influenced a century of Western fashion, whether African batiks or the Chinle geometrics of the Navajo Indian. Each decade has adapted global traditions in ways to match the fashion of their time, creating trends that display both heritage and the contemporary: original pieces offering a rich array of patterns and details.

3, 4 The end of the fifties saw
an increase in affordable foreign
travel. Women in the United
States, in particular, were able
to experience the glamour of
nearby Hawaii. The vibrant
Aloha prints showing tropical
flowers, exotic fruit, birds and
feathers were brought home
as holiday souvenirs and the
sarongs and cool cotton dresses
were enjoyed as fashionable
summer wear, as well as cocktail
and evening wear. COTTON.
c. 1960s.

5 Polyester was first patented
in 1941 and slowly developed
through the fifties and sixties to
become a fabric celebrated for its
durability and ability to reflect
the vibrant colours of printing
dyes. Eastern influences inspired
both silhouettes and decorative
details during the late sixties and
early seventies, and free-flowing
designs blurred the differences
between day and evening wear:
outfits like this could be worn
anywhere, anytime. POLYESTER.
c. LATE 1960s.

1 Twiggy models the outfit especially designed for her by Bill Gibb to wear to the première of her first major film, Ken Russell's 1971 *The Boy Friend*. The design displays the influence of traditional European dress.

2 Eastern fashions were a huge influence on hippy fashion and more prevalent in the late sixties to early seventies era than in any other decade. A contrasting mix of prints and fabrics added to the opulent overtones. EMANUELLE. VELVET AND COTTON. c. 1970s.

3 This heavily embroidered jacket is traditionally worn by the nomadic Banjara cattle herders of Pakistan and Afghanistan. These jackets have been made the same way for hundreds of years, always using 4½ metres (14 ft 9 in.) of cotton and hand-embroidered. They have also been sold in London's Portobello Market for many years, and are particularly associated with the 'boho' trend at its height in 2004 when they were worn by celebrities such as Anna Friel and Sienna Miller. Their intricate stitchwork and pleated shapes have inspired many fashion brands, notably Gap, Abercrombie & Fitch and Tracey Boyd. COTTON. 19TH CENTURY ONWARDS.

4 Elizabeth Taylor's wardrobe, drawn from several decades, was sold by Christie's New York auction house in 2011. The garments included a stunning collection of kaftans by Thea Porter, of whom Taylor was a loyal customer.

5 The late sixties fascination with India and its culture was fuelled by the hugely publicized visit by the Beatles to the Maharishi in 1968. The anti-establishment style of the group helped promote the use of original fabrics, then imported and made up for high street fashion. British retailers Dollyrockers teamed up with Dolcis shoes for a combined publicity campaign fronted by Patti Boyd, then-wife of George Harrison. DOLLYROCKERS. COTTON. c. LATE 1960s.

6 Of the many ethnically inspired patterns fashionable during the seventies, the woven designs of Navajo Indians have been reinterpreted for contemporary fashions. The woven diamond and cross-stitch patterns created for the famous blankets translate easily to printed and knitted fashion fabrics. Despite criticism that fashion has plundered a traditional craft, Navajo Indian-inspired designs are as popular today as they were in the seventies. POLYESTER. c. 1970s.

1 Paisley was a very popular print of the late sixties, again influenced by the Beatles' 1968 trip to India. Although the motif has many historical influences, its strong association with India meant it was adopted by wearers of hippy fashion, worn with accessories such as love beads and delicate gold filigree jewelry. SYNTHETIC. c. 1960s.

2 The Afghan coat is traditionally made of sheep or goat skin, turned inside out so that the fur appears on the inside, and embroidered in chain stitch. They were at their height of popularity in Western markets in the sixties. It has been claimed the owners of the famous boutique Granny Takes a Trip on London's King's Road first imported them into the UK, but they were popularized when the Beatles were seen in them after purchasing them from the shop. These coats have to be maintained very carefully as the tanned leather has a tendency to disintegrate. GOATSKIN. c. 1960s.

3 The seventies in the United States saw a revival of the craft of marbling, a practice thought to have started in the Middle East in the 15th century. Although it suited the bohemian silhouette, designers of youth fashion also adopted the look. HANDMADE. POLYESTER. c. 1970s.

4 Rows of Moorish-style houses create the printed design on this cotton dress by designer John Bates for his label Jean Varon. The print was not exclusive to the label, being used by other fashion houses in other colourways, all using a Mediterranean colour palette.
JEAN VARON. COTTON. c. 1970s.
WORN WITH GOLD LEATHER
BUTTERFLY BELT. c. 1980s.

5 Traditional European embroidered garments have been adopted for fashionable wear since the twenties. By the seventies, embroideries from earlier decades were being worn as vintage fashion as well as being an influence on design in the period. As a result, it is often hard to date a garment. The clue to this Hungarian gold silk dress being a seventies interpretation is that traditional designs were rarely embroidered in one colour.
SILK. c. 1970s.

1 This day jacket uses traditional Western satin-stitch embroidery and rickrack braid edging. Villages and communities developed their own floral motifs and colorations to appeal to holidaymakers enjoying the freedom of newly affordable travel. HANDMADE. WOOL. c. 1930s.

2, 3 Many capes of the sixties had military details, such as epaulettes and metal buttons, inspired by the uniforms worn by the police force. Others, such as the styles worn by the flower children of San Francisco, were painstakingly embroidered in folk-influenced styles. This style of embroidery came to be used on everything from handbags to leather belts and boots. HANDMADE. WOOL. c. 1960s.

4 This hand-knitted cardigan has been embroidered with French knots and slipstitch to make up the German or Swiss edelweiss flower. As holidaymakers admired the handiwork of traditional crafts, women's magazines began to offer patterns and transfers imitating the style. It is often difficult to tell if the design is original or made closer to home. HANDMADE. WOOL. c. 1930s.

5 This front cover of a sixties craft magazine advertises a free rose embroidery transfer that displays an oriental influence.

6 Traditional dresses of Hungarian and Czech origin are, like the blouses, handmade with smocking and embroidery work that is a true labour of love. Though each design is beautiful, the stitches are traditional to communities that use them in every decade, making it sometimes difficult to determine the correct age of a piece. Irregularity of stitch and fine early cottons are indications of early samples. HANDMADE. COTTON. c. 1920s/1930s.

7 Vintage Carven pieces are perfect for petite females. Carmen de Tommaso was only five foot one and, although trained in interior design, established her couture house because she struggled to find clothes that fit. An avid traveller, Madame Carven (as she renamed herself) designed collections that were inspired by trips to Portugal, Egypt, Brazil and Asia. The white-on-white embroidery on this summer evening dress references the delicate and fresh quality of Swiss embroidery and is very fitting for her extremely successful teen eveningwear line. CARVEN. COTTON. c. EARLY 1960s.

8 Traditional-style embroidery has been added to the opening and shoulder line of this late thirties evening dress. The padded shoulder of the thirties is softer and rounder than that of the forties. HANDMADE. CREPE. c. LATE 1930s.

1 Three girls pose in traditional Ruthenian (Ukrainian and Belarusian) blouses from the early twenties.

2–8 These embroidered cotton peasant blouses range from the twenties to the seventies. Traditional wear in countries such as the former Czechoslovakia, Hungary, Austria and Germany, and the embroidery often reflected national emblems or flowers. Czechoslovakian blouses were embroidered with geometric shapes and angular florals, patterns taken from the country's renowned Art Nouveau architecture. They were hand-embroidered by their owners and worn for special occasions, such as a Saturday night dance. These blouses became so fashionable in the United States that they were soon imported.

2 COTTON. c. LATE 1920s.

3 HANDMADE. SILK. c. 1930s.

4 HANDMADE. COTTON. c. 1970s.

5 POLYESTER. c. 1970s.

6 COTTON. c. 1930s.

7 COTTON. c. 1970s.

8 HANDMADE. COTTON. c. 1960s.

3

4

5

6

7

8

1 Chinoiserie-inspired woven jacquards were used for cocktail wear in the fifties and early sixties. Made in richly coloured or subtle tones, they created the ideal hostess gown. HANDMADE. SILK. c. EARLY 1960s.

2 Vibrant kimonos were a key item of twenties fashion, perfectly suited for the decadent loungewear worn around the house before an evening out. The shape of the kimono inspired coats of the period and, much later, during the bohemian fashions of the seventies, the kimono influence can be seen on dresses and blouses. SILK AND COTTON. c. 1920s.

3 East Asian garments have been imported for Western wear since the beginning of the 20th century. Their embroidered motifs have changed little over the intervening years and today they provide striking eveningwear just as they did in earlier years. SILK AND LAMB'S FLEECE. c. 1950s.

4 President Nixon's 1972 visit to China is often cited by fashion historians as sparking the seventies trend for oriental-inspired textile designs and fashion, as seen on the print on this maxi dress. WOOL. c. EARLY 1970s.

5 The influences of natural fabrics, embroidery and beadwork from Morocco, India and Turkey on fashion were evident from couture to the high street. Many textile designs also reflected the landscape and wildlife of these countries. The deep horizontal border print on this Italian maxi skirt and matching top illustrates Japanese mountains, and is typical of a popular seventies style for non-repeating prints. SILK CHIFFON. c. EARLY 1970s.

6 Japanese imagery has been especially popular throughout Western 20th-century fashion. This twenties fine silk sleeveless top and cardigan would probably have been part of a lounge suit, worn with matching palazzo-style trousers. The print is inspired by Japanese chrysanthemums (the flower adopted by the Imperial Family as their emblem). The black border shows the influence of Art Deco. SILK. c. 1920s.

LITTLE BLACK DRESS
TIMELESS STYLE

'WHEN THE LITTLE BLACK DRESS IS RIGHT, THERE IS NOTHING ELSE TO WEAR IN ITS PLACE.' WALLIS SIMPSON, DUCHESS OF WINDSOR

The 'Little Black Dress' (LBD) has not always been little. Its style has been dictated by changing fashions and it has been variously lengthened, shortened, flared and tapered throughout the decades, as fashions have changed around it. The LBD is simple and elegant, a dress that can be worn anywhere, at any time. The many variations to this straightforward template that can be found in each fashion era ensure the continued appeal of the Little Black Dress.

The concept of the Little Black Dress is usually accredited to Coco Chanel. First revealed in American *Vogue* in 1926, Chanel's original design for this classic wardrobe staple was a simple crepe dress for daywear, not the time-honoured evening dress it swiftly became. At this time, black was a common sight but as a colour worn for mourning, not fashion, as seen on the many widows created by the First World War. It was a colour associated with a loss of innocence and a grown-up sophistication and therefore not considered a suitable colour for the young and fashionable.

The Jazz Age was a time of change. For the first time women could vote and serious consideration was given to fashionable dress for the increasing feminine presence within the workplace. American *Harper's Bazaar* noted that, as women became more important in a commercial world, their dress became more streamlined and functional. Even so, Chanel's design was without precedent. It was possibly created in reaction to the rich Ballets Russes-inspired fashions of the time and the lavish creations of Poiret. It has also been speculated that inspiration for the design came from the uniforms of Chanel's orphanage childhood, or her own mourning dress after the death of her beloved Arthur Edward 'Boy' Capel in 1919. The commercial success of the dress was not anticipated. The popular uptake of the style was an endorsement of its designer's undeniable chic.

1 After working as a hat designer, Hervé Léger became assistant to Karl Lagerfeld at Fendi before following him to Chanel. The Hervé Léger label was established in the mid-eighties and is renowned for its sensual use of stretch fabrics. HERVÉ LÉGER. SILK JERSEY AND VELVET. c. LATE 1980s/1990s.

2 Rae Spencer-Cullen was the designer behind the Miss Mouse label. A publicity-shy former student of fine art, she is known for her kitsch prints and for naming her designs with catchy phrases such as 'Walking the Dog'. The black, circular-skirted dress looks to the fifties, a decade referenced by a selection of seventies designers, and is made in a highly polished synthetic satin. This was one of the favourite fabrics of glam rock, a style led by international music icons, notably David Bowie, Roxy Music, the New York Dolls and Iggy Pop. MISS MOUSE. SYNTHETIC SATIN. c. 1970s.

3 The British high-street chain Wallis was first established in London in 1923. This simple dress displays the full circle skirt of the fifties and is made from heavy ribbed grosgrain combined with fine 'spaghetti' shoulder straps. Wallis labels of the fifties were printed with a pink rose. WALLIS. GROSGRAIN. c. 1950s.

4 This forties evening dress carries a CC41 label, marking it as being manufactured to the British government's wartime austerity regulations. A dress like this would have cost approximately seven coupons of a citizen's yearly sixty-six coupon allowance. RAYON. c. 1941.

5 This is probably one of the most famous Little Black Dresses of the 20th century. The producers of the 1961 film *Breakfast at Tiffany's* disapproved of Hubert de Givenchy's initial design for Audrey Hepburn's Holly Golightly for showing too much leg. The film's costume designer, Edith Head, subsequently lengthened the dress.

American *Vogue* compared it to Ford's Model T car of the time, a simple and affordable design that was accessible to most social classes.

Long and glamorous and not so 'little' during the thirties, many Little Black Dresses were inspired by the costumes of Hollywood film, specifically designed for black and white viewing. The gowns worn by stars of the screen such as Gloria Swanson, Jean Harlow, Joan Crawford and Marlene Dietrich were, on occasion, created by significant fashion designers of the day, notably Chanel, Hattie Carnegie and Schiaparelli. But the real power behind the screen silhouette was the studio costume designer. Each studio contracted a designer for the many films they produced. One of the most influential, Gilbert Adrian, head of costume design at MGM, saw copies of his black and white designs for screen licensed for sale in department stores, their release timed to coincide with the relevant film. Couturiers such as Schiaparelli included black dresses in their collections, too, recognizing their commercial appeal. Schiaparelli modelled her own first design for eveningwear, a low-backed, long crepe de Chine sheath in black.

Shorter and more serviceable during the austere years of the Second World War, the LBD upheld its name while imposed restraints resulted in higher hemlines and the use of alternative manmade fabrics, in addition to material such as crepe, rayon and satin that was unrestricted. The refined tailoring of the era that appeals to so many today saw dazzling relief in the eveningwear, exploiting the appeal of decorative sequins and bugle beads that were unconstrained by wartime rationing.

The Little Black Dress of the fifties portrayed a variety of messages. While, during the early twenties, in the aftermath of the First World War, black had symbolized mourning, it now became associated with the femme fatale and the unabashed sexuality of starlets such as Marilyn Monroe and Jayne Mansfield – a look far removed from the wholesome cotton florals of the housewife who favoured feminine colours for social occasions. As the decade moved on, the mode for cocktails and home entertaining created a backdrop for a sophisticated hostess and guests clad in the socially acceptable uniform of Little Black Dresses and arrangements of pearls that have accessorized the classic since its first inception.

At its shortest during the sixties, the LBD really came into its own after the mid-fifties. It was perfectly suited to

1 Gabrielle Chanel is the originator of the Little Black Dress. Captured here by Man Ray in 1937, she has styled a dress of timeless elegance with her trademark pearls. She noted, 'Black comprises everything; so does white. They possess absolute beauty. They are in perfect harmony.'

2 This late thirties evening dress is embellished with bronze bugle beads that follow the line of the shoulder. A gentle emphasis on the rounded shoulder is often seen on evening dresses of this time. HANDMADE. CREPE. c. LATE 1930s.

3 An illustrated fashion plate for an elegant little twenties dress by Madeleine Vionnet.

4 A rare forties evening dress of beaded net is too fragile to wear today. However, like twenties chiffon evening dresses, heavy with beading, the net and chiffon can often be backed with a modern fabric to support the weight of the jewelled textiles. SILK NET. c. 1940s.

5 Austerity measures in the
United States limited yardage
and restricted the addition of
details such as pockets, copious
buttons or elaborate collars
and cuffs. Belts were reduced
to a quarter of an inch wide,
yet sequins, which were not
rationed, could be added in
abundance. This resulted in
many otherwise spartan evening
dresses of the early forties
sparkling with embellishment.
MOSS CREPE. c. 1940s.

the simplistic, Lolita style of the new youth fashion, yet also flattering for the figure-hugging 'wiggle' dresses worn as sophisticated eveningwear. This era saw one of the most iconic of all Little Black Dresses: Hubert de Givenchy's design for Audrey Hepburn's character, Holly Golightly, in the 1961 film *Breakfast At Tiffany's*. Styled in conjunction with the film's costume designer, Edith Head, the look was immortalized with a mass of pearls, long elegant black gloves and oversized Ray-Ban Wayfarer-style sunglasses and is one of the most emulated of more recent eras. Ironically, Givenchy's original design was redesigned by Head, as it was criticized by the film's makers for showing too much leg. The image used on the film's poster is the longer version, with the pasted addition of Hepburn's leg delicately emerging from a front split in some publicity images.

As the sixties evolved, and a modernist mood prevailed, white was often added to detail the LBD. The designer at the forefront of the progressive significant youth fashion of the period, Mary Quant, noted that 'the Little Black Dress

Merry Widow Silhouette

1941 look — feminine, feline, from the era of pink champagne and soft-gowned Merry Widows. Soft fullness everywhere. Delicate shoulders and smooth, long waists. Draped hips. And your figure, your walk — willowy and languorous. In black satin, 49.95 Merry Widow Day and Evening Dresses, exclusive with The Designers' Shop, on the Third Floor

LORD & TAYLOR

Only at our New York store.
Fifth Avenue at 39th Street

1 Three Little Black Dresses display the feminine lace jabots and collars used with fitted tailoring to create the elegance of the thirties so admired today.

2 An advertisement for US department store Lord & Taylor illustrates the changing silhouette of the early forties. The name of the fashion house 'Merry Widow Silhouette' appealed to the widowed status of those who had lost their husbands during the war.

3 Beaded embellishments applied to look like jewelry, as on the neckline of this cocktail dress from the United States, are a common feature of early forties eveningwear. WOOL. c. EARLY 1940s.

4 A handmade dress from the United States features the peplum that appeared on many jackets, blouses and dresses. The sequinned bows help to identify it as American, as this playful touch was not as common in British or French styles of the period. MOSS CREPE. c. 1940s.

5 Decorative fringing was a trimming frequently used in the twenties and more selectively during the thirties and forties. Using a surprise flash of colour, in this case a red velvet belt hidden beneath the fringing, was a design technique seen in the work of couturiers such as Paquin, Schiaparelli and Lanvin during the thirties and early forties. SILK. c. 1940s.

that goes anywhere and everywhere is the most appreciated garment in a woman's wardrobe, and the most fun to design. Because it has such precise limitations, it is an interesting problem to design one's way out of... The most successful LBD I ever designed was called the Banana Split. It was made of black jersey, always a good start for any time of day... It danced, this dress ... had a white stand-up collar with points to the ears, and a zip running down the centre... It was tough, sporty and dressy – all at the same time, in black and white.'

The LBD was perhaps least worn in the seventies, the decade that embraced both nostalgia and freedom. The colour black was not suited to the sheer, flowing maxi dresses and patchwork bohemian styling of the period. However, in the eighties it was once again moved to the forefront of women's wardrobes. The power dressing style of the decade demanded bold solid blocks of colour that were contrasted with collars and cuffs and oversized buttons. Black suited the glamorous feel of the period and the Little Black Dresses of the decade, sculpted from stretch jersey, velvets and taffeta, made an ideal canvas for the ostentatious accessories of vibrant jewelry, gilt buttons and rich, heavy embroidery. Azzedine Alaïa, Jean Paul Gaultier, Yohji Yamamoto, Moschino, Comme des Garçons and Kenzo are some of the most celebrated designers of this era, each renowned for their individual take on the Little Black Dress.

Rarely has one item of fashion become so revered that it can be identified by just a set of initials. The 1926 observation by American *Vogue* that the LBD would become a 'sort of uniform for women of all taste' remains true today, as it has throughout every subsequent decade of fashion history. But the power of the Little Black Dress is pertinently demonstrated in the design worn by Diana, Princess of Wales to the 1994 *Vanity Fair* dinner at the Serpentine Gallery, London, an event that coincided with the media announcement that admitted her husband's adultery. Her off-the-shoulder LBD of pleated chiffon designed by Christina Stambolian caused a photographic frenzy. The following day news of Prince Charles's confession was eclipsed by hundreds of photographs of a sensational Diana wearing an LBD.

1 In the sixties, jersey was a fabric more often used for easy-care daywear and the drapery on this mid-sixties cocktail dress is unusual for its time. Little is known about the label, Chafil London, but dresses bearing this label date from as early as the thirties, with very few found after the sixties. CHAFIL LONDON. SILK JERSEY. c. 1960s.

2 Diana, Princess of Wales skilfully used clothes to capture the mood of the moment. This figure-hugging LBD by Greek designer Christina Stambolian was dubbed 'the Revenge Dress' and featured on newspaper front pages the following day.

3 John Bates brought modern youthfulness to his early designs for the label Jean Varon. Considered by some to be the 'other' originator of the mini skirt, he designed many of Diana Rigg's costumes for her Emma Peel character in the 1965 TV series *The Avengers*. Several designs were later sold promoting the series. He is also known for designing the famous backless sequinned gown worn by Julie Christie in the 1975 film, *Shampoo*. JEAN VARON. SATIN-BACKED CREPE. c. 1970s.

4 The decorative placement of diamanté resembles a belt on this British sixties cocktail dress. REMBRANDT. WOOL. c. 1960s.

5 Italian-born Franco Moschino worked for Giorgio Armani as an illustrator before launching his own company in 1983. Known for his humorous and sometimes outrageous designs, he used his training as a tailor to ensure that all designs were cut with expertise and sophistication. MOSCHINO. SILK AND LACE. c. 1990s.

6 Cerruti began as an Italian fabric manufacturer in 1881 – hence the label 'Cerruti 1881'. It was established as a fashion line in Paris during the sixties; a womenswear line was added later, in 1976. CERRUTI. SILK. c. LATE 1980s/EARLY 1990s.

1 Leslie Fay was a United States clothing label founded by Fred Pomerantz. As a manufacturer of army uniforms during the Second World War, he was given the results of a government statistical study on the female form to enable him to fit uniforms properly. This information helped him to produce designs for women after the war. The label is named after his daughter. LESLIE FAY. SEQUINNED POLYESTER. c.1980s.

2 The silhouette of the eighties was deliberately exaggerated: shoulders were padded and powerful and the fifties batwing sleeve was revived and combined with cowl necks and boat necks. POLYESTER JERSEY. c.1980s.

3 Inexpensive seventies LBDs often have a sophisticated styling achieved using pleating and embroidery techniques easier to realize in slinky polyesters that could be permanently heat-set. PLEATED POLYESTER. c.1970s.

4 The Little Black Dress of the eighties was powerful. The genius of the period is found in the use of unusual fabrics and new cutting techniques to create statement pieces reflecting the mood of the era. Here a section of the sleeve is replaced with net stiffened with metallic gold thread. The sleeves add drama to the sleek body of stretch velvet. KAREN OKADA FOR DAVID HOWARD. VELVET. c. 1980s.

5 Norman Hartnell designed several wedding dresses for the British royal family and received the royal warrant in 1940. He was famous for the elaborate embroideries used on his couture garments. At the insistence of his sister and business partner, Phyllis, he also introduced simpler, more everyday designs into his collections to ensure and satisfy a regular stream of customers. NORMAN HARTNELL. SILK. c. 1960s.

1 True sophistication reflected in the chiffon train of a sixties cocktail dress with beaded décolletage. SILK CHIFFON. c. EARLY 1960s.

2 An early sixties advertisement for Courtaulds fabric places a beautiful LBD in a home setting. Dinner parties, cocktails and home entertaining had become the fashionable evening activity and the role of hostess was taken very seriously.

3, 4 The Little Black dress was a firm fashion fixture by the mid-fifties. Any dubious connotations had been dismissed and many dresses can be found from this date and well into the sixties. Black lace has always been one of the most popular fabrics of choice, evocative of bygone eras, and remains one of the most copied styles by designers of today. A successful style needs little reinterpretation.

3 HANDMADE. COTTON. c. LATE 1950s.

4 COTTON. c. EARLY 1960s.

5 As sixties trends moved on from the simplicity of futuristic design, a penchant for antique clothing gathered momentum. While more adventurous dressers were happy to wear original 19th-century nightdresses and twenties flapper dresses, many preferred the less flamboyant mainstream fashion interpretations. Historical influences can be seen on this mid-sixties Little Black Dress with a 16th-century-style lace collar. SHUBETTE. VELVET. c. 1960s.

6 Ribbon embroidery (also known as Rococo embroidery) can be found as early as the 17th century and is thought to have originated in France. It can be found on early bags, shoes and anything worn as eveningwear. In the fifties an all-over ribbon stitch was fashionable, creating a lustrous texture on simple cocktail dresses. The ribbon was often dyed to the exact colour of the dress fabric. SILK RIBBON. c. LATE 1950s.

4

5

6

1 British designer Gina Fratini, known for her romantic designs, became firmly established when the British Princess Anne wore one of her dresses for her twenty-first birthday portrait. Fratini also created many dresses for Princess Diana and designed for Ossie Clark's little-known lingerie label Rustle. GINA FRATINI. SILK JERSEY. c. 1970s.

2 Here John Bates combines flowing, transparent silk chiffon with a butterfly sleeve to create an LBD in keeping with the bohemian mood of the seventies. JEAN VARON. SILK CHIFFON. c. LATE 1970s.

3 Many notable designers began their careers under the umbrella of the British manufacturer Alfred Radley. Although this garment doesn't carry Ossie Clark's name, the interesting construction of the dress, with front-crossing straps, bears the hallmarks of his design, while the print is by Celia Birtwell and can be seen on other designs that carry an Ossie Clark label. RADLEY. MOSS CREPE. c. 1970s.

4, 5 Janice Wainwright launched her own label 'Janice Wainwright at Forty Seven Poland Street' in the early seventies. Later in the decade, the 'Forty Seven Poland Street' was dropped and designs became simpler, although still in sophisticated jersey shapes. The appliquéd gold arrows, seen on these two Little Black Dresses from this era, were a popular motif used on all sorts of items, including shoes and tights. JANICE WAINWRIGHT. SILK JERSEY. c. LATE 1970s.

6 Embroidered satin-stitch roses, the flower so associated with the fifties, effectively highlight the waistline on this simple cocktail dress. WOOL. c. LATE 1950s.

7 Indian influences provided inspiration for sixties evening dresses. The heavy turquoise and silver embroidery on the upper part of this dress has been applied to resemble a necklace of Indian origin, such as would have been worn by the likes of Elizabeth Taylor, Brigitte Bardot and the wealthier jet set who enjoyed a luxurious interpretation of bohemian style. MARJON COUTURE. WOOL. c. 1960s.

1 A border print, often seen on the maxi dresses of the seventies, in a style influenced by the films of the era *The Boy Friend* and *The Great Gatsby*. LADIES PRIDE. COTTON. c. 1970s.

2 A hand-tinted photograph shows a painterly plum design used on a thirties chiffon evening dress. While the colours have undoubtedly been exaggerated to enhance the image, a textile design of this imagery was still unusual, particularly for an evening dress.

3 Horrockses commissioned or employed many artists and illustrators for their fashion brand to keep their celebrated prints fresh and ahead of trends. The giraffe print is attributed to Pat Albeck, a graduate of London's Royal College of Art, who worked for the company during the fifties. HORROCKSES FASHIONS. COTTON. c. EARLY 1950s.

NOVELTY PRINT
NARRATIVE FASHION

3

The whimsical pictorial textile designs that began to decorate the newly fashionable leisurewear of the late twenties are affectionately referred to as 'novelty' prints. These figurative designs were mostly printed on lightweight fabrics, such as silk, cotton, rayon and crepe, and were a welcome change from the florals and geometrics that women had become so used to wearing. These illustrative prints were intended to be fun and frivolous and a distraction from a depressed economic climate. Inexpensive to purchase, they were picture-perfect for this new, rapidly emerging area of fashion in Europe and North America. The promotion of picturesque holiday resorts, cruise ships and steam trains, as well as the introduction of a week's paid annual leave for all in Britain, helped drive demand for a fashionably informal way to dress and to parade beside the sea. 'Playtime Prints' depicted holiday pleasures, and nautical novelty prints featuring starfish, shells, anchors, bobbing boats, sailors' lanterns and ships' wheels were common alongside scenic landscapes and tropical scenes.

Pictorial designs had been fashionable since the 18th century in the form of Toile de Jouy. This figurative style incorporated images of plants, animals and realistic scenes. It is a style often accredited to Christophe-Philippe Oberkampf, an 18th-century textile manufacturer, whose intricate pastoral scenes in monochromatic blue, red or black on white were produced as wallpaper and furnishing fabrics, decorating notable homes and much admired by Marie Antoinette.

By the early 20th century, the pictorial printed image had been developed for mass production, commercialized to appeal to an image-hungry market. Many designs were developed to appeal to children, with images representing well-known nursery rhyme and storybook characters. Pictorial prints seem to be at their most fashionable at times

5, 6 Even knitwear designs were not exempt from the delights of novelty. Both Weldons and Bestway patterns were British. Bestway seems to have been prevalent from the forties, while Walter Weldon established a paper pattern business as far back as 1888. Knitting and needlework patterns provide an inspirational record of everyday fashion history.

1, 2 Rae Spencer-Cullen, who was behind the Miss Mouse label, was declared by *Harper's Bazaar* to be a 'leading style innovator'. Her deceptively simple conversational print designs referenced fifties kitsch. MISS MOUSE. SYNTHETIC SATIN. c. 1974.

3 The wives of two competing tennis players arrive at Wimbledon for Ladies Day in 1954. One has appropriately found a dirndl skirt with a strawberry border print to wear.

4 The historical reference is unusual in this nonetheless witty mid-century American conversational. Illustrative prints of the era tended to reflect topics such as hobbies, travel and sporting activities. PETIT LEIGUE BY CHERBOURG. COTTON. c. MID-1950s.

of trouble and the American stock market crash of 1929, and subsequent Depression, fuelled a demand for escapist imagery and focused on the cartoon characters that emerged in thirties animated films. Disney's Mickey Mouse and friends, and Snow White and the Seven Dwarves, were some of the many immortalized on fabric. Manufacturers took advantage of a trend for commercialized fabric design to advertise products such as Planters Peanuts and Maxwell House coffee, all reproduced for fashionable wear.

As mass production became more sophisticated and screen-printing techniques replaced traditional engraved roller printing, fashionable imagery began to include landscapes, towns and houses, intricate woodland scenes, birds, dancers, luggage stickers, stamps and coins: basically anything that reflected cheerful pursuits. The patterns, full of frivolity, were never meant to be enduring classics, instead offering an everyday reflection of current trends. These fabrics were in such demand that it was not unknown for large textile manufacturers to include more than 800 novelty designs in their annual repertoire. The topical images were always light-hearted, designed to be affordable and printed on durable fabrics.

These witty designs are now historical documents, in particular the garments produced around the Second World War. Patriotic prints became a familiar sight throughout the Western world, but especially in Britain and the United States, attempting to raise morale and brighten the dull, utilitarian fashions of wartime. Skirts, blouses and scarves were made from fabric printed with sailors, airplanes, battleships, maps and flags reproduced alongside popular

7–11 The dirndl skirt, fashionable throughout the fifties and sixties, was traditionally made from a full circle, providing the perfect canvas for the prints of the day. Imagery covered everything from hobbies to aspirational scenic destinations. Pop memorabilia was also a common theme, initially unhampered by copyright. As Beatlemania made its mark on everything, even the Dutch department store C&A released a series of dresses. This skirt (8) is handmade, suggesting that fabric could be bought printed with images of the Fab Four.

7 RICHARD SHOPS. SATINIZED COTTON. c. MID-1950s.

8 HANDMADE. COTTON. c. 1960s.

9 COTTON. c. 1950s.

10 ASSOCIATED AMERICAN ARTISTS. COTTON. c. MID-1950s.

11 HANDMADE. APPLIQUÉD FELT ON COTTON. c. EARLY 1950s.

propaganda slogans such as 'Dig for Victory' and 'Careless Talk Costs Lives'.

Elsa Schiaparelli's collaboration with surrealist and friend Salvador Dalí also had an impact on mass-market novelty prints in the thirties and forties. The resulting designs included her well-known 'Tears' dress (a sophisticated evening dress printed in carefully placed rips resembling torn flesh) and the 'Lobster' dress, famously worn by Wallis Simpson, a loyal patron of her work. Her 'visual jokes on textiles' also resulted in a collaboration with textile manufacturer Charles Colcombet to create satirical prints based on imagery including newspaper articles. (In true Schiaparelli style, all the articles were about her.) Her renowned 'Circus' collection of 1938 included images of circus horses, trapeze artists, clowns and small dogs, manifested in appliqué, embroidery, beadwork and buttons.

The novelty print became even more prominent post-war, chiming perfectly with the jubilant fashions of the time. The prints were used extensively on leisurewear, a more prevalent trend in North America than in Europe. Leisure-time activities such as playing cards, cocktail drinks, rock 'n' roll and even French poodles decorated all kinds of clothing, including men's shirts. The full-circle skirt, a classic of fifties fashion, was the perfect canvas for these new, often gaudy prints. They were not always printed in the usual all-over repeat, as the border print allowed much larger-scale imagery than in previous decades. Novelty images were also embroidered and appliquéd, as home sewing increased with the post-war baby boom.

The textile industry in Europe did not recover from wartime austerity as quickly as it did in the United States. Many international artists were invited to design for fabric in an effort to revitalize a flagging textile industry. 'Artists Quit Easels' was one of the newspaper headlines announcing the initiative. At the forefront of the trend was the textile firm Ascher, under the helm of Zika and Lida Ascher, which commissioned many notable artists, including Henry Moore, Feliks Topolski, Cecil Beaton, Philippe Jullian and even Henri Matisse, to produce a limited range of designs for fabric. Many of the resulting famous Ascher Squares (large headscarves) and fabric designs were narrative, and, while it might appear demeaning to reduce the work of such artists to the level of a lighthearted novelty print, the impact on the British fashion market was so successful that a trend ensued for whimsical painterly narrative prints, a

1

1 Schiaparelli's infamous lobster dress was made in collaboration with the surrealist artist Salvador Dalí and was one of the first novelty images to make fashion headlines. The dress was suggested to Wallis Simpson by Cecil Beaton when he photographed her for *Vogue*. The magazine then devoted eight pages to the sitting and the print became part of mainstream fashion, inspiring styles for decades afterwards, rather than being the surreal comment with sexual overtones that Dalí had intended.

2 This housecoat depicts rows of medieval minstrels between a stripe of florals. Housecoats, lounge suits and pyjamas were indoor wear to be seen in and were therefore made from elaborate printed or embroidered fabrics. RAYON. c. 1930s.

3 This is a rare early example of the novelty print. Fruit prints were not common and were usually reproduced on a diminutive scale. HANDMADE. SILK CHIFFON. c. 1920s.

complete contrast to topical American style. Ascher followed his artists' prints with a range of novelty designs under the 'Bourec' label, priced to appeal to the mass market. The British manufacturer Samuel Sherman (under his Sambo label) made the designs – featuring luggage, Victorian outdoor scenes and rows of houses in stripes – into full-skirted shirtwaister dresses.

Novelty prints of the sixties pared down as streamlined fashions took hold. However, the work of Pop artists Andy Warhol and Roy Lichtenstein and Surrealist Max Ernst inspired visual textile design that realized their artwork on fabric. Icons of the era appeared in print, and the fad for paper dresses provided a backdrop for images such as Warhol's Campbell's soup tins. These Pop patterns remain as appealing for designers today as they did in the sixties and in 2014, for example, Diane von Furstenberg issued a collection of her signature wrapdresses decorated in a selection of Warhol prints. In London, the boutique Mr Freedom used Disney and other childhood characters such as Rupert the Bear alongside appliquéd stars, thunderbolts and ice creams for their deliberately kitsch designs.

Mainstream seventies design embraced an ethereal style referencing historical imagery in line with the fashion silhouette of the era. The illustrations of Aubrey Beardsley were hugely influential, inspiring designs of swirling mermaids, butterflies, birds and other romantic imagery that trailed over blouses, skirts and dresses. Another trend in the twenties was also a trend mid-seventies, a likely consequence of two influential films – Ken Russell's *The Boy Friend*, starring Twiggy in a musical pastiche of the twenties, and the 1974 film adaptation of *The Great Gatsby*. Despite average reviews, *Gatsby* became a cult film and won an Academy Award for best costume design. Subsequent large-scale novelty prints recreated fashionable ladies of the twenties accompanied by stylish automobiles or dogs.

Good novelty prints from any of these eras are easy to spot but hard to find today. Known as 'conversationals' by fashion professionals, designs from the forties and fifties and seventies, the heydays of the 'novelty print', frequently reoccur in contemporary collections, requiring little reinterpretation to be successful. The kitsch of fifties Americana has been interpreted by Miuccia Prada who used American Chevrolets on shirts, while Victoria Beckham's cat print made fashion headlines. Both Gucci's umbrella print and Tory Burch's straw-hat pattern, included in their 2014

resort collections, have a nostalgic resonance. Many consider the colloquial novelty print best reserved for youth fashion, but there are plenty of sophisticated versions that are evident of great artistry. Aside from the famous Ascher collaborations, many painters and illustrators have seen their work realized on cloth, either as commissions or while employed by textile-producing fashion companies. The British company Horrockses, which started making fashionable dresses in 1948, utilized the talents of artists Alastair Morton, Eduardo Paolozzi, Pat Albeck, Graham Sutherland and Henry Moore. Consequently a beautifully narrative dress could turn out to be quite an investment and, as the artist rarely signed the garments or fabrics, familiarization with their illustrative style is paramount.

Of all vintage fashions and trends it is the novelty print that is the most indicative of its era. The stories that are visualized on printed cloth not only highlight the travels and pastimes that were popular in each era, but the artistic influences that became interpreted by fashions of the day. Be it jubilant balloon prints that signified the end of war, or psychedelic pig prints indicating the drug experimentation of the sixties, the stylized narratives not only allow easy identification of a decade but they also make wearing history particularly poignant.

1, 2 Blouses of the sixties and early seventies can be found with imagery that varies from beautiful representations of illustrative fashion to cute storybook animals. The elephant print has humorous overtones. 'Seeing pink elephants' was the euphemism used to describe the hallucinogenic effects of drug-taking that began to impact society in the sixties and early seventies.

1 LUREX. c. 1970s.

2 BRUSHED POLYESTER. c. 1960s.

3 A forties dress printed in a repeating Parisian scene. This was a popular design motif after the liberation of Paris. GAYETTE. CREPE. c. 1940s.

4 American style, particularly that of the forties and fifties, is easy to distinguish from European fashion. Colours were bolder and fashion prints developed a graphic style ahead of European trends. CREPE. c. 1940s.

5 A quirky Lowry-style dancing ladies design by Radley. Radley had their own fabric mills and production factories. RADLEY. RAYON. c. EARLY 1970s.

6 This joyful balloon print was purchased by its owner before the Second World War. Subsequent textiles were more muted, as dyes were needed for the manufacture of uniforms. RAYON. c. EARLY 1937.

1

1 Jean Patou opened his first fashion house in 1912 in Paris. His early success was based on sportswear (tennis dresses and knitted swimming costumes), but he became well known in the United States after the First World War. The red silk dress pictured dates from the early forties, when the fashion house was under the direction of Patou's sister Madeleine. It features an elaborate puff sleeve cut on the cross, an open seam known as 'faggotting', and an unusual conversational print based on the fairy tale, 'The Three Little Pigs'. This dress was bought for only twenty Euros in the famous Parisian flea market Les Puces at Porte de Clignancourt. The unusual print, elaborate sleeves and sophisticated seamwork indicate the work of a couturier. Happily for its present owner, the Jean Patou label is attached far down inside the dress and was unnoticed by the seller. JEAN PATOU. SILK. c. EARLY 1940s.

2 The umbrella motif is surprisingly common from as early as the Art Deco period. Early designs are beautifully executed, but the motif was briefly revisited in the seventies revival when it was commercialized on cheap synthetics. LINEN. c. 1940s.

3 This dress uses a dainty nursery-style conversational print, making for a typically quirky design from designer Rae Spencer-Cullen. MISS MOUSE. COTTON. c. 1970s.

2

3

1

2

3

1 An early sixties dress by the British company Alice Edwards Italians. The novelty print, featuring foreign newspapers and fruit, captures some of the delights of summer holidays. ALICE EDWARDS ITALIANS. SATINIZED COTTON. c. EARLY 1960s.

2 This late forties cotton dress is decorated with a pattern featuring rows of Staffordshire-style pottery figurines. 'Stripes', or rows of novelty print motifs, were common to the forties and early fifties, although there are earlier examples. COTTON. c. LATE 1940s.

3 Affordable flights made travel to far-flung destinations increasingly possible in the late fifties and early sixties. This in turn influenced fashion and is reflected in designs such as the tribal print on this dress. BLANES. COTTON. c. LATE 1950s/EARLY 1960s.

4 The souvenir-style travel print was a popular motif throughout the forties and fifties. The prints reflected holiday pastimes, such as Spanish flamenco dancing, which were now more accessible. RAYON. c. 1950s.

5 A cotton dress printed with cancan dancers, typical of post-war novelty patterns. Hobbies, travel and all sorts of enjoyable pursuits were reflected in print. LONDON TOWN. COTTON. c. LATE 1950s.

6 This early forties advertisement for US brand Catalina shows a nylon taffeta swimsuit that could be made into a sundress with the addition of a dragonfly-pattern printed skirt.

MADE EXCLUSIVELY FOR
BERGDORF GOODMAN
· ON THE PLAZA – NEW YORK ·

Marcel Fenez

IT IS RECOMMENDED
THAT THIS GARMENT
BE DRY-CLEANED.

LEE BENDER

Mr Freedom
MADE IN ENGLAND

THIS GARMENT
SHOULD BE
DRY CLEANED

CREAZIONI MADE IN ITALY
ANNA GIOVANNOZZI
BORGOGNISSANTI 28R – FIRENZE

Thea Porter
14

miss
carven
paris
for Marcel Fenez

FREDERICK STARKE
L O N D O N
Made in England
DRY CLEANING RECOMMENDED

Miss Mouse
12
LONDON

REAL SUEDE
100% RAYON

·Ann·
Buck
MADE IN ENGLAND

10

LEATHER CLEAN ONLY

BIBA

YUKI
Designs for REMBRANDT

DESIGNED BY
OSSIE CLARK
MOSS CREPE
DRY CLEAN ONLY
WARM IRON WHEN DRY. DO NOT STEAM.

Ui-Maikai
RN 26300
100% ALL COTTON
MADE IN HAWAII

HAND WASHABLE OR MACHINE
WASHABLE AT MILD SETTING.
USE MILD DETERGENT ONLY.
DO NOT BLEACH, RUB,
WRING OR TWIST.
DRIP DRY OR TUMBLE DRY
AT WARM SETTING.

Jancourt
PETITE Sports

FIND OUT MORE

There is a wealth of information available about vintage clothing: the problem can be to know where to start! The books below either offer a good general overview or else more detail on a specific aspect of vintage clothing, presenting it within a modern context. Original magazines are also a fantastic resource to learn about the way fashions were originally worn, the shapes, colours and fabrics of each garment. The Vintage Fashion Guild website offers a valuable label and fabric resource – useful for helping to date specific garments. Finally, there are many vintage blogs. While these can provide inspiration as to how to wear vintage clothes, the examples listed below focus more specifically on interesting aspects of vintage fashion history.

BOOKS

Nicky Albrechtsen, *The Printed Square*, London, 2012

Nicky Albrechtsen and Fola Solanke, *Scarves*, London, 2011

Thomas G. Aylesworth, *The History of Movie Musicals*, London, 1984

Andrew Baseman, Harold Charlton and Robin Nedboy, *The Scarf*, New York, 1989

Emma Baxter-Wright, Karen Clarkson, Sarah Kennedy and Kate Mulvey, *Vintage Fashion*, London, 2010

Alexandra Black, *Evening Dress*, New York, 2004

Danièle Bott, *Chanel: Collections and Creations*, London, 2007

Christine Boydell, *Horrockses Fashions: Off-the-Peg Style in the '40s and '50s*, London, 2010

Caroline Cox, *Vintage Shoes: Collecting and Wearing Twentieth-Century Designer Footwear*, London, 2008

Lilly Daché, *Talking Through My Hats*, New York, 1946

Design Museum: Fifty Dresses That Changed The World, London, 2009

Design Museum: Fifty Bags That Changed the World, London, 2011

Christian Dior, *Little Dictionary of Fashion*, London, 2007 (rev. ed.)

Marnie Fogg, *Vintage Knitwear*, London, 2010

Marnie Fogg, *Vintage Handbags*, London, 2012

Vanessa Friedman, *Emilio Pucci*, Cologne, 2010

Paul Gorman; introduction by Paul Smith; foreword by Malcolm McLaren, *The Look: Adventures in Rock and Pop Fashion*, London, 2006 (rev. ed.)

Carolyn Hall, *The Forties in Vogue*, London, 1985

Edith Head, with Joe Hyams, *How To Dress for Success*, London, 2009 (rev. ed.)

Amy Holman Edelman, *The Little Black Dress*, London, 1997 (3rd ed.)

Georgina Howell, *In Vogue: Sixty Years of Celebrities and Fashion from British Vogue*, London, 1978

Barbara Hulanicki, *From A To Biba*, London, 2007 (rev. ed.)

Brigid Keenan, *Dior in Vogue*, London, 1981

Sarah Kennedy, *Vintage Swimwear*, London, 2010

Lawrence Langner, *The Importance of Wearing Clothes*, London, 1959

James Laver, *Taste and Fashion: From the French Revolution to the Present Day*, London, 1945

Harriet Love, *Harriet Love's Guide to Vintage Chic*, New York, 1982

Valerie Mendes, *V&A Pattern: Novelty Patterns*, London, 2010

Simon Murray and Nicky Albrechtsen, *Fashion Spectacles, Spectacular Fashion*, London, 2013

Colombe Pringle (trans. Jane Brenton), *Roger Vivier (Fashion Memoir)*, London, 1999

Mary Quant, *Quant by Quant*, London, 1967

Geoffrey Rayner, Richard Chamberlain and Annamarie Stapleton, *Artists' Textiles in Britain 1945–1970*, Woodbridge, 1999

Giorgio Riello and Peter McNeil, *Shoes: A History from Sandals to Sneakers*, Oxford, 2006

Nancy Schiffer, *Eyeglass Retrospective: Where Fashion Meets Science*, Atglen, PA, 1999

Opposite A collection of labels from garments of different ages. Labels not only add to the history and charm of vintage clothing but also help date a garment. The era can frequently be identified by the script used on the label: for instance, garments dating to the fifties often have labels with embroidered or sloping italic lettering, while by the sixties and seventies printed labels became more common, often in the 'groovy' font popular at the time. Generally, although the main label of garments up to the mid-century do not give sizing, they do offer more information such as country of origin and fabric than later styles.

Cameron Silver, *Decades: a Century of Fashion*, London, 2012

Valerie Steele, *Shoes: A Lexicon Of Style*, London and Hong Kong, 1988

Kerry Taylor, *Vintage Fashion & Couture: From Poiret to McQueen*, London, 2013

Tracy Tolkien, *Vintage: The Art of Dressing Up*, London, 2002

Jo Turney and Rosemary Harden, *Floral Frocks: A Celebration of the Floral Printed Dress from 1900 to the Present Day*, Woodbridge, 2007

Jonathan Walford, *Shoes A-Z: Designers, Brands, Manufacturers and Retailers*, London, 2010

Jonathan Walford, *Forties Fashion: From Siren Suits to the New Look*, London, 2011 (rev. ed.)

Judith Watt, *Ossie Clark 1965–74*, London, 2003

Claire Wilcox, ed., *The Golden Age of Couture; Paris and London 1947–57*, London, 2008

Harriet Worsley, *100 Ideas that Changed Fashion*, London, 2011

WEBSITES

Fashion Encylopedia
www.fashionencyclopedia.com

Vintage Fashion Guild
vintagefashionguild.org

Vogue Italia Encyclo
www.vogue.it/encyclo

Vogue Magazine Archive
www.vogue.co.uk/magazine/archive

Voguepedia
www.vogue.com/voguepedia

BLOGS

Advantage in Vintage
advantageinvintage.co.uk

Clothes on Film
clothesonfilm.com

Last-Year Girl
lastyeargirl.blogspot.com

Queens of Vintage
www.queensofvintage.com

Tuppence Ha'penny Vintage
blog.tuppencehapenny.co.uk

The Vintage Traveler | Fuzzylizzie's Fashion & Travel: Vintage Style
thevintagetraveler.wordpress.com

Vintage-a-Peel blog
emmapeelpants.wordpress.com

Jonathan Walford's blog
kickshawproductions.com/blog

1–3 Three very different floral decorations from varying fashion eras. **1** uses silk-stitch embroidery with diamanté stones on a bespoke cocktail dress from the cusp of 1959/60. The single-stemmed rose or similar full-blown flower is a typical embroidery reference of this era. **2** shows machine embroidery on the pockets of a linen day dress from the early fifties. The irregular stitch is indicative of a mass-produced garment from this time and not a sign of wear and tear. The handmade corsage decorating the bodice of **3**, an early twenties evening dress, displays the effort spent on homemade clothing.

SOURCING AND BUILDING A VINTAGE COLLECTION

There was no pivotal moment when the term 'vintage' was created to encompass everything sold as second-hand clothing. The collective noun for fashion of all decades – antique, retro, or even at a push, last season's designer – became an acknowledged fashion category during the nineties. Although the sixties, seventies and eighties explored different trends using second-hand clothes, it was not the mainstream, all-decade-encompassing style that has grown in popularity steadily since the nineties.

Everyone has a favourite decade to which they are naturally drawn: the rule of thumb from the fashion professionals (the stylists, editors, personal shoppers, anyone and everyone involved in the business of looking good) is to wear the colours and shapes that one is instinctively attracted to. But while each decade has a distinctive colour palette and a characteristic silhouette that will suit different figure shapes, dressing completely from one decade can give a dressing-up box appearance. It is far better to concentrate on a few select vintage pieces, such as a beautiful sweater or an embroidered blouse that will always be relevant to a contemporary wardrobe. Vintage shopping, whatever the price of the garment, is investment dressing. Dresses, coats or separates selected for their own unique beauty are timeless classics that can be worn repeatedly, whatever the current trend.

Author James Laver devised the table to the left. Laver was a fashion historian and curator at the V & A Museum. He was also a theorist and, in an effort to make sense of the ever-turning cycles of fashion, he composed a table that was first published in his book, *Taste and Fashion*, in 1937. With a little modern interpretation and substitution of contemporary vocabulary, the table's comparative observations form a light-hearted but relevant guideline for today's vintage shopper.

The many vintage fairs and markets that exist in the world's fashion capitals can easily be found through the internet and shopping guides. Even Dubai now has a tiny selection of vintage fashion shops.

As they are constantly changing, including a guide here would not be appropriate. The famous international vintage fashion sources such as California's Rose Bowl, Clignancourt in Paris and London's Portobello Market are constant and it is always worth looking up market dates when visiting a city or on holiday to find new sources. Every antique market or flea market has a clothes section. On the whole, dealers are keen to help and many have pitches in different markets, exhibit at fairs or even have their own shops. Different shops and dealers have their own selective hallmark and some have become deliberate curators of a particular style so building relationships, finding a selection of preferable sources and tapping in to a style that suits you all helps in the search. But it should be an exciting search, and looking in different countries will reveal an eclectic mix of styles: France is known for its beautiful 'whites', cotton underwear that is suitable for summer dressing; Italian markets reveal exquisite printed silk jersey garments – alternative Puccis; and the many vintage fashion sources in North America have an abundance of everything, particularly forties and fifties fashion.

4, 5 Two scenes from the popular London vintage fashion fair, Frock Me. Well-established fairs such as this are havens of reputable and knowledgeable vintage clothing dealers, many of whom are experts in their specialities.

Indecent	10 years before its time
Shameless	5 years before its time
Outré (Daring)	1 year before its time
Smart	'Current Fashion'
Dowdy	1 year after its time
Hideous	10 years after its time
Ridiculous	20 years after its time
Amusing	30 years after its time
Quaint	50 years after its time
Charming	70 years after its time
Romantic	100 years after its time
Beautiful	150 years after its time

HOW TO DATE VINTAGE FASHION

While the original date of a garment should not be the governing factor in deciding what clothes to wear, it is certainly important to be aware of the different characteristics of each period, as this will influence both price and aftercare. Among the most common errors are mistaking eighties floral summer dresses for earlier fifties designs and believing the popular moss crepe dresses of the seventies to be original forties pieces. With so many reinterpretations of fashion's themes and patterns, not just today but in earlier decades, even reputable vintage shops can fall into the last trap, an indication of how difficult it can be for the average shopper.

Nothing can replace the first-hand experience of examining a garment, and there are plenty of opportunities to do this with the abundance of vintage fashion fairs, markets, shops and even high-end department stores that specialize in retailing fashion from all eras. Handling original garments, examining seams and zips, and feeling the texture of cloth are imperative in learning to date garments correctly. Ephemera such as original magazines, paper patterns and fashion plates also help with identifying the silhouettes and details, such as dress length, that typify each era.

There are several obvious clues for identification:

Overlocking: The machined edging seen on most contemporary garments was only put into practice in manufacturing during the late sixties and early seventies. Overlocking from these eras is looser and the stitches wider apart than today.

Fastenings: Hook and eye fastenings are most common during the twenties and thirties. Garments up until the fifties were also made with covered, wooden, plastic and Bakelite buttons, as well as metal press-studs which take the same format as those of today but are either much larger and heavier (forties and fifties) or else tiny (twenties and thirties). With metal needed for the Second World War effort, press-studs are rare on forties garments. The zip was introduced to clothing in the thirties, but many garments from this era

will still have buttons, press-studs or hook and eye fastenings. Generally the heavier, thicker and chunkier the zip, the earlier it is. Coloured plastic-looking zips are also early – usually thirties. However, it must be remembered that much fashion was handmade and the stash of the sewing box was a big asset, with women utilizing older fabrics, trimmings and fastenings, which can add to modern-day confusion. Zips were made from metal well into the fifties and it wasn't until the sixties that plastic zips with closed, fitted teeth were introduced, and even these are heavier and fairly easy to distinguish from modern ones. Zips also tended to be fitted in a side seam into the fifties.

Fabrics: Learning the different feel of fabrics from different decades is easier than it sounds and an instant way to check a date. As textile manufacturing has improved over the years, fabrics have become more polished, with smoother, skin-friendly finishes. This even applies to knitwear and is important in distinguishing the many modern recreations knitted from old patterns. Print styles are an obvious clue, with the floral of the fifties often looking much more elementary and printed in fewer colours than designs from the eighties, for example. Early silks and 'artificial silks' have a sheeny finish but, compared to modern silks, have a fragility that is easy to see. The synthetics that flooded manufacturing during the sixties and seventies are thick and heavy. Jersey fabrics are hardest to distinguish but,

again, became more refined and polished as time went on.

Labels: The styling of a label is one of the most obvious indicators of date, with sloping italics, old-fashioned graphics and a lot of information potentially available. Sadly many old labels have been removed over time or even swapped by disreputable dealers. The Vintage Fashion Guild has compiled a very useful online label resource, with different collectors contributing their finds and knowledge (see 'Find Out More', p. 420). Designer houses often change their label style over the decades and, once one is familiar with this, it is a way to pinpoint the era or distinguish between ready-to-wear and couture. More generally speaking, cleaning care instructions and sizing were rarely included on labels before the very late fifties. Most garments found today dating before the late forties will have been handmade and will therefore have no label.

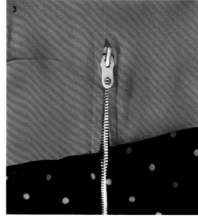

LOOKING AFTER VINTAGE

All vintage clothing, unless you are very lucky or are paying exceptionally high prices, will show signs of wear and tear. While there are certain types of stains that may never be removed and rotting areas of fabric that are past repair, small holes, tears, drawn threads, missing buttons and belts and fading are all the marks of time and should not discourage a purchase of a fabulous garment. Historical clothing has a story and these signs of wear and tear can be the distinguishing mark of vintage, just like the 'shabby chic' of antique furniture. Why else do manufacturers of modern fashion emulate the ageing appearance of leather or the fading of a floral, or utilize an endless variety of denim washes to sell contemporary clothing under the banner of 'vintage style'?

However, vintage clothing is becoming increasingly scarce and, as fast as garments of past decades are becoming more rare, prices are increasing, so care should be taken that any investment is worthwhile and the garment will not disintegrate in the first wash. Signs of rotting and disintegrating fabric are a warning, particularly under the arms (although these are small sections that can be replaced) as old deodorants (if even worn) had a very different chemical base from those of today. Such signs can be seen on anything from silks or wools of the twenties to cheaper Lurex jerseys of the sixties and seventies, which can have a tendency to shed their sparkle.

Although dry cleaning is often advised against, it does work. However, it isn't always effective at removing bad odours from vintage clothing. Trimmings may also need to be removed. Early sequins (twenties and thirties) were made from gelatine so can melt during washing and dry cleaning. Gentle hand-washing in suitable detergents is how vintage garments were intended to be cared for.

Bicarbonate of soda is a good neutraliser of old, musty and even damp smells. Garments such as furs should be turned inside out, inserted into a plastic bin liner, doused in bicarbonate and shaken. Left for a few hours, this treatment can be more effective in smell removal than expensive dry cleaning.

Some stains can be removed but it is so dependent on identifying what they are and what the fabric content of the garment is. Brownish 'age' or 'rust' spots are very common, as are the marks of old oil-based make-up, such as lipstick. Age spots are relatively easy to fade but hard to remove from natural fabrics such as silk and cotton. Lemon juice and bicarbonate of soda are natural bleaching agents. Combined together in equal parts to form a paste before adding a few drops of vinegar, this paste can be applied with a cotton wool bud and left in natural sunlight to boost the bleach. Glycerine is another agent that can help to loosen stains. Both pastes should be washed off after about an hour to avoid excessive bleaching. Old oil-based make-up stains are best removed with a small amount of colourless washing-up liquid and warm water. Ink stains can sometimes be removed from pale fabrics by soaking in milk. It will turn the fabric the colour of the milk if it is going to work. For darker fabrics that may be stained by the milk itself, spraying the ink and other severe stains with hairspray can be surprisingly effective. Brush away carefully with a soft cloth. Tea and coffee stains are difficult to remove, particularly tea (although it is itself a very useful and effective dye if an 'old'-looking camel colour is the desired shade for a white cotton blouse or camisole, for instance). These stains are best removed with a 5% hydrogen peroxide solution, or glycerine followed by white vinegar, rinsed in warm soapy water.

1 Mother of pearl buttons fasten this hand-smocked blouse from the late twenties. Tiny buttons were commonly used on the front, back and sides of garments from this era before zips were adapted for clothing use.

2 A collar handmade from interwoven Rouleau loops adds decorative interest to this wedding dress from the twenties. Collars and cuffs were often made separately so these ornamental accessories could be reused on other garments.

3 Heavy metal zips are an obvious clue to dating a garment, seen in fashion from the thirties onwards. As the decades progressed, zips became more refined, becoming an invisible fastener by the eighties. Contemporary fashion has borrowed the heavy exposed zip as a feature.

4 Vintage fabrics, particularly fine silks, lace and knitwear, can be delicate and padded hangers provide a support frame that won't distort shoulders. Old dyes tend to fade in natural light so clothes should be kept covered or in the dark.

4

The most common defect of knitwear is moth holes or dropped stitches that cause a run in the fabric. Dropped stitches are quite easy to restore using a small, ratcheted hook such as a rug hook. Find the first stitch that has invariably worked its way down to the welt, pick it up with the hook and pull through the loose yarn to form the next stitch, knitting a single vertical row. Moth holes can only be darned or covered with a button, embroidery or similar, but care must be taken that no moth eggs still remain, as they have a long incubation period. Cedar chip products are good moth deterrents and have a more pleasant odour than mothballs.

Hats are surprisingly easy to restore in terms of lost shape. Holding a straw or felt hat continuously over the full steam of a kettle is very effective. Turn the hat continuously while teasing it back into the original form and the shape will remain firm. This can always be repeated to freshen a hat or to help one that has been caught in the rain, and will have the same effect on ribbons, fabric flowers and corsages.

It's often suggested that garments should be folded in acid-free tissue paper in the dark. However, unless garments are frequently taken out and worn, permanent fold lines can develop. Rolling the garment is more effective, or consider hanging it on a padded hanger.

Steaming can be more effective than ironing, as ironing can change the colour of a fabric, particularly on dyed crepes and rayon. In past decades, many women hung their clothes over the steam of a warm bath to remove creases.

Leather handbags, shoes, gloves and belts may need specialist attention from a traditional cobbler. Coloured leather polish covers most scuffs and scratches, while saddle soap is a good restorative cleaner, but loose stitching and broken straps need the attention of a leather specialist. To prevent cracking and peeling, plastic bags and shoes need nourishment too: Vaseline is a good rub-in and any marks or scuffs can often be removed with a soft, good quality eraser. Shoes and boots will always benefit from the use of a wooden or plastic shoe block to encourage a firm shape for an over-worn shoe. Spraying with a leather restorer first will soften the leather before inserting the block.

Old sunglasses and spectacles are best washed in warm soapy water with a small amount of vinegar, but it is vital to dry and polish with a soft lint-free cloth to avoid scratches. Advice should be taken from an optician if you are considering replacing the existing lens with a modern prescriptive one. Generally old lenses were glass and much heavier than modern equivalents and therefore most frames are able to support a modern prescriptive lens. Opticians can also supply a variety of different-sized screws for arms that have become detached.

1 There is no better way of storing a fragile hat, keeping it safe from moths and helping to retain its shape than to utilize a beautiful vintage hatbox. Hatboxes that display their maker's name or a well known department store can be as collectable and valuable as the hats themselves.

ALTERING AND ADAPTING VINTAGE

It is important to remember that vintage sizing (even if stated) does not compare to modern fashion. A very rough indication is to go two sizes up from the stipulated size, if there is one, i.e. a vintage size 14 will be the equivalent of a modern 10. But trying on or at the very least knowing your measurements is important, particularly when buying at fairs and markets.

As women have grown taller and become healthier over the decades, our body shapes have changed and many vintage garments will be too small. It is always worth looking to see if seams are the double French seams that were common between the twenties and late thirties. If these can be successfully let out without leaving a fade mark or substantial stitch holes, they can add as much as four inches to the overall width of a garment. If things are too big they can easily be altered and may not need the expense of a dressmaker. As so many vintage garments were homemade, little hand alterations can easily adapt garments to create a better fit and can even improve on the look. Because garments were made to fit their wearer, little idiosyncrasies will often need to be altered anyway.

Wide shoulders can be adapted with the introduction of a series of pin tucks or pleats running vertically across the shoulder seam. The voluminous shoulder pads of the eighties are often far too excessive for today's wear, but removing them can cause droopy shoulders that will benefit from chic pleats (*Fig. 1*). If there isn't one already there, the addition of a small shoulder pad may be enough to take up the excess volume of fabric, particularly on a hand-knitted sweater that can't be sewn like fabric. The little half-moon shoulder pads of the forties, often made

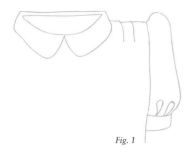

Fig. 1

in delightful scraps of fabric, are easy to emulate and need only three stitch points to hold them in place.

Sleeves that are too tight on the cuff may need to have the cuff removed and left with a simple hem if short, or gathered onto elastic if long. Sleeves that fall short of the wrist can be turned into a three-quarter-length or short sleeve by unpicking the cuff if there is one, measuring the desired length, cutting and reapplying the cuff or hemming. If the sleeves are too long they can be shortened in the same way, or it may be enough to turn back the cuff (if the fabric is not too thick) and stitch down creating a double or higher cuff and catching in excess fabric.

Busts are that too big or, more often, too small can also be altered. Depending on the volume of fabric, horizontal darts can be increased by unpicking the original seams. Vertical darts can be inserted from a shoulder seam with one row of machine stitching, tapering out at the waist, or above waist level or even continuing right down to a hem on a dress shape such as an early smock. Taking out volume by curving in side seams is also effective.

Belts, of course, can be used to pull in a waist but removing a waistband enables darts to be properly adjusted and is easier than expected. This is particularly useful for adjusting men's trousers for women's wear. Unpicking a waistband front and back is necessary; increasing the gathers, decreasing or increasing existing darts will also involve unpicking them and restitching. The waistband will then need to be realigned and taken in at the centre back seam to decrease the size (*Fig. 2*). The waistband can be increased by finding a small piece of the same fabric from an unseen area, such as the pocket or inside leg seam, to be added as a small placket, or square, to the centre back (if it is to be covered by a belt) or to the front, where the fastening clip will need to be moved over onto the new piece of fabric.

Generally the look of garments can be easily improved. Buttons can be changed if one or two of a set are missing (make sure the new choice is not too heavy for the existing fabric). If only one is missing from an obvious place, it may be possible to replace it by taking the top one from a collar (if it is never to be worn done up), a button from a pocket, or the last one on a shirt that will be worn tucked in. Covered buttons, if worn or rusted, can be recovered by matching a colour in the print

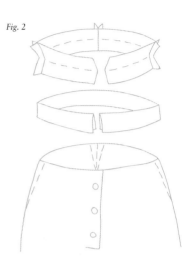

Fig. 2

or taking a small piece from the side seam, inside pocket or hem (which, even if it is just the right length on the inside hem, can be replaced with a matching strip of bias binding). This is also a useful technique if a narrow belt is missing and needs to be made to match the print. Excess fabric taken from the side seam can also be used to remake a missing belt, or this can simply be replaced with a vintage belt that is sympathetic in colour. Wide coloured ribbons in grosgrain or petersham also make good replacement belts.

Printed square scarves can be made into fabulous inexpensive linings for early unlined jackets and can also be added to cuffs, even if the sleeves are not lined. They also make beautiful summer halternecks by turning on the triangular and folding the top corner over a metal hoop, necklace or even a ribbon. The two remaining corners can then be knotted at the back if the scarf is a large one, such as an Hermès, or stitched. Two scarves of the same print can make a simple square blouse by joining them at the shoulder and side seams.

Camisoles and teddies with insertion lace or embroidery can be improved with the addition of coloured ribbons, which also make them look less like lingerie. Long cotton nightdresses can be shortened to dress or blouse length, as can the long maxi dresses of the sixties and seventies that sometimes can be overpowering in their vibrant prints. Reducing the length reduces the impact of the print and makes them more wearable for day rather than just for evening.

PICTURE CREDITS

SECTION OPENERS

pp.2–3 (left to right) Handmade printed silk evening dress, c. 1930s; handmade nursery-print rayon dressing gown, c. 1930s; handmade printed spot on cotton dress, c. 1950s; Louis Féraud printed silk evening dress. c. 1970s.

p.15 A model photographed in 1927 wears a dress decorated with a bold Art Deco motif.

p.33 Greta Garbo is photographed on the film set of *The Painted Veil* in September 1934, as the character Katrin.

p.53 Two models photographed on Louisburg Square, Boston, in 1946. The herringbone suit to the left is by Claire McCardell, while the one to the right is in gabardine wool by Eisenberg.

p.71 A winter coat and matching hat with hound's-tooth trim are modelled in a café in Rome in 1957.

p.91 Twiggy and other models showcase sixties fashions for Marks & Spencer.

p.111 An outfit from the 1974/5 ready-to-wear collection by Pierre Cardin is modelled on a French street.

p.132 Top row: (2) detail from Pierre Cardin wool dress; (3) detail from Bruce Oldfield dress. **Second row:** (2) detail from Zandra Rhodes evening dress; (3) detail from Escada jacket. **Third row:** (2) detail from Zandra Rhodes evening dress. **Fifth row:** (2) detail from Moschino jeans.

p.133 The model Abyan is photographed wearing an outfit from the Pierre Balmain haute couture collection, spring/summer 1990.

IMAGE CREDITS

All material is collection of Nicky Albrechtsen unless otherwise stated. All garments are photographed by Drew Gardner (assisted by Marie Absolom) unless otherwise stated.

Bill Gibb bee brooch © Aberdeen Art Gallery & Museums Collection: 332 (3)
© Matthew Adams Frock Me Vintage Fashion Fair: 421 (2, 3)
Photography by Nicky Albrechtsen: 14, 32, 52, 70, 91, 110, 418–20, 422, 427
The Art Archive/Tate Gallery London/Eileen Tweedy. © David Hockney: 127 (5)
Private collection of Atelier Mayer: 137 (2, 3), 149 (4), 188 (3), 272 (2), 325 (4)
Courtesy of Elaine Bell: 251 (2), 252 (1, 2), 254 (2)
Courtesy of Lizzie Bramlett: 254 (1)
Collection of Broadbase: 161 (7, 8)
Courtesy of Chanel: © All Rights Reserved 336; © Man Ray Trust/ADAGP Paris 2012 394 (1)
Private collection of Daphne Corbin: 5 (4), 18 (1), 154 (1), 155, 156 (2), 157 (all), 158 (2), 159 (all), 160 (1–3), 161 (1–5), 162 (all), 163 (all)
Corbis: © H. Armstrong Roberts/Corbis 31 (5); © Bettmann/Corbis 19, 38 (2), 45 (4), 172 (1), 184 (1), 298 (1), 408 (3); © Fabian Cevallos/Sygma/Corbis 133; © CinemaPhoto/Corbis 267 (4); © Condé Nast Archive/Corbis 55 (2), 115 (4), 191 (9), 282, 304, 323 (3), 342 (1), 380 (2); © Russ Einhorn/Splash News/Corbis 367 (4); © Andrew Gombert/epa/Corbis 383 (4); © Jacques Haillot/Apis/Sygma/Corbis 108 (1); © Hans Hildenbrand/National Geographic Society/Corbis 374 (2); © Hulton-Deutsch Collection/Corbis 15, 264 (1), 359 (4); © Rob Latour for LE/Splash News/Corbis 224 (4); © Genevieve Naylor/Corbis 53, 208 (1); © Paramount Pictures/Sunset Boulevard/Corbis 393 (5); © Mark Peterson/Corbis 183 (5); © Philadelphia Museum of Art/Corbis 410; © Scheufler Collection/Corbis 388 (1); © John Springer Collection/Corbis 24 (1), 373 (4); © Pierre Vauthey/Sygma/Corbis 111, 146 (1)
Private collection of John Day & Andi Smith: 5 (8), 77 (2), 86 (2, 3), 168, 169 (4), 170, 171 (2, 3), 172 (2), 173 (4), 174 (1, 2, 4), 175 (5, 9), 178 (1, 3, 4), 182 (2), 183 (1), 185 (9–12), 186 (1–4), 187 (4, 5, 8–10), 189 (10), 209 (9)
Private Collection of Liz Eggleston: 105 (7), 122 (1, 2), 127 (4), 131 (6), 415 (3)
Marilyn Monroe's bra courtesy Huw Rees, Frasers Autographs.com: 221 (9)
Getty: Apic/Getty Images 34 (2); Archive Photos/Getty Images 95 (2), 364; Archivio Cameraphoto Epoche/Getty Images 71; Autrey/NBC/NBCU Photo Bank via Getty Images 349; Dave M. Benett/Getty Images 39 (4); Terence Donovan Archive/Getty Images 201; Evening Standard/Getty Images 161 (6); Nat Farbman/Time Life Pictures/Getty Images 214 (6); Jayne Fincher/Getty Images 398 (2); © Mimi Haddon/Getty Images 236; Dave Hogan/Getty Images 114 (3); Hulton Archive/Getty Images 125 (5); Kurt Hutton/Picture Post/Getty Images 324; Imagno/Getty Images 244 (1); Georges De Keerle/Getty Images 141 (4); Keystone/Getty Images 284 (1); Keystone-France/Gamma-Keystone via Getty Images 287; David McNew/Getty Images 270 (3); Michael Ochs Archives/Getty Images 77 (4); Mondadori Portfolio via Getty Images 86 (1); NBC/NBCU Photo Bank via Getty Images 353 (2); Popperfoto/Getty Images 59 (3), 335; Bill Ray/Life Magazine/Time & Life Pictures/Getty Images 94; Ebet Roberts/Redferns/Getty Images 138; Silver Screen Collection/Hulton Archive/Getty Images 203 (4); Clarence Sinclair Bull/John Kobal Foundation/Getty Images 33; Justin de Villeneuve/Hulton Archive/Getty Images 382 (1); Kevin Winter/DMI/Time Life Pictures/Getty Images 218; Chaloner Woods/Getty Images 333 (5)
Private collection of John Hamilton: 211 (5)
Courtesy the House of Dormeuil: 318 (3)
© Laura Ashley Ltd: 101 (6), 118 (3)
The Estate of Antonio Lopez and Juan Ramos: Pat Cleveland, Paris, 1973, © The Estate of Antonio Lopez and Juan Ramos. Courtesy The Suzanne Geiss Company 134 (1); 143 (5)
© M&S Company Archive: 85 (7) c.1959, (91) c.1967, 92 (2) c.1967, 96 (4) c.1969, 97 (5) c.1967, 108 (2) c.1969/70, 230 c.1930s

Private collection of Su Mason: 314 (2, 3: jodhpurs)
Private collection Simon Murray, Onspec Ontic: 192–9 (all glasses)
Private collection of Sheena Napier: 18 (2), 20 (all), 23 (3,4), 24 (2–6), 26 (1), 27 (3), 28 (1), 31 (4), 34 (1), 36 (2), 37 (4), 39 (3,5), 40 (2), 41 (4–6), 42 (2), 43 (3, 5), 44 (2, 3), 45 (5), 47 (4, 5), 51 (5), 184 (2–4), 187 (7), 188 (6, 11), 189 (14), 190 (3), 191 (6, 7, 8, 10), 328 (2), 411 (3)
© Ted Polhemus/PYMCA.com: 181 (7)
© Radio Times Archive: 36 (3), 50 (3)
Courtesy Rebekah Gilbertson © Rainy Day Films: 312 (2, 3)
Rex: Everett Collection/Rex 84 (3)
Private Collection of Sharon Selzer: 125 (6), 214 (2)
Courtesy Silhouette: 198 (1)
Private collection of Liz Tregenza: 85 (6), 365 (4), 407 (3), 408 (1, 2, 4), 409 (7–10), 413 (3, 4, 6), 416 (1, 3), 417 (5)
Victoria & Albert Museum, London: 154 (2), 161 (9)
Dagmar/*Vogue*. © Condé Nast: 69 (4)
WireImage: Nick Harvey/WireImage 298 (3)
Courtesy Sarah Kenny Ackerman © Whiting and Davies: 182 (1)

REFERENCES

p.7 'Fashions Fade', *Interview*, 13 April 1975; **p.16** 'The twenties', email correspondence with author, January 2014; **p.28** 'Owing to this craze', American *Vogue*, 1921; **p.34** 'I never came', Pamela Golbin, *Madeleine Vionnet*, New York, 2009; **p.35** 'What Hollywood designs', Jane Mulvagh, *Vogue History of Twentieth Century Fashion*, London, 1988, p.123; **p.37** 'The Garbo girl', *The Herald*, 18 March 2013; **p.54** 'Forties fashions', email correspondence with author, January 2014; **p.54** 'Il faut skimp', British *Vogue*, October 1941; **p.54** 'Every woman in Paris', Lucien François, *Votre Beauté* magazine, May 1940; **p.57** 'Fashions do not die', Edna Woolman Chase, 'Morale', American *Vogue*, 1 March 1942; **p.58** 'For half a century', Rare Vintage blog, rarevintage.blogspot.co.uk/2012/12/quote-of-day-5-treasuring-norell.html; **p.72** 'It was the time', Vanessa Friedman, Alessandra Arezzi Boza, Armando Chitolina, *Emilio Pucci*, Cologne, 2010, p.49; **p.76** 'Squalor and solitude inside', Brunello Rondi quoted in Peter Bondanella, *The Cinema of Federico Fellini*, Princeton, 1992, p.134; **p.92** 'What was different', Watt, 2003, p.32; **p.98** 'Instant age', *The Miami News*, 19 June 1970; **p.98** 'Ugly, ugly', *Boca Raton News*, 17 July 1970; **p.112** 'You can find', Howell, 1978, p.305; **p.114** 'He dressed the woman', Watt, 2003, p.18; **p.116** 'You are only as good', *Design Museum*, 2009, p.58; **p.125** 'Left nothing to the imagination', www.vogue.it/encyclo; **p.134** 'The new money': York, 1984, p.23; **p.134** 'It is terrible to say', 'Off The Street', American *Vogue*, April 1994; **p.139** 'I wasn't born this way', Modern Art + Style, www.modernartandstyle.com/2012/06/08/the-grace-jones; **p.154** 'A hat makes clothing identifiable', Stephen Jones, *Hats: An Anthology* exhibition webpage, www.vam.ac.uk/content/articles/h/hats-an-anthology-by-stephen-jones; **p.154** 'Hats have never before', 'Cloche Hat Will Prevail This Spring', *New York Times*, 7 February 1926, XII; **p.158** Glamour is what makes a man', Daché, 1946; **p.160** Advice on hat styles from 'Made for Each Other – and for you!', *Every Woman* magazine, March 1940, reproduced on blog.tuppencehapenny.co.uk/2010/02/if-hat-fits-wear-it.html; **p.160** 'I truly believe', Lilly Daché, 1946, p.168; **p.165** 'Handbags, gloves and shoes', Head with Hyams, 2009, p.136; **p.168** 'Give a girl', widely attributed; **p.182** 'The handbag, an article of utility', Langner, 1959, p.325; **p.186** 'I was fed up', Coco Chanel, quoted in Justine Picardie, 'Chanel Handbags: Quilt Trip', *Telegraph*, 27 March 2009; **p.193** 'To me, eyewear goes way beyond', *2020 Mag*, February 2002, http://www.2020mag.com/story/16; **p.200** 'With a stretch belt', Beth Ditto, 'What would Beth do?', *Guardian*, 25 May 2007; **p.211** 'A scarf to a woman', Dior, 2008, p.99; **p.218** 'Lovely lingerie', Dior, 2008, p.73; **p.218** 'British girls', Kate Finnigan, 'The Survival of the Fittest', *Telegraph*, 15 January 2013; **p.219** 'Lingerie is part of my DNA', Press release, 2010,

quoted on main.stylelist.com/2010/06/28/jean-paul-gaultier-la-perla-lingerie; **p.230** 'Nothing inspires my creativity more than', Melissa Odabash, swimwear designer, email correspondence with author, December 2013; **p.241** 'I'm interested', speaking in video installation at *Schiaparelli and Prada: Impossible Conversations* exhibition, The Metropolitan Museum of Art, 10 May–19 August 2012; **p.241** 'When I was a child', Anne Sebba, *Laura Ashley; A Life by Design*, London, 2013; **p.250** 'Knitted clothes', Bernandine Morris, 'Shop Talk: Status Symbol Couple Arrive to Show Styles,' *The New York Times*, 15 November 1973; **p.265** 'Finding a beautiful vintage gown', email correspondence with author, January 2014; **p.265** 'An evening dress', speaking in *The Last Emperor*, 2009; **p.267** 'When a woman smiles', www.vionnet.com/madeleine-vionnet; **p.282** 'The history of bridalwear', email correspondence with author, January 2014; **p.294** 'A feminine brand', email correspondence with author, January 2014; **p.296** 'The Paris Collections this season', British *Vogue*, June 1939; **p.313** 'Designers revisited', Lucy Hutchings, 'Countryside Alliance', 5 July 2012, www.vogue.co.uk/fashion/trends/2012-13-autumn-winter/countryside-alliance; **p.316** Howell, 1978; **p.319** 'There are so many', Dior, 2008, p.21; **p.322** 'The tiger in the jungle', Laver, 1937; **p.324** 'Madame Bricard', Keenan, 1981, p.20; **p.330** 'By their sales', Alison Settle, *Observer*, 8 February 1953; **p.330** 'All my inspiration comes from nature', 'Diane von Furstenberg on the Meaning of Luxury', *Time*, 17 June 2010, http://content.time.com/time/arts/article/0,8599,1997006,00.html; **p.337** 'Over the last 150 years', Amy Miller, *Sailor Chic* exhibition webpage, www.rmg.co.uk/about/press/archive/sailor-chic-summer-exhibition-at-the-national-maritime-museum-2007; **p.338** 'Give a fashionable salute', *Ellensberg Daily Record*, 28 August 1940; **p.349** 'I consider lace to be one of the prettiest imitations' *L'Illustration* newspaper, 29 April 1939, cited in Marianne Carlano, *French Textiles*, USA, 1985; **p.352** 'Coquettish', www.vogue.com/voguepedia/Nina_Ricci_(Brand); **p.352** 'Sensuous element of surprise', 'Lace is Dominant in Cocktail Mode', *The New York Times*, 23 October 1954; **p.352** 'She had an eye for design', Stanley Donen, 'Obituary', American *Vogue*, April 1993; **p.363** 'I don't think', The Bazaar Blog, 20 June 2012, www.harpersbazaar.co.uk/blogs/new-purfumes-chanel-guerlain-marcjacobs; **p.364** 'According to their colour', Dior, 2008, p.34; **p.374** 'Every time Schiaparelli', 'Schiaparelli Among the Berbers' American *Vogue*, 15 August 1936; **p.376** 'Masked parties, Savage parties', Evelyn Waugh, *Vile Bodies*, London, 1930; **p.392** 'When the little black dress is right', Holman Edelman, 1997; **p.396** 'The Little Black dress', Mary Quant, *Mary Quant: My Autobiography*, London, 2012, p.162; **p.407** 'One of Liberty's', email correspondence with author, January 2014; **p.410** 'Visual jokes', Mendes, 2010; **p.410** 'Artists Quit Easels', *The Coaticook Observer*, 20 June 1941

1 Embroidered paisley and floral motifs create the border on a twenties wool shawl.

2 A refined paisley forms part of the diagonal border on a seventies wool dress by Jean Varon.

INDEX

Page numbers in *italic* refer to illustrations

Designer names are indexed only where specifically discussed in texts or captions

ACKNOWLEDGMENTS

Angela Jeffrey, Archivist Laura Ashley Ltd

Atelier Mayer, www.atelier-mayer.com

Avril Broadley, broad-base.co.uk, for her design prowess

Cecile Goddet-Dirles, Chanel

Daphne and Pete Corbin, williamcassie.tumblr.com

Drew Gardner and Marie Absolom for photography

Emma Bosh, Rebekah Gilbertson, Rainy Day Films

Frances Ambler for her perceptive editing and endless patience

Huw Rees, frasersautographs.com

John Day and Andi Smith, bimptulipvintage.tumblr.com

Katherine Carter, Archivist Marks & Spencer Company Ltd

Liz Eggleston, vintage-a-peel.co.uk

Liz Tregenza, advantageinvintage.co.uk

Lizzie Bramlett, thevintagetraveler.wordpress.com

Maria Ranauro for support and picture research throughout

Assistant photographic stylists and additional picture research: Kezzia Albrechtsen, Tyler Archard, Francesca Caicedo, Iona Spencer, Holly Weldon and, above all, Jo Murphy for additional research, enthusiasm and endurance skills

Roger Dixon, Picture Editor *Radio Times*

Rootstein, www.rootstein.com

Sarah Kenny Ackerman, bollare.com for Whiting & Davis

Sharon & Michael Selzer at The Shop

Shea Goli, Associate Director, the Suzanne Geiss Company

Sheena Napier, Costume designer

Su Mason, Bluelinencupboard.tumblr.com

Victoria Ward, Curator Museums and Galleries Aberdeen

1 Rarely seen in any other era, atomic textile designs are indicative of the early fifties.

2 Covered buttons are a common feature of thirties and forties garments, regardless of whether they are handmade or mass-produced.

3 Vertical seams contrasting with horizontal decorative faggotting are identifying feature on fashions up to mid century.

4 This detail of a psychedelic sixties fabric comes from a Marcel Fenez evening dress.